Skunk Ranch to Hollywood

The West of Author Hal Evarts

by Hal Evarts, Jr.

CAPRA PRESS
SANTA BARBARA

Copyright ©1989 by Hal G. Evarts, Jr.
ALL RIGHTS RESERVED
PRINTED IN THE UNITED STATES OF AMERICA.

Cover design by Francine Rudesill
Design and typography by Jim Cook/Book Design & Typography

LIBRARY OF CONGRESS CATALOGING-IN-PUBLICATION DATA
Evarts, Hal George, 1915–
  From skunk ranch to Hollywood.
  Bibliography: p.
  1. Evarts, Hal G. (Hal George), 1887–1934—Biography.
2. Authors, American—20th century—Biography. 3. West
(U.S.)—Biography. I. Title
PS3509.V443Z65 1989   813'.52[B] 88-7941
ISBN 0-88496-297-0

Published by CAPRA PRESS
P.O. Box 2068
Santa Barbara, California 93120

For Hal and Sylvia
in loving memory

1887–1934
1890–1977

"You did a good job in selecting your parents!"

Horace M. Albright,
letter, November 5, 1986,
Studio City, California.

ACKNOWLEDGMENTS

For their support and encouragement I owe special appreciation to Edward Kemp, former Acquisitions Librarian, University of Oregon, Eugene, and to the "light of my life," Dorothea.

Grateful acknowledgment is made to Robert Parrish for permission to incorporate into Chapter 12 quotations from his book, *Growing Up in Hollywood*, copyright ©1976. Originally published: Harcourt, Brace, Jovanovich, Inc. Reprint: Little, Brown & Co., 1988.

To Betsy Sanders and Rosemarie Fiebig, who volunteered their editorial expertise to proof read the final manuscript, my profound thanks.

And to my son Bill, without whose patience and good humor, word processor and photographic skills, this book might never have made it to the finish line, a heartfelt *muchas gracias*.

LA JOLLA, CALIFORNIA
AUGUST 1988

1.

"... the mass circulation magazines were the television screens of their day, the first half of this century. The 'big slicks' were then the central fixture of American culture, the despair of all right-minded intellectuals. But it was a valid culture and the mass magazines virtually created it, perpetuated it and expanded its influence." —W. H. HUTCHINSON

IN MIDSUMMER of the year 1929, a few weeks before the October stock market crash on Wall Street that plunged the United States and much of the world into the Great Depression, my father completed his thirteenth novel. There was, of course, no correlation between these two events, one to have dire global consequences, the other affecting only our small family. In any case the unlucky aura of thirteen would have been lost on my father, even if he had possessed a crystal ball and occult powers to foretell the future. What he did possess was a robust skepticism coupled with boundless confidence in his own opinions.

As a matter of recorded fact, he *did* predict the crash; not the depth or extent of it, but the approximate date. All through the final throes of the Roaring Twenties and the go-for-broke bull market, he had predicted a catastrophic drop, and backed up his forecast with gobs of cash. He was playing the market on margin, a paltry ten percent in those halcyon days before federal regulation, and selling short against the grain. And losing his shirt as the Dow Jones averages surged ever Onward and Upward. Investing for a rainy day, he called it. My mother, Sylvia, had a harsher term: gambling.

In their divergent ways perhaps they were both on track. As my father was to declare later, often and heatedly, "I was right, Sylvia, but dammit, I was right too soon!"

Christened Harry George Evarts, a name abbreviated in childhood to Hal, he turned forty-two that August. By then a veteran of the freelance fiction wars, he had no literary pretensions (I'm only trying to tell a story) but he took his work, if not himself, seriously. This particular story titled *The Shaggy Legion*, dealing with the slaughter of the last major buffalo herd on the American continent, underscored a theme very serious indeed to Hal: the protection of wildlife.

Back in that pre-TV era, the target of every writer who aspired to money and/or the widest possible audience was the Big Slicks. The biggest, highest-paying, granddaddy slick of them all was a weekly magazine, a national institution known as the *Saturday Evening Post*. It sold for five cents a copy, annual subscription two dollars, had a circulation close to three million, an estimated readership of millions more, and was to be found in nearly every barber shop and board room across the land. The editor-in-chief of this august publication, George Horace Lorimer, once described as a "five button mandarin," occupied a niche in Hal's personal pantheon higher than that accorded President Herbert Hoover, ranking well above God. Fortunately for our household Lorimer shared most of Hal's views on conservation.

My earliest picture of the author at work encompasses a scarred and ancient rolltop desk, stacks upon stacks of yellow unlined paper and a smoke-filled bedroom called Dad's Den, in whatever house or apartment we happened to be residing at the time. That a stage, rather than a physical image of the author himself, should have been imprinted so vividly upon my youthful memory explains much about our daily life, for my father always wrote at home, not in a separate office "downtown." Sylvia frequently had to field the question from inquisitive friends and relatives: How could she *stand* having him underfoot all day, every day, including Sundays? Worse still, for lunch? Looking back, I suspect that she secretly favored the arrangement. At least she knew where her sometimes erratic and unpredictable husband was and what he was doing.

There was another more pragmatic reason. Hal's handwriting, to put it charitably, left much to be desired. He composed in longhand, using the softest lead pencils available, scribbling with furious concentration and intensity, lighting one Camel cigarette from the stub of another, slashing out entire paragraphs, balling up pages and hurling them on the floor. At the end of a productive session, the den smelled rather like a pool hall, and resembled a *Front Page* version of a newspaper city room after the final edition had been put to bed. Someone had to gather up the day's copy, decipher and transcribe it. This role fell to Sylvia by default.

My mother was one of the few persons who could read Hal's scrawl with comparative ease. The discipline of Palmer's Penmanship drill, to which he had been subjected in grammar school, proved a failure. To the uninitiated his chirography was virtually illegible. Early in his career Sylvia became his amanuensis, his secretary, his indispensable Girl Friday at his beck and call for a hasty revision or second draft. During their life together she typed and retyped fourteen of his novels, hundreds of short stories, articles and columns, and thousands of letters. They were, whether they realized it or not, a team, quarrelsome and embattled much of the time, but a team nevertheless.

So in that parlous season *The Shaggy Legion*, which Hal referred to semi-jokingly as "my buffalo yarn," underwent its creative progression, from conception through gestation to term and finally birth. And thence into the marketplace. A few days later he received an airmail letter, postage one nickel, which in those more leisurely times indicated a communication of some urgency. "Dear Hal: Erd and I have read your new book and like it very much. I am sending it on to Philadelphia and will let you know the verdict as soon as possible. Cordially yours, Carl."

Translation: The brothers Brandt—Carl and Erd—Hal's literary agents in New York City, had approved his story as it stood, *in toto*, and forwarded the manuscript to the desk of that potentate of popular taste, inheritor of the mantle of Benjamin Franklin, George H. Lorimer, Independence Square, City of Brotherly Love, Pennsylvania. *Keep your fingers crossed, old friend.*

That was the situation when I rejoined the family fold in Los Angeles after several weeks in a boys' camp on Catalina Island off the southern California coast. At fourteen I was a charter member of an earlier "me generation," as were most of my peers. Collectively we were as self-centered, self-indulgent and narcissistic as any child of the 1980s. Spoiled? Possibly. It was, so social historians remind us, a hedonistic decadent age, not unlike Babylon before the Fall.

In retrospect, my chief preoccupations of the moment would seem to have been fairly typical: (1) enrolling in a strange new school, (2) trying out for the football team, (3) grades, and (4) girls. In due time item four would supplant the first three on the list, but at no time then were my priorities those of my parents. The fate of Hal's novel did not unduly concern me. At this late juncture I am ashamed to admit that I had a "So what?" attitude. After all, he had never written a failure since Day One. He was in constant demand as a speaker. He could crank out money as if by machine, according to his mood or need. He was in *Who's Who in America*. He was famous, wasn't he? So how could he miss this time around?

He didn't miss. The day after I entered Los Angeles High, a lowly tenth grade "scrub," he received a telegram. In 1929 the arrival of a telegram, delivered to the front door by uniformed messenger, usually portended the death of a loved one or a major disaster. This one, however, read: SWELL NEWS. POST BUYING LEGION THIRTEEN FIVE. CONGRATULATIONS. BRANDT. Which meant that my father had sold the first and second North American serial rights to his book for the then princely sum of $13,500, a substantial increase over the price he'd received for his previous book. Two weeks later Lorimer, returning from vacation, liked the story so much that he raised the ante another $1,500.

How did my parents react to what should have been a joyous occasion, the culmination of a full year's shared endeavor? One would like to report that they celebrated somehow, kicked up their heels sedately, or at the minimum breathed a prayer of thanks to the bitch goddess of all free-lance fictioneers. But my memory draws a blank. Probably not. They were not demonstrative people, both descendants of colonial New England Yankees who seldom displayed their emotions in public. Or maybe they too, like their only child, took success for granted as their just due, a slice of the American dream of pie-in-the-sky that soon was to self-destruct.

By November I had achieved one of my goals: I was a second string guard on the "Junior B" football squad, a ragtag band of inept but hopeful, would-be future All-Americans. As a mini reward Hal kept me out of school for a week and took me camping in a remote area near Death Valley, where we encountered not another human being (unimaginable today). He was an expert trapper; as a teenager he had once supported himself trapping fur. On this occasion he caught four desert foxes and a lynx, not for their pelts but to learn their habits. During that brief span, by sheer power of observation and retention—I never saw him jot down a note in his life—he acquired the material for two animal short stories, *Swift the Kit Fox* and *Jerbo the Jumper*, both of which shortly appeared in the *Post* at his going price of $2,000 apiece and later in book form. To greet us on our return Sylvia left the latest issue of the *Post* prominently displayed on the hall table. Across the bottom of the cover, where the names of several contributors were customarily listed, only one name leaped out: "Beginning THE SHAGGY LEGION by Hal G. Evarts." In capital letters, solo billing! Whatever he felt, and he never mentioned the matter to me, at that moment I was supremely, glowingly proud of my old man.

The story appeared in what was then standard serial format: six consecutive installments, each of the last five headed by a brief plot synopsis so that any reader could refresh his memory quickly or pick up the threads. Two or three black and white illustrations with titillating captions accompanied each segment, a school of painting ridiculed by critics as calendar art. But Hal, for the most part, loved *his* illustrations. W.H.D. "Big Bill" Koerner, a popular commercial artist who came to specialize in western subjects, had illustrated several of his earlier serials. My father decided he must have an original for his own and wrote the *Post* to inquire if it were possible to obtain one particular painting that he much admired. Shortly into the new year a large flat package arrived at our house, with a card: "Courtesy of G.H. Lorimer and staff." It was a brilliant full color 30" x 42" oil on canvas, a scene depicting a horde of Comanche warriors attacking a trader's post on the Texas plains. A gift.

Hal wrote the artist: "Many thanks for the picture of the 'Dobe Walls fight. It's a marvelous picture and will have the place of honor in my den right over my desk. I want to take this opportunity to express my admiration for all of your illustrations. They're great. Many people have congratulated me on my good fortune in having you to illustrate my stories."

Big Bill and Hal never met, never corresponded again, but were to collaborate long distance on two more serials. Koerner paintings today hang in galleries around the country, notably the Whitney Gallery of Western Art in Cody, Wyoming, and command handsome prices.

Three months after "Black Tuesday" the stock market was still on its ruinous toboggan slide. Panic-stricken brokers were said to be leaping out of Wall Street windows, words of hollow cheer were issuing from the White House, and the national mood had altered abruptly from one of whoopee to gloom. My father, his bleakest predictions fulfilled far more grimly than he ever imagined or could have wished, was holed up once more in his den, mulling over a new yarn. Meanwhile, half way around the world another admirer of W.H.D. Koerner's work was leafing through some back copies of the *Saturday Evening Post*. Lightning was about to strike.

What happened next is according to Hal, his version, a tale

he recounted many times, one replete with variations, embellishments and, no doubt, downright creativity. It never came out quite the same way twice. This was a practice of his that greatly embarrassed me as a child. (That's not true, I would protest silently. He's lying, lying! Why doesn't he tell it the way it *really* happened?) I had much to learn about the story teller's art, the freewheeling technique of poetic license.

A few days before my fifteenth birthday, he received a phone call from a woman he understood to be the secretary of "some big mucky muck at Fox Studio" who wanted to discuss a motion picture deal. "I forgot to ask," my father said as he hung up. "Where's this Fox outfit located?"

"I know where it is," said my mother, ever practical. "This could mean a lot of money."

Two of his previous books had been made into films, both with considerable box office success, but his attitude toward the movie industry was atypical for a writer, especially one who had lived on the fringes of Hollywood for some time. Movies did not attract or interest him whatsoever, with one exception: any picture starring comedian Harold Lloyd. In contemporary parlance Hal was a Harold Lloyd "freak." He saw them all. I remember attending the classic *Safety Last* with him and a scene in which hapless Harold dangled from the hands of a giant clock high atop a skyscraper, the city streets far below. Hal burst into such gales of laughter he had to grope his way out of the theater, gasping, his eyes streaming with tears.

In truth, he did not much care for the town itself, any town for that matter. If he'd had his druthers he, essentially an outdoor creature, would have bought a ranch somewhere in the mountains and raised animals for experimental breeding purposes. But Sylvia had journeyed that route with him before. As she firmly pointed out, they had a teenage son to raise and educate. Proximity to what she considered a "good" school was uppermost among her concerns. So my father, somewhat grudgingly, continued to live in, but not of, Hollywood.

He welcomed the additional income from the sale of motion picture rights but his curiosity, or ambition, ended there. He had no desire to hobnob with movie elite or watch the cameras roll, although both avenues were open to him. Nor did he ever voice the complaint, almost universal among writers, that some Hollywood hack had butchered his work, bastardized it into so much celluloid trash. To Hal a movie was a movie was a movie, ho-hum, including his own. Aside from Harry Carey, a Western actor who owned a horse breeding ranch out in the Saugus hills, he knew nobody in the industry. He had never set foot inside a studio until the afternoon he drove up to the ornate Fox front gate on Pico Boulevard, a lamb cast among the cinema wolves. That evening at the dinner table, I heard Episode One of what was to become his next serial, a real life soap opera before the term was coined.

Dinner at our house was what might be labeled the "family hour." Promptly at six o'clock we sat down. Throughout the meal, served by our maid, my father would hold forth on the subject of General Motors or Allied Chemical or whatever stock had skidded to a new low; my mother would discuss her latest interests, usually of a social nature. Probably I talked track, the next sport on my agenda. By seven o'clock I was upstairs in my room geared for Homework, a college preparatory course charted by my counselor at L.A. High. For the next three hours I wrestled with Caesar's *Gallic Wars*, English literature, modern European history and geometry, the last of which I loathed. At ten o'clock I closed my books, switched on my Spartan console radio and for half an hour listened to the sweet brassy music of George Olsen and his band emanating from a supper club in Culver City. Ten-thirty, lights out. Such was my routine five nights a week.

But on this eventful evening Hal, returning from his first studio conference, had a fresh topic for dinner conversation: the offer of a job. If he accepted, it would be his first in some eighteen years, an interval during which he had fiercely resisted working for anyone but himself, minus a five-month hitch in the U.S. Army in World War I. Above all, my father treasured his independence. They, he informed us—"they" being the nameless mucky mucks of Fox—wanted him to write a screenplay based on *The Shaggy Legion*.

"Oh, Hal, that's wonderful!" my mother said. "But you've never written a screenplay before." Which, in hindsight, was a kind of prophecy.

"They'll pay me a thousand a week," he said. "One thousand dollars each and every week." Under stress he spoke slowly and emphatically, enunciating each word. "Starting tomorrow."

With that announcement he had our undivided attention.

"You remember the Koerner painting? The Indian one? Well—"

Of course we remembered. It was the show piece of his den.

And he then unfolded the following improbable scenario: By coincidence a director under contract to Fox (whom Hal could identify only as "some fellow named Walsh—never heard of him"), while on vacation in Paris had happened on the Fight at 'Dobe Walls illustration, liked it and so read the serial by an author *he* had never heard of. No Evarts had ever been to Paris but the three of us around the table attempted to visualize the mysterious Walsh in some elegant Champs Elysées hotel, transported by *The Shaggy Legion*, suddenly grabbing one of those funny French phones and shouting, "Find that man! Now!" Actually it took Walsh three days to run the author to earth, via a complex circuitry from Paris, New York, Philadelphia, Hollywoood, New York again, back to Hollywood and finally to our new home on South Lorraine Boulevard. The message was, more or less: "Locate a writer named Hal Evarts and sign him up for my next picture."

2.

Los Angeles, California, August 1, 1887
"Dear Bro: . . . some people seem to be stuck on San Diego. Everybody to their taste but a country or town that has no water privilege or good soil is N.G. [no good] in my estimation, and that is what San Diego has to get. They have got a big boom down there but nothing like this place."

So WROTE EUGENE EVARTS to his brother George in their home town of Topeka, Kansas. A recent arrival in southern California, Eugene had been severely bitten by the booster bug. In 1887 San Diego was a waterless wasteland, boom or no boom; for an ambitious young man who hoped to make his fortune in real estate, Los Angeles, City of the Angels, Elysium of opportunity, was the place to be. Eugene, one of thousands of Americans who swarmed west that year to cash in on the Second Gold Rush, never went home again.

As a postscript he added: ". . . learned that Nellie was no better. I hope by this time she is a great deal better and will improve fast and that you all will have good health. I guess that it has kept you busy taking care of her as I know what typhoid fever is myself."

The stricken Nellie was the ten-year-old daughter of George and Emma Evarts. Emma was pregnant with her second child, expecting any day, and in no condition to look after a desperately ill little girl. In that crisis George took leave from his job and pitched in to succor his beleaguered family. Nursemaid, cook, laundress, all-everything, he struggled through a sweltering Kansas heat wave that broke records across the Middle West. Nellie recovered and lived for another seventy-seven years. On August 24 Emma delivered a healthy eight-pound boy. But poor, devoted luckless George, five weeks after his brother's benediction, died at thirty-three, a victim of typhoid fever contracted from his daughter. The fatherless, future author, Hal to be, was twelve days old.

Maxwell Evarts Perkins, the celebrated editor at Scribners, who first brought to public attention such writers as Ernest Hemingway, F. Scott Fitzgerald and Thomas Wolfe, characterized his, and my, New England Evarts forebears as "dour, stern and God fearing." As an adult Hal was definitely none of the above. Replying to a stranger who claimed kinship, he wrote, "... certain parties told me that if I did not know my ancestry to look at myself in the glass and if I had thin lips and light green eyes it was almost certain that I sprang from the original Connecticut family. The description fitted. So you might consider my application to the family tree as a thin-lipped green-eyed Evarts." The earliest existent photograph, taken in lacy bonnet and white christening robe, reveals a solemn, chubby and slightly popeyed baby, thereby formalizing the acknowledgement of his small self as a tenth generation Evarts in the New World.

Throughout his life Hal had no interest in his or anyone's genealogy. An unconscious egalitarian, he never sought to trace his ancestral roots. "You can choose your friends," he said frequently, "but you're stuck with your relatives." One aunt, eager to qualify for membership in such organizations as the Colonial Dames and Daughters of the American Revolution, hired a professional genealogist in Boston to research the bloodlines of what Hal referred to with indifference as "my tribe."

The key name was John Evarts, "founder of that family name in New England." Delvers into historical archives differ on a few details but this much seems reasonably certain: John Evarts, of Dutch ancestry, was born in Hertfordshire, England, early in the 17th century, lived for some while in Wales and emigrated to America from the port of Bangor in 1631. Seven years later he was officially "made a freeman" in Concord, Massachussetts, which is to say that he had crossed the Atlantic as an indentured servant and worked off the indebtedness of his passage, a common practice of the times. Still later he settled at Guilford, Connecticut where he bought property, was "appointed tillingman," raised a family and died in 1669.

From these bare bones there emerges a solitary, human flesh-and-blood event, this chilling entry: In 1665 John's daughter Elizabeth married one Peter Abbott, an itinerant farm worker who, according to the Colonial Records of New Haven, had been insane for several years. "Coming thither to help his father weed corn, he was taken the same day with lunacy; which occasioned much charge and exercise to the town, which they conceived should be bourn by the publique." Within two years of the marriage, Abbott murdered his wife and attempted to kill their only child, Hannah, "for which offence he was tried and executed October 16, 1667, in Fairfield," a tragedy that must have shocked the community and hastened John Evarts into his grave. Across the gulf of time one can only speculate. Why did Elizabeth marry a man seen by her neighbors as a "lunatic?" Whatever became of their infant daughter? But on that score history is silent. The stern God fearing Puritans buried their closet skeletons along with their dead.

Evarts men sired large families, a biological necessity in those days of epidemics and limited medical knowledge. My own grandfather, George Alfred, the eldest of eight children, lost three of his siblings to such diseases as typhoid, diphtheria and brain dropsy. For their women, the mothers and child bearers, life must have been physical and emotional hell. Of the first eight male Evartses in my line, six outlived their original wives and remarried, usually within a year or two. Only the hardiest, or the lucky, survived into middle age.

The great majority of this proliferating clan remained in Connecticut for several generations—farmers, artisans, merchants, minor public officials. One, according to family legend, took part in the Boston Tea Party and several soldiered in the Revolutionary War. About my seventh generation ancestor, Eben Bishop Evarts, a few facts are known from his obituary: He was a veteran of the War of 1812, an active Master Mason, father of seven children, died at the age of seventy-eight, "a wiry man large of stature, honest, fearless, independent and true as steel." Eben's son, my great grandfather, George Sylvester Evarts, became the first to quit the Atlantic seaboard permanently.

G. Sylvester's wife, born Harriet Humphrey, came from a more venturesome strain. Two of her Humphrey antecedents fought in the French and Indian War at the capture of Montreal in 1760, and in the Revolution at the siege of Boston and the battle of Long Island. Another, General David Humphrey, served on George Washington's staff and became U.S. Minister to Spain. It might have been this heritage that fortified her willingness to leave the secure family nest with husband and six children for a remote frontier town halfway across the continent. But what enticed G. Sylvester to make such an unprecedented move?

A staunch pillar of his community, he received this farewell accolade from the Hartford, Connecticut, Court of Common Council October 28, 1867: "Whereas Alderman Evarts is about to take his Departure from amongst us and establish his future home in the new and growing state of Kansas and Whereas, during his long residence in this City he has established an enviable reputation as an honest, industrious and skillful Business Man and Fellow Citizen of the Hightest Worth, BE IT THEREFORE RESOLVED that he bear with him our warmest hopes for his future prosperity."

Once arrived in Topeka the ex-alderman left no memorable mark. But Harriet did. A leader in the temperance movement, precursor of the redoubtable Carry Nation, she occupied the position of Grand Worthy Vice Templer of the state and twice was delegate from the Grand Lodge of Good Templers to their National Council. All of which would have amused her future grandson, my Hal, a noted non-templer in ultra "dry" conservative Kansas.

When asked about his background G. Sylvester would reply with that purported sly Yankee wit, "I'm a full blood Mohawk Indian. Not a drop of white blood in my veins." Presumably this was an allusion to his Boston Tea Party ancestor, the participants in which were said to have daubed their faces with paint as a disguise. Harriet bore him two more children, then joined the Great Templer in the sky, shortly after which he remarried, unsurprisingly, a much younger woman and became a speculator in real estate.

To quote again his son Eugene in far off California: "I have not heard from Father since last spring but I expect that Lizzie and him are getting so much real estate in hand that he doesn't find time to write. I wish him all the profits he can get. I guess now is his time if he ever expects to make anything, as Topeka is booming." Like father, like son, boomers both. Like millions of their fellow citizens, they were caught in an irresistible undertow, lured by a dream of all those empty miles, all that unclaimed land stretching to the Pacific. What did flow in Great Grandpa's veins was the westering urge, Manifest Destiny if one prefers; it nurtured the national psyche throughout the 19th century. But whatever "profits" he made therefrom, if any, none trickled down to his Evarts heirs.

Hal knew his father only by hearsay. Later he described George Alfred Evarts as a "professor of languages with a mechanical bent," a bit of pardonable hyperbole. In fact, George did *study* languages; he completed a three-year preparatory course at Washburn College in Topeka in 1871, concentrating on Latin, Greek and mathematics which, for that era and locale, represented a high level of academic achievement. But his pursuit of formal education and a scholarly career ended there. To help support a large family George quit school at seventeen and went to work for the railroad.

As a child of another century, vaguely aware that Grandfather George had been an "engineer" long ago, I had a mental picture of him in bib overalls and a gray billed cap, his face grimy with coal dust, at the throttle of a mighty steam locomotive thundering across the Kansas prairie, framed in the open cab window, blasting a long mournful "hooo-oo-oo-oo" with a yank on the whistle cord. A fanciful image to my boyish mind, one which paled into disillusionment as I grew up and came to realize that Grandfather had been a construction engineer and surveyor, not a hotshot "hogger" on the Atchison, Topeka & Santa Fe.

In the 1870s Topeka was a major division point and the Santa Fe was rapidly expanding its lines into the west. George grew with them, often away from home for months at a time, mounting the ladder of promotion and responsibility. Five years later he married my grandmother, Emma McLaughlin, and in 1881 took her and their daughter on an odyssey that four-year-old Nellie would long remember. They traveled by work train, a private car their home on wheels with a cook to prepare the meals. At night the train parked on sidings, often far from any settlement on the high, lonely western plains. During frequent and protracted halts Nellie would play and pick wild flowers in fields alongside the tracks, until a warning toot summoned her scurrying back aboard. At Isleta in the Territory of New Mexico, as remote then to most Americans as the farthest reaches of Cathay, she and Emma were the first females "to cross the Rio Grande by railroad, riding in the cab of the first engine to feel its way across the newly completed bridge that spanned the river."

Railroading was regarded as a glamorous career for young men in that day and George might have gone far. An early member of the fledgling labor movement, he became treasurer of the local chapter, a so-called "knight" of the Ancient Order of United Workers. But the following year further ecomonic pressures forced him to relinquish his ambitions and quit the Santa Fe to help bail out a struggling short-lived grocery business started by his father. His untimely death in 1887 left his own small family, if not destitute, than genteelly poor.

Widowed at thirty-one, Emma had to scrimp and scrape, hoard every penny. An expert seamstress, she made many of the clothes for herself, Nellie and Hal. Pert, pretty and gregarious, she loved parties and card games and telling stories about her girlhood on an Indiana farm. Her favorite was an account of how she had filed in solemn procession past the open crepe-hung casket of Abraham Lincoln when his funeral train stopped in Indianapolis en route from Washington to Springfield, and she looked down upon the face of the Great Emancipator. This became, in time, *my* favorite story, Honest Abe my first and abiding hero.

To shepherd her little flock through those lean times, Emma had the aid of numerous female relatives, but males on both the Evarts and McLaughlin sides had suffered a high rate of attrition in that generation. As my father put it: "There I was, the sole male infant in a large relationship copiously supplied with girls. Therefore, the surroundings of early family life could scarcely be held accountable for my pronounced preference for outdoor pursuits." One man who did play a vital role in his life was "Granfaddy," Emma's father, John Alexander McLaughlin, a genuine combat infantry colonel in a day when bogus complimentary titles were handed out like passes to the county fair.

About his maternal grandfather Hal wrote: "It is said that he could never be content indoors. As a youth he left the fringes of settlement in Indiana and made his way westward to Texas, there to throw in his lot with the Texans and to fight throughout the Mexican War." This was an example of my father's fertile imagination at work; records show that John McLaughlin was a sergeant in the Fourth Indiana Volunteers in 1847, serving alongside his fellow Hoosiers. Be that as it may, after the war he married the granddaughter of another soldier, Lieutenant John White. White, a Virginia-born Irishman, survived four years of cavalry campaigns during the Revolution, including capture and prisoner exchange by the British, only to be ambushed, tomahawked and scalped by Indians in the Western Border warfare near what is now Lexington, Kentucky. All these twice-told tales Hal absorbed from sundry aunts and senior cousins, which provided grist for a future novel, *Tomahawk Rights*.

But Granfaddy was his principal inspiration, the font of military lore. Elderly and ailing, bedridden most of the time, John McLaughlin enthralled his grandson hour after hour with accounts of the watershed event of his life, the Civil War. For three years he had commanded the 47th Indiana Regiment through some of the fiercest, bloodiest engagements of the western theater, climaxing in the siege of Vicksburg. The great names and battles rolled off his tongue: Grant, Sherman, Pemberton. Yazoo Pass, Fort Pillow, Champion Hills. An old soldier yarning to a rapt, fascinated little boy. I can still visualize my father long years later, then a grown man of thirty-eight, his hand clutching mine, in the National Cemetery on the Mississippi bluffs above Vicksburg beside a monument erected to the memory of the 47th Indiana and Colonel John A. McLaughlin. With tears in his eyes.

Shortly before Hal's fourth birthday Granfaddy died, leaving him a gold watch, his ceremonial sword and dress uniform sash, and to his daughter Emma a bequest of several thousand dollars which considerably eased her financial struggles. He appears to have been the only family member to prosper during those Topeka years, acquiring several lots, a store near the state capitol and a firearms and sporting goods business that became the biggest in Kansas. Which left Hal still another legacy: a lifelong love affair with guns.

In 1891 Topeka was essentially a two-industry town— government and railroads—with a population of some 30,000 clustered in the Kansas (or, as it is called locally, the Kaw) River Valley. Decades before urban sprawl, the surrounding hills were thickly wooded, laced with creeks, abounding in wildlife, with a farm tucked away here and there among the hollows. Described by an early resident as a "Tom Sawyer kind of world," the countryside exerted a magnetic pull on my father from earliest childhood.

". . . of my father's studious tendencies there seemed not a trace," Hal wrote in *On Inspiration's Trail*, an autobiographical piece for the *Saturday Evening Post* in 1926. "My mortal body might be cramped into an undersized school desk upon which reposed the geography or spelling book that should have claimed my undivided interest, but my thoughts were always elsewhere, scouting along some creek in search of a likely place in which to set a trap, flushing imaginary coveys of quail from the hazel brush or jumping cottontails in favored cornfields, lurking in a blind or marsh or sandbar in wait for the hiss of wings that presaged a flock of incoming mallards. Instead of being fired by my father's passion to learn much of everything I refrained from learning much of anything. Many were the pelts of muskrat, possum and civet, many were the squirrels and ducks that I proudly carried home—never once a report card upon which my anxious relatives could discern a trace of hope fulfilled that I might yet become a brilliant scholar. But each year I handed them a pleasant surprise by slipping through by a narrow margin."

Long before Hal attained such wide ranging freedom, he displayed certain nonconformist, somewhat anti-social inclinations. "Brat" seems to have been the family consensus, except for his doting mother, who excused his pranks as "mischievousness." In her fashion Emma tried to cope by withdrawing Nellie from school to baby-sit and oversee little brother. Nellie, a shy, fragile girl, who did inherit her father's scholary inclination, deeply resented this and with just cause. But early on, Hal managed to circumvent most restraints, seeking out a male-only sanctuary at the neighborhood firehouse, where he became a kind of mascot. He listened to the salty talk of the fire laddies, helped groom their horses, shoveled out manure, smoked his first hand-tailored cigarette and gained some elementary knowledge about the birds and the bees, education he never would have received at home or school.

Here is how he recalled his first trapping venture, at the age of six: "The first powerful ambition that claimed me was the desire to possess a gun. In lieu of better armament I went alone with a slingshot and rusty steel trap acquired by barter, and hastened to a small limestone cave about a mile from town that I had discovered earlier. I modestly christened this unpretentious cavern 'Evarts Cave' in honor of myself and carefully placed the trap on the floor. The next day, charged with hopes of bagging anything from a chipmunk to a panther, I approached the spot cautiously with the slingshot held at the ready. Nothing."

After weeks of failure Hal shifted the scene of operations "to a cavity under the roots of a giant elm tree. But hope never died, even though the trap occupied perhaps a dozen different sets in the ensuing six months without yielding a single pelt. Likewise, the desire for a gun, instead of waning, mounted daily, and on occasion I would repair to the gun store that once had belonged to my family and peer enviously through the windows at the noble array of firearms on display."

In his ignorance, my father was nothing if not persistent. As a second grader ". . . my one indoor pastime was the reading of outdoor stories and through this medium I learned for the first time that using bait was a material help in luring fur bearers to a trap. But even this knowledge proved unavailing, and continued lack of success led me to study woodlore. It occurred to me that the principle upon which I had been operating—the larger the hole the larger the prey—was of doubtful value. While meditating upon such matters, I espied a hole scarcely larger than a baseball in the butt of a tree, and observed that it was well worn with much matted hair around its edges. Approaching the tree the following evening with Fox, the alleged hound dog who accompanied me on all my rambles, I riveted my gaze on a moving object there. Fox anticipated me, charged forward with an exultant clamor, disregarding my frenzied commands, and slew a trapped rabbit. I had never before considered a rabbit as a tree-dwelling creature, so this, my first catch, also added another shred of knowledge to my slender store. Swinging the cottontail in one hand and carrying the slingshot in the other, I returned to town covered with rabbit fur, blood and glory—the triumphant huntsman."

Launched now, Hal extended his range, exploring several miles from home. Evarts Cave became his hidey-hole, his secret base, in which he kept a cache of candle stubs and matches, food and a blanket, where he could camp at night, using the ever-loyal Fox as a pillow. This led to frequent truancies, added no luster to his performance at school. He spent more time in the principal's office, he claimed, than in the classroom. But from another source he was learning his first lessons of commerce. "The crisp days of autumn touched the hardwood hills with magic wand. Hackberries, wild grapes and paw-paws ripened under the pinch of frost and I feasted thereon. The hulls of walnuts turned soft and yellow, then black, and my attention veered to gathering them, pounding the outer hull away, spreading the kernels in the sun to dry. Occasional finds of hickory and hazel nuts also fell to my lot. These I peddled to neighbors for twenty-five cents a bushel, immediately invested my returns in another trap and an implement known as a Barlow knife."

At length indulgent, tender-hearted Emma succumbed to his entreaties and agreed to let him have a gun for his ninth birthday, provided he earn the purchase price himself, confident that he would falter and lose interest. But she underestimated her son's single-minded determination. In his words he became a "professional forager of the woodlands." He gathered baskets of dandelions, dock and lambsquarter greens for sale. In the river he caught perch, bullheads and channel catfish that commanded up to a quarter a pound in butcher shops, frogs a dime apiece, and trapped rabbits and squirrels at a nickel per. He met the deadline easily and so became the owner of a single shot .22 rifle. Within the year he added a cheap shotgun to his arsenal and taught himself how to load his own ammunition, enabling him to bag wild ducks for the market at the heady price of forty cents each. The following year he and a friend invested in a rowboat, set up camp along the Kaw far from parental supervision, and passed a glorious profitable summer fishing with set lines several hundred feet long. No steady, plodding town jobs for Hal, no newspaper routes or mowing lawns, the traditional employment of his peers. By age twelve he was in business for himself.

Gradually the environment through which he moved began to pique his curiosity, not merely as a resource to exploit, but as an intellectual challenge. Struck with wonder, he asked himself more and more questions. Why this? Why that? How does such-and-so work? He knew no naturalists, if indeed any existed in Topeka, so he had to provide his own answers by the empirical method.

"The woods were full of interest," he wrote. "Birds congregated in flocks preparatory to flying south. Redwing blackbirds wheeled in smoky clouds above the cattails of the marshes. Most thrilling of all were the strings of ducks and geese that winged down from the north, following the course of the river and lighting on the ponds and sloughs. These mysterious migrants fascinated me. I frequently encountered birds whose names were unknown to me but no books of reference were available. It was impossible to determine which birds constructed nests in tall trees and which in the rank grass of the meadows except through personal observation and careful spying upon their domestic life. Bit by bit I learned their ways."

Later he would study Audubon, Darwin, Huxley and the other greats, but at this stage he was groping for some philosophy, some master scheme that would square with his perception of his tiny cosmos: "I soon became a skeptic, aware that much popularly accepted natural history was actually unnatural. Porcupines did not shoot their quills in self-defense. A hoop snake did not inflate itself and roll downhill, tail in mouth, to assault a victim. The ground hog and his shadow were no longer on the payroll of the Weather Bureau." Later still, near the end of his life, he made this comment in an interview: "I am not by any stretch of the imagination a qualified naturalist. I do not know the scientific name of any creature extant. Much of my knowledge of nature is incomplete and spotted, but what I do know is rooted in my own experience."

Topeka was growing and changing too, but hatreds from the Civil War still ran deep. In the pre-war 1850s, before statehood, Kansas had been "Bleeding Kansas," cockpit and battleground of bitter pro and anti-slavery foes, from whence sprang John Brown and the raid on Harper's Ferry. Topekans did not easily forget that in 1863 her neighbor town of Lawrence had been sacked and burned by a mob of Secesh raiders from Missouri. The Grand Army of the Republic, GAR, veterans of the Union Army, which Granfaddy had staunchly supported, was a potent force in local politics. WASPs ruled the statehouse. Popery, Demon Rum, Populists and Democrats were the enemies. The triple flag of God, Free Enterprise and Republicanism waved over the Valley of the Kaw except for two brief interludes. Many years later I asked my Aunt Nellie if, to her knowledge, any member of our family had ever voted for a Democrat. "Never!" she assured me. "Personally, I would sooner vote for the Devil."

Duly liberated from her bondage as Hal's nominal guardian, Nellie never returned to school but revealed hitherto unsuspected literary talent. "Jingles," she deprecatingly called her first efforts. Self-conscious about her minimal education, she submitted samples to the leading daily newspaper, the *State Journal*, under the pseudonym "Nels Yingle" and became a regular, if unpaid, contributor. Later she wrote some good serious poetry which was not taken seriously by the family. Composing verse—"dabbling"—was considered a suitable activity for Victorian maidens, like crocheting or painting china plates; that a male Evarts should contemplate writing in any guise as a legitimate occupation was unthinkable. Nellie married young, an insurance agent, Edwin C. "Ted" Fox. For Hal's eleventh Christmas the newlyweds gave him a pocket edition of the Bible, which to this day remains in mint unused condition.

His literary tastes ran to Beadle Dime Novels, the "penny dreadfuls," which he traded among his friends and read avidly at the firehouse or behind the barn. He played football with enthusiasm, acquired the nickname "Tack," short for "tackle." He collected bird eggs and U.S. postage stamps, which latter included entire sheets of Confederate issues that Granfaddy had saved from burning by his troops and brought home as wartime souvenirs. He discovered alcohol; on one occasion he and a pal, tipsy on hard cider, were trapped and nearly decapitated by a speeding freight on a railway trestle west of town. But at last he graduated with his eighth grade class from Clay Street Grammar school as he said, "by the skin of my teeth and with great sighs of relief from all concerned."

He labored through his freshman year of high school but then, again in his words, "My affairs took a sudden sharp turn for the worse. Perhaps because I had learned so little that, by reasoning in reverse, I had already acquired all the wisdom that could be taught me. . . . I deserted school forever with the first flight of ducks in the fall." The basic reasons for this decision, or impulse, were more complex.

He was fifteen when his mother remarried, a wealthy widower from Hutchinson, Kansas. The couple departed on an Alaskan honeymoon and shortly thereafter for a trip around the world that lasted some three years, leisurely even in an era of slow boats and horse drawn vehicles. Hal was left behind for safe keeping in the care of Emma's sister and brother-in-law, Aunt Mamie and Uncle James Penney, also of Hutchinson, who ran a much tighter ship than he was accustomed to. This arrangement was a mismatch from the day my father moved in with his traps, precious guns, duck decoys and assorted gear. Sticklers for punctuality and orderliness, the Penneys observed the Sabbath in the fullest sense of the word. Tobacco and spirits were strictly taboo, profanity unheard of, betting on games of chance such as marbles or mumblety-peg in the back yard a sacrilege. Aunt Mamie was not amused by her nephew's life style and deportment. So he soon moved out, out of the house and out of town, severing all family ties, and took off for less circumscribed horizons.

By 1903 the "frontier," that mythic land, the fantasy never-never world beloved by legions of *Leslie's Weekly* Wild West buffs, had vanished, a victim of progress, faded that-away into a sunset of nostalgia. The buffalo were gone, the Indians too, except for a few pitiful remnants penned on reservations, the old cattle trails webbed with fences, the marshals and the gunslingers already enshrined in legend. It was a West in transition, somewhere between the realm of storybook anachronism and harsh reality, ripe for the 20th century Deity of Development. A latecomer to this historical stage, Hal had the curiosity to question senior citizens who enjoyed reminiscing with an impressionable kid gifted with almost total recall.

His flight was not unique. The American West was still sparsely populated; into its vast spaces young males often submerged without trace, then resurfaced years later. Two of my father's uncles did exactly that. One of my mother's cousins, a troubled teenager, ran away from home in the

Chicago suburbs. His father, an affluent doctor, spent thousands of dollars hiring Pinkerton detectives who, nine years later, tracked him down on a Montana ranch. This turn of the century West, so long a kind of national safety valve, now a rapidly filling vacuum, still lured the restless and the romantic, the dispossessed and the delinquent. Which was Hal? Although he never said so, verbally or in print, I am sure he must have felt a hurt, a sense of rejection and possibly failure, a compulsion to prove himself, if only to himself. For better or worse, he was embarked on a course of footloose adventure that led him far afield from his taproots during the next four years.

3.

AFTER A DISAPPOINTING duck hunting season, Hal and a friend made camp on the Arkansas River in the Great Bend region. "Fur sign was plentiful," he wrote, "and one afternoon we put out our traps, an even dozen, all within a half mile of camp in sure-fire muskrat sets. We sat late before the campfire, discussing future prospects, and decided to make a winter of it, moving to new localities as we trapped out the thickest of the fur. My companion had never trapped before and sometime after midnight could restrain his curiosity no longer. So we set out in our boat with a lantern and ran the line. The twelve traps yielded eleven muskrats and one raccoon, the highest percentage of catches in my career."

For the next two months the boys worked their way upriver and "... one memorable morning we bagged two big boar mink within 100 yards of our tent. The weather was cold with occasional flurries of snow and we decided to make one more move before ice closed the river. We pulled the traps and struck camp, packed for an early getaway... but that night snow fell to a depth of 18 inches before dawn. My companion decided to quit trapping forthwith. With our guns and two blankets, each containing a huge bale of furs, we set out for the railroad on foot, caching the rest of our outfit for later retrieval." Much of that experience he later fashioned into *Fur Sign*, which appeared as a magazine serial and became a popular book for boys.

His next move seems out of character but in one context it conformed to family tradition. He signed on for a job with his father's old employer, the Santa Fe, and joined a railroad survey crew in Indian Territory, the last so-designated parcel of land in the continental United States, which soon was to be annexed to the state of Oklahoma by an act of Congress. Oil had been discovered and the northeast corner of Sooner country swarmed with drillers, riggers, shell game promoters and bootleggers trafficking with the original owners, to whom intoxicating liquors were sternly forbidden by the Great White Father. Whiskey running was a major industry. Hal entered this lively milieu with his usual zest and inquisitive turn of mind.

"For seven months," he wrote, "I was faithful custodian of a 12-pound sledge hammer for which I received a recompense of 30 dollars a month, board and free transportation, which last consisted of my chauffeuring a pump handcar from one point to the next. Copan was no more than a tent town and the jail at Ochelata was a one-room affair built by spiking 2' x 4's flatwise upon one another. I was never in it. But I was one of a parched group that watched a federal officer smashing bottles of liquid against it." Evidently my father had graduated from hard cider to stronger beverages. Here he accumulated the material for perhaps his most important novel, *Tumbleweeds*, the story of the great land rush into the Cherokee Strip, which had taken place fifteen years earlier.

By the summer of 1904 he was on the move again with another partner to "gypsy around the country" with a team and wagon. They followed the harvest north into the Dakotas, working eighteen-hour days with threshing and haying crews until, at the onset of cold weather, they split up and Hal returned to the Arkansas when trapping season came round once more. And then? After that, what? Where did he go next? "By the age of 19," he wrote, leaving a three-year hiatus, "I had tracked over much of the West, hunting in the mountains of several states and acquired a store of information about the ways of wild creatures and the workings of nature." About that interval he was maddeningly vague, short on specifics, almost rueful in tone, as though he had some secret or youthful misconduct he preferred to gloss over. He did drop one facetious hint: "...should there occur a reunion of my associates from that period the good townsfolk would turn in a general alarm and call out the militia."

At some point he discovered the Colorado Rockies which "...afforded me the opportunity to cruise the high country with gun, blanket, a pot and frying pan, a little bacon, salt and flour and baking soda, with a fishline wound round my hat. There I saw my first beaver sign and first bear track, shot at my first deer and was so badly afflicted with buck fever that, although I could toss walnuts into the air and break them with a rifle nine times out of ten, I missed an unsuspecting buck at a range of 15 yards. Having known the charm of the hardwood hills in autumn, the subtle drawing power of limitless prairies, the game coverts and salt marshes of the sandhill country, I now felt for the first time the irresistible appeal of the mighty ranges exerting a spell that calls me to this day." I doubt that he ever suffered buck fever again. Before he finally put aside his guns for a camera, he had shot at least one specimen of nearly every big game variety in North America. As for his marksmanship, he became a dead shot, a veritable Daniel Boone with rifle and shotgun, skills I never managed to master, much to his disappointment.

Unquestionably, he spent most of those "missing" years in northwestern Wyoming in the shadow of the magnificent Absaroka Range. This became the setting of his first novel and the site of my first remembered home, and the seed bed for another novel, *The Passing of the Old West*. The one person now alive—he was a small boy then—who knew Hal in that period remembers him as a "likeable kid who could tell wonderful stories" and recalls a rumor that he was "sort of a teenage remittance man" financed by monthly checks from his family to keep him out of trouble. This version falls within the realm of conceivability but seems unlikely. Another old-timer who should know, told me that Hal possibly, even probably, took part in a failed holdup of a small-town South Dakota bank with four daredevil pals. The father of my informant, a member of this quintet, went to his grave with a mysterious unexplained bullet embedded in one kidney. Whatever the truth, Hal's sixteenth, seventeenth, and eighteenth years remain a contradictory muddled chapter.

To borrow a phrase from the California gold rush, I assume he "saw the elephant," meaning that he sampled life in the raw, not just as spectator but as an eager partaker, a spectrum that would have included: saloons, whorehouses, gambling joints, shooting elk for their tusks and consorting with varied gentry who "rode the hoot owl trail," namely on the nether side of the law. In his quintessential novel about Wyoming, *The Cross Pull*, he introduced a character, Teton Jackson, who was an idealized rendering of Butch Cassidy. Butch left the Absaroka country for South America shortly before my father's arrival, but Hal knew many intimate details of his life decades before that outlaw became a national folk hero.

Wyoming's wild and woolly era of range wars, train robberies, bank holdups and wholesale homicides was drawing to a close. But that same year a young man from Troy, New York, Fred Richard, who had come west to make a fresh start and was soon to befriend my father, on his first night in the cow town of Meeteetse witnessed a gun battle that left three men dead on the street. The following year, 1903, Tom Horn, Wyoming's notorious contract killer who bragged of bushwhacking suspected rustlers for $500 fees, was hanged in Cheyenne after a sensational trial. A few months after that Hal, age sixteen, first appeared on this sometime violent scene. Another young man, who shall be nameless, widely believed to have been Horn's sidekick, who himself had shot six men at an early age, became one of my father's lifelong friends. "One of the nicest fellows I ever met," Hal wrote about this individual some twenty years later, praising him in the pages of the *Post*.

The man who had the most profound influence on Hal's life was Ned W. Frost, son of a professional bear hunter. By the age of ten Ned had become a commercial hunter himself for his father's stagecoach station on the Meeteetse road. His job was to provide fresh meat, deer and elk and antelope, daily table fare for the stage line's hungry passengers. Once every winter he and his brother filled two freight wagons with frozen carcasses, made the rugged drive north to Billings, Montana, and traded their cargo for a year's supply of staples. In retrospect the thought makes any conservationist shudder but in those days game abounded in seemingly inexhaustible supply and, so went the rationale, why not make use of what the Lord provided? After the stagecoach era ended Ned acquired his own ranch in partnership with Fred Richard and became a guide. He took Hal under his wing and taught him the art of conducting moneyed eastern sportsmen on hunting forays into the mountains. The mystique of big game trophy bagging in the wide-open West, glamorized by the exploits of such as "Buffalo Bill" Cody and Teddy Roosevelt, was at its height. So my father, too, became a guide, a fast learning novice, and fell in love with what he called the "Land of Many Rivers," much of it then a semi-wilderness.

One of these, the Stinking Water, so called because of sulfurous fumes emitted by thermal springs along its lower course, had been renamed "Shoshone" by an act of the state legislature in 1901, to which one official objected as "a gross injustice to the truth." Here in the valley of the North Fork, the eastern gateway to Yellowstone Park, a scenic wonderland of red sandstone formations, volcanic dikes and towering snow-crowned 12,000-foot peaks, Hal found his Nirvana. It was remote, sparsely settled, far from any urban center, served by an execrable single-track road. There were no stores, no mail delivery. The few valley dwellers bought their supplies in the county seat of Cody, a two-day roundtrip. During these outings, often family affairs, the men customarily bedded their wives and children at the storied Irma Hotel and "went out on the town." As late as 1920, when I was five years old, upstairs with my mother one night, a drunken celebrant shot up the lobby. More extensive shopping sprees, involving a ride on the Chicago, Burlington & Quincy spur line to the metropolis of Billings, might occupy as much as a week.

The majority of North Fork residents were reasonably sober, peaceful-minded, industrious ranchers, but the valley's isolation inevitably attracted a certain element who valued their privacy and, for reasons best known to themselves, kept a low profile. There was, for example, Billy Green, some of whose land Hal was to buy years later; Billy sold out in 1907 and moved to Alaska because of "too many people moving in, getting too crowded." And a cast of characters that included: Sam Barry, an alleged human bounty hunter; Jimmy "The Tough" Tuff, convicted horse thief; "Hurricane" Bill Herrick, who answered to more than one name, died with his boots on and was left refrigerated in a snow bank by his buddies until the conclusion of a three-day poker game; Hardy Shull, moonshiner, who made "really good whiskey, not rotgut"; Hardy's rival, Jack Spicer, who died with three bullets in his chest in a shootout with a nephew; Earl Crouch, gold miner, who "took one drink too many, went to bed and never woke up." All of these and more, with whom my father had at least a passing acquaintance. Jack Richard, Fred's son, a photographer and historian, who probably knows the area and its people as well as anyone, put it this way: "Back then it was every man for himself, any way to survive and make a dollar. There was no law in Park County west of Cody."

Hal seems to have thrived in this atmosphere and acquired his ultimate education. So why did he go back to straight-laced flatland Kansas from which he had fled four years earlier as a rebellious juvenile? His memoir provides not even a clue: "I returned to the town where my mother was living, a prodigal with no great evidence of material success, and settled down to a more or less normal business career. Hope for my case was slightly revived in the breasts of friends and well wishers." He once told a Los Angeles *Times* columnist that he had saved $200 with which to make an impressive triumphant reentry, but lost it all within an hour on "galloping dominoes" (*i.e.*, shooting craps).

Emma and her second husband, Leander Adams Bigger, had returned from their extended honeymoon and this remarkable man took an interest in his fiddle-footed stepson. Born on an Ohio farm, Lee Bigger enlisted in the Union cause in 1861 as a sixteen-year-old schoolboy. At war's end he was mustered out as a battle-hardened first lieutenant of infantry, after a brief incarceration in the infamous Confederate Libby Military Prison in Richmond. He studied law at the University of Michigan and later followed his star to the budding hamlet of Hutchinson, became a real estate developer, co-founder of the town's first bank and, later, four-time mayor. As he told Hal, "In my day I made three fortunes and lost two-and-a-half of them." Now in his sunset years, he was engaged in compiling a four-volume account of his foreign travels entitled, "Around the World with a Businessman," which he had printed at his expense. Three-quarters of a century later this work—his own, not the by-product of some literary ghost—is still eminently readable, learned, sparkling with dry humor.

In a rare personal note Lee Bigger added: "I have met and shaken hands with all the Presidents from Lincoln to Roosevelt and have enjoyed each meeting. When I grasped Lincoln's hand the shadow of civil war hung heavy over the land. He was not then the great man he became, but the touch of his fingers and one glance from his eyes made me more loyal and I felt I had a friend in Court. Plenty of epaulettes and gold lace were there; he was the only man plainly dressed. I was little more than a boy then, and regretted not having bought a new suit of clothes for the occasion."

My father was welcomed back into the family bosom but the path of his conversion to solid citizen was one of zigs and zags. Rather than move into the Bigger household, he helped set up a residence known as the "Bachelors' Roost"—named after Butch Cassidy's Utah hideout—for himself and other congenial young blades. The parties and goings-on at the Roost raised eyebrows all over town. He went to work for the Hutchinson *Daily Gazette* which, according to a fellow employee, was a "one horse paper edited by Sheridan Ploughe. Ploughe was author of *The Chisholm Trail* and other historical notations. Hal was the print shop's devil during the day until the sheet went to bed, and then he was the mail clerk. But he didn't take to the mechanics of the print shop. His whole soul and thoughts were out in the hills, down by the river or out in the fields—with nature. He had visions of stories he wanted to tell. Maybe Hal got his first ideas about writing from Ploughe."

Hal inherited his mother's gift for impromptu story telling. Endlessly inventive, he could entertain guests at the dinner table or strangers anywhere. One turn of the spigot and he gushed forth. His use of language was decorous, spiced with an occasional "hell" or "damn" to capture the vernacular. The explicit vocabulary of his grandchildren, born years after his death, would have shocked him, the women's liberation movement have defied his comprehension. The female characters in his stories, the mandatory love interest, were stick figures on a pedestal, scatter-brained but paragons of virtue, invariably "ladies" or "good scouts." The only real woman in his adult life, Sylvia, he did not regard in any such simplistic terms but, like his heroes, he remained a straight arrow, nonphilandering, monogamist. The depth of his feeling for her I cannot judge but, so far as I know, he never had an affair or even a flirtation after his marriage. His self-image as an iconoclastic maverick notwithstanding, Hal was a conservative at heart, true to his class in terms of morality, sexuality and politics; in many respects an old-fashioned "square."

After six months in the newspaper business, he turned to greener pastures. "... it was conceded that as a real estate salesman I gave promise of some moderate success. I took a small flyer and for some time speculated on a shoestring, but when the local market slackened I disposed of my few holdings.... my way led on through several live western towns where booms were in progress." His mother must have thrown up her hands in resignation, or despair.

His first port of call was Billings, where a subdivision fell through, and then on to Twin Falls, Idaho, again too late. The bubble there had burst. He saw a potential, however, filed on a homestead and invested some of his slender capital—his capital was always "slim" or "thin" or "meager"—in that year's bumper crop of potatoes. "My prospects seemed rosy," he wrote, "and I stopped rolling my own cigarettes and occasionally sported a prosperous looking cigar." But this venture failed when a temporary shortage of freight cars developed and left him, literally, holding the bag. There were other towns, other schemes, involving real estate bonds and irrigation projects and, in one unlikely instance a washing machine franchise, all of which seemed to tiptoe along the tightrope of legality. From these enterprises came one solid if long delayed dividend: a *Saturday Evening Post* story about con game land swindles. It had the ring of authenticity; the author knew whereof he wrote.

For a second time he returned to Hutchinson, somewhat wiser, perhaps, but in no way bowed, lured by another "opportunity." "Certain people," he wrote, "were floating a chain department store proposition, and they discerned in me the makings of a future merchant prince." He invested some more of his capital and became the local assistant manager. But after a few months, convinced that his boss was a crook, Hal threatened him with public exposure in the press, and possibly worse, and got his money back.

"Can you imagine your father as a clerk waiting on ladies in a department store?" my mother once asked me, years later. Sylvia, on her first visit to Hutchinson, a guest of the Biggers, had stopped by her future husband's place of business and saw "... his mouth full of pins, his face like thunder, scowling at some silly woman who had made him undo half a dozen shirtwaists she had no intention of buying. He could have strangled her."

No, I couldn't imagine it then, nor can I now. Nor can I see him in the next scene, his own shoe store, straddling a stool all day fitting shoes on customers. "He hated it, every minute," Sylvia told me. That I can believe, especially his reaction to women who, in his jaundiced view, "could never make up their damn minds!" My father a misogynist? I think not. He was, simply and understandably, more comfortable in male company. After all, he had grown up in a "relationship copiously supplied with girls."

About 1887 Lee Bigger had constructed a large handsome house (since designated an historic landmark of the Ute Pass area) at 7,000 feet in the Front Range above Colorado Springs as a retreat in which to escape the blistering Kansas summer heat. Here, near the village of Cascade on the flank of Pikes Peak, Hal discovered another sanctuary of sorts. He came often, in all seasons, whenever possible, to work at self-assigned chores and tramp about the mountains, with or without a gun. He found peace, quiet, majestic beauty and freedom from day-to-day anxieties about the future of a young man going nowhere. It was an appropriate setting for the first and only love story of his life.

While building a rock wall one July afternoon in 1910, he happened to glance across Cascade Creek and noticed two young women strolling along the path. He took a second look, turned to a friend and declared, "You see those two over there? The short pretty one, that's the girl I'm going to marry."

Apocryphal? Love at first sight? Fairy tale or fact? Did he actually say that, out of the blue? I have it on good authority that he did. On the other hand it seems improbable, the romantic improvisation of a future fiction writer, given my father's penchant along those lines. Who knows? But, sentimentalist that I am, I like to believe the story contains a nubbin of truth.

Sylvia Abraham was nineteen that summer, three years younger than Hal. She had completed her freshman year at Kansas University, following a year at National Park, a private "finishing" school for young ladies in Washington, D.C. A 1908 graduate of Kansas City, Kansas, High School, she was depicted in her senior annual the *Jayhawker* in this highfalutin poesy:

> A damsel of high lineage, and a brow
> May blossom and a cheek of apple blossom,
> Hawk eyed; and lightly was her slender nose
> Tip-tilted, like the petal of a flower.

In the humor section her favorite song was listed as "Waltz Me 'Round Again, Willie."

Hal became her instant Willie. He was smitten.

Somehow he wangled an introduction and was in turn introduced to her family, vacationing in Cascade—Mother, Father and Big Sister, who quickly sized up Sylvia's first "serious beau." She had been overshadowed all her life by her older sister Lillian, "Lala," nine inches taller, regal in manner, brainy, a smashing beauty who attracted suitors galore. But this was to be Sylvia's season in the sun, her turn to glow in the aura of a man whose background, tastes and outlook were alien to her own. She was a sheltered city girl; as the expression went, "in society."

Delighted, the Biggers threw open their home and Lee made his chauffeur-driven Winton Six available to her relatives. There were picnics, horseback outings, supper parties with games and dancing to Victrola records, an overnight junket to the summit of Pikes Peak by tallyho. Hal was in his element as a tour guide, knowledgeable about the flora and fauna and the history of Colorado's ghost town mines, stepson of the resident squire showing off for his beloved. Sylvia's cousin, Evan Browne, then twelve, remembers the summer well. "I met Hal first, before the family," he said, "when he took me and another boy rock climbing. He knew everything about nature, was kind and patient and never condescending to a kid. He loved the outdoors. I thought he was great. After he met Sylvia, though, he didn't have much time for me."

Sylvia's mother, Cora, had some reservations. Born a Leland, daughter of a distinguished judge and proud of her Colonial credentials, Cora had lofty standards where her daughters were concerned. As prospective in-laws the Biggers passed with high marks, but Hal rated about C- on her scale. He was reputedly "fast," had a murky past and in no respect measured up to the bright, promising young business and professional men who came calling back in Kansas City. His relationship with Cora was to be thorny for the duration. Emma, less exacting, was entranced by the prospect of Sylvia as a daughter-in-law. Was her son about to forswear his nomadic ways, marry a respectable girl, settle down at last and raise a family? But she did have one latent doubt. Sylvia, raven-haired, doe-eyed, with a somewhat prominent nose and what might be described as a Mediterranean complexion, was patently no fair Anglo-Saxon flower. Abraham? Wasn't that a Jewish name?

The forebears of Andrew Abraham, Sylvia's paternal grandfather, were as Dutch as Edam cheese, faithful of the Dutch Reformed Church. Andrew graduated from Amherst Seminary in 1849, married fellow seminarian Sarah Biddle so they could embark as man and wife upon a life of missionary devotion among the heathen, and sailed for South Africa one week later. After a harrowing six-month voyage, they reached the nascent port of Durban on the Indian Ocean and set up the mission station of Mapumulo fifty miles back in the bush. There, among the Zulus, my grandfather Charles Edward was born and his parents died, as he said, of "sheer loneliness."

As a teenager during the Zulu War, he drove an ox team hauling freight for the British Army, and made enough money to return to his native land. He studied pharmacy at the New York State Normal School in Albany and opened a drug store in Kansas City. For years one wall of this building bore the prominent numerals "64," the commercial logo of an effective and popular laxative Charles developed in his basement. This was a matter of vast embarrassment to his wife and daughters, one never mentioned in my presence. About his life in Africa my grandfather was even more reticent than was Hal about his early Wyoming years. Whenever the subject arose he spoke in terms of melancholy, as if he harbored a host of painful memories. Missionary-born, he became a conspicuous and dedicated abstainer from all church activities, another source of embarrassment to my grandmother Cora.

In 1904 he took his womenfolk to the Louisiana Purchase Exhibition in St. Louis, which coincided with the third International Olympic Games being held in that city. He watched the marathon, described by an observer as "the most bizarre race ever to take place on American soil." It was the first Olympic event in which black Africans participated; of the two Zulu runners entered, one—a tribesman named Lentauw—finished ninth, even though he was chased off the course and through a cornfield by two dogs. Afterward my grandfather visited the so-called Zulu Village, part of the British Boer War exhibit, a sad little assemblage of black men and scruffy grass huts, not unlike a "Wild Man from Borneo" freak sideshow. When Charles spoke to the poor bewildered souls in their mother tongue and tried to comfort them, they burst into tears, creating such a commotion that police had to be called in to restore order.

Sylvia's other grandfather, Pardon Kimball Leland, also departed the eastern seaboard by sailing vessel in 1849 but marching, one might say, to a different drummer. Bound for California around the Horn at twenty-one, he spent two years grubbing for gold on the North Fork of the American River near Auburn and, like the great majority of '49ers, found only disappointment. Broke and homesick, he returned by Nicaragua, crossing the isthmus in a dugout canoe where he nearly died of yellow fever. During this entire period he wrote a daily journal which, once home, he kept under lock and key. A quarter century after his death my grandmother and her sister burned the only copy because, as they announced to our astounded family, it contained what these two pious ladies considered some "objectionable" material. Thus was lost a first-hand report on one of the great American experiences by a literate, educated—Amherst and Brown University graduate—observer. Hal was livid when he learned of this; of a long list of grievances against his mother-in-law it was the heaviest.

Grandpa Pardon, descendant of Lelands who arrived at Plymouth Colony aboard the Mayflower II, went west again, this time only as far as Illinois. He studied law, became absorbed in politics and was elected a county judge. An organizer of the Lincoln-Douglas debates of 1858, he stumped the state for Douglas and knew Lincoln well. Of his three children the eldest, my great-uncle Kimball, established a successful medical practice in the Chicago suburbs and then—horror of horrors—committed an unforgivable solecism: he married a Catholic. Thereupon he and his unmentionable wife became not only family outcasts, but non-persons. I was sixty years old before I learned that an Uncle Kimball and his runaway son had ever existed.

Such was the nature of the strictly orthodox Protestant family that Hal hoped to enter. He was on the threshold of another "investment" that summer. "Why it seemed that fortune still beckoned me into merchandising is now obscure," he wrote, "but I purchased a bill of shoes and opened a small retail store. For several years this afforded a moderate livelihood and served to double my capital." To relieve the tedium he hired a local pugilist to instruct him and a few chums in the manly arts of self-defense during the lunch hour in his storeroom. But during the next two years most of his energies were devoted to the pursuit of Sylvia.

That fall she returned to college, joined her sister's sorority and, universally popular, was swept up on a social merry-go-round of dates, dances, fraternity hi-jinks and chaperoned house parties—a world unknown and inaccessible to Hal. He must have writhed with resentment and jealousy. And Sylvia, on her part, may have been a deliberate tease, blowing warm and cool, confident in her new-found power to ensnare a man.

The following summer Cora shunned Cascade and installed her family on the western slope of the Front Range at Grand Lake. But Hal turned up there, with or without an invitation, to escort Sylvia on hikes and horseback rides, along with a mountaineer known as "Squeaky Bob." Under an alias, Squeaky Bob appeared in the *Post* in several reincarnations. Throughout that year and the next love letters flowed in spate between my future parents, from Hutchinson to Kansas City and back, with Hal pressing his suit, Cora pressing her daughter to say nay. Sylvia, a dutiful, compliant child, was torn. Later, after he sold his first story, she made a part-time career of record keeping, saving every letter, clipping and memento, down to and including my school report cards. But of their courtship correspondence not one scrap remains.

For the summer vacation of 1912 Cora mapped her strategy well in advance. Avoiding the state of Colorado, she established herself and her daughters in southern California, at a hotel overlooking Santa Monica Bay. Now, far away, she had that pesky, tenacious young Evarts at a geographical disadvantage vis-a-vis sweet Sylvia. But then, as they used to say in old-time, silent movie captions: "Fate intervened."

Nearby Hollywood, recently incorporated into Los Angeles, was a sleepy little enclave of bungalows, orange groves, pepper trees and dusty roads. It was also the western cradle for the infant motion picture industry. On the second day Sylvia was approached by two glib young men who introduced themselves as movie producers. They had seen her at the beach and, *mirabile dictu*, came to the conclusion that she had promise as an actress. Would she try out for a role in their new two-reel epic? Flustered by this overture, which could have been a scene from some flickery melodrama, she obediently reported the incident to Mother. In time it became a family joke, one in which Sylvia could laugh at herself. Did she have star quality? *If* she had accepted, gone before a camera in costume and grease paint, would she have become another Mary Pickford, say, or a slinky vamp like Theda Bara? She never had the chance to find out. Thoroughly alarmed, Cora packed up her two girls and moved a hundred miles south to a more secluded beach resort, beyond the reach of temptation and corruption. Eighteen years later, Sylvia earned five dollars as a sun-bonneted extra in a mob scene for a day's work in one of Hal's movies. But by then opportunity had passed her by.

Big sister Lala, "Sis," was twenty-four that August, still unbetrothed, which in some eyes qualified her as an old maid. Today, we'd say she was waiting for Mr. Right to come along. On her first day in the village of La Jolla, she met her future in the person of a handsome bank cashier. Their romance blossomed overnight. Before the month was out they announced their engagement, with Cora's blessing. "Sis would have married almost any man who would take her out of Kansas City," my mother told me later, not without a touch of malice. "She felt smothered there, ashamed of it. She could never understand why Father, of all places, chose Kansas City, Kansas."

However Sylvia felt about the Sunflower State, a submissive mouse she was not. Some time during those weeks in La Jolla her resolve hardened. She determined that this once she would not let Sis upstage her, would not play second fiddle in the mating game. They were a Mutt and Jeff odd couple, these two sisters, both physically and psychologically. At 5'10" Lala towered over most of her schoolmates. On her high school basketball team, she was so overpowering the coach made her sit on the bench the second half of every game to give the other girls a chance. Sylvia never went out for sports. In the classroom Lala earned straight A's; Sylvia B's. Lala had the admirers; Sylvia won the friends. It could not be called a sibling rivalry because my mother was a non-competitor, but a modified love-hate relationship, unspoken and probably unrecognized, existed between them throughout their long lives, exacerbated to a state of red alert when they lived together as widows in their eighties.

"Your mother married me out of pure spite," Hal once told me. And laughed.

On the last day of November Lala married her banker. On New Year's Eve Sylvia married Hal. For three solid months a seamstress had been at work in the house making the two trousseaux. Cora and Charles must have been reeling from this one-two punch, emotionally, physically and financially, after staging two big, expensive weddings so close together. So, on New Year's Day, 1913, my parents set out, not into the sunset, but on the midnight train in a Pullman lower berth. The second night, their first in their Hutchinson home, Hal's cronies from the Bachelors' Roost welcomed them with a rousing shivaree that rattled the windows.

4.

AS A WEDDING GIFT Lee Bigger gave them rent-free occupancy of his house for an indefinite stay, while he and Emma resumed their travels. Two weeks later he wrote from Los Angeles, "I hope each of you is enjoying married life, which is the only sane life to lead." Hal never heard from him again. Not long afterward Lee died of a cerebral hemorrhage in California, a few years too soon to see the young vagabond whom he had grown to love as a son, on whom he had lavished his encouragement and support, burst upon the national arena as a best selling author.

Sylvia could have lived out her life in contentment as the wife of a small town merchant. Due both to the Bigger connection and her own sunny personality, she won immediate acceptance by the "right" people, the "in" crowd, the movers and shakers whose doings filled the news and society columns. No social climbing necessary, thank you; she was already there. "There" in the second decade of this century was a county seat of some 17,000, its economy fueled by wheat and salt. Less parochial and partisan than Topeka, Hutchinson had a certain ambiance unusual in the central farm belt, often noted by visitors. The well-to-do sent their children to private schools, traveled abroad, subscribed to eastern newspapers, bought books in quantity, furnished their homes from shops in New York and San Francisco. A small island of the privileged few, placid and self-satisfied, it suited my mother perfectly.

Hal, however, grew increasingly restive. He hired an assistant to operate the store during his frequent absences and, that fall, introduced his bride to duck hunting at Little Salt Marsh west of town. In the dead of winter he took her trapping along the Arkansas where, surprised by a storm, they spent a snowbound week in a tent. If "good sport" Sylvia uttered any complaints I never heard. Their next outing, a honeymoon postponed for one reason or another, would have occurred only to Hal. Niagara Falls? Atlantic City? The Grand Canyon? To some other idyllic spot favored by young lovers? Not on your tintype. In the spring of 1914 he took my mother, who had never held a rifle in her hands, on a bear hunt in Wyoming. They headquartered at the guest ranch of his old mentor, Ned Frost, twenty-five miles west of Cody, his favorite stamping ground of yore. For three weeks they crisscrossed the mountains with a pack string, camping each night in freezing temperatures. Unsuccessful at first, on the final day they struck a bonanza: four bears. Hal insisted that Sylvia shot one her very own self, which had to be a fabrication.

During that trip two further events that were to alter their lives took place: (a) Sylvia got pregnant. (b) Hal changed careers. The latter was a ticking bomb that when detonated almost blew their marriage apart. The honeymoon, he wrote, "... brought on my complete relapse. The shoe business was sold and I went to Wyoming to start what was probably the first fur farm in the northwest United States ... at that time the only one within a thousand miles. At the age of twenty-six, at which period most men are contemplating entering business, I retired." And there his autobiography ends.

In less elliptical language this is what happened: Hal bet his entire stake on one longshot, all-or-nothing roll of the dice. He bought 120 acres of sagebrush and meadowland, plus a ramshackle structure lacking every amenity but four walls and a quaint gambrel roof that leaked, on the market because the lady of the house found the location too lonely and refused to live there any longer. The package included partial riparian rights to Green Creek which flowed, when not frozen, through the property, and the mailing address of Wapiti, the Indian word for "elk." He then contracted with an eastern breeding farm for delivery of 250 six-month-old skunks and 250 red and silver fox pups. The verdict of friends and family was unanimous: an idiotic scheme doomed to failure.

Hal was present for my birth in Hutchinson in early 1915, then hurried back to Wapiti to build pens for his animals and ready the house for Sylvia and me. His one attempt at hanging wallpaper was a fiasco, and the cellar furnace broke down, never to be repaired. His mother had bought and shipped ahead by rail an automobile, his first, a four-cylinder Buick open touring model with isinglass panels that could be snapped on during bad weather which, according to Hal, meant "eight months every year." He taught himself to drive on the wicked cliff-hugging shelf of a road that led up Shoshone Canyon toward our ranch, backing up whenever he met oncoming horse teams which had inviolable right of way. Our infrequent visitors from Kansas were terrified by that canyon passage (described in a 1982 Cody Chamber of Commerce brochure as an "unforgettable experience") and so was I when I grew older.

Six weeks later in chilly March, my mother and I arrived aboard the one-a-day mixed jerkwater train that linked Cody to the outside world. All I can say with certainty about that landmark day is that my father did not carry her over the threshold of our home.

We lived there for three and a half years. My earliest memories, obviously, do not run on an orderly, continuous time track with cause and effect melding into a sequential whole. I have, instead, a kind of mental mosaic of bits and pieces, random snippets, far from complete. Our house had no plumbing; chamber pots and a privy served. Water came from the creek, in buckets, often in the form of ice that had to be melted. No electricity, no telephone. A wood burning kitchen stove with upstairs vents provided heat; Hal provided the wood with saw and axe, a never ending task. A Holstein cow, Old Pet, provided fresh milk—another of Hal's daily chores. One of my most vivid pictures is of Sylvia boiling huge pots of cornmeal mush fortified with chunks of elk liver, which he carried out to feed the skunks and foxes behind the house. I do not recall the winter weather specifically but temperatures of 40 degrees below zero were not unknown.

That June, when all roads were hub deep in mud from spring runoff, we had our first visitors, Charles and Cora, who came to inspect what their son-in-law had wrought. It far exceeded Cora's darkest expectations; she was appalled to see her dear little Sylvia and four-month-old grandson subjected to such privations. Margaret Richard, co-hostess of the Frost and Richard ranch down the road, where my grandparents were domiciled, witnessed the final showdown.

"Your grandma was in tears," she told me. "Sylvia was in tears. Hal and your grandpa were trying to calm their two hysterical women. You were just a little bundle asleep in a basket. Your grandma begged Sylvia to pack up and bring the baby back home to Kansas City where she belonged. Sylvia wept and clung to your father. She said she had to stick by him. I was proud of her."

So Sylvia stuck. That crossroads behind her, she would always remember her Wyoming years as the happiest, richest and most exciting of her life. Hal's long-range plan called for a four-year holding pattern until his stock matured; their fur would then be prime, ready to sell. Meanwhile his cash flow was nil. To earn a few extra dollars he ran a trap line each fall. In the summer he raised alfalfa. All year long, as occasion required, he poached out of season, a practice widespread among North Fork residents, game wardens being nonexistent.

In winter social concourse slowed to a trickle; winter was survival time. But summer brought an influx of guest ranch dudes and swarms of tourists who were transported to Yellowstone Park, forty miles west of Wapiti, in boxy Service buses that churned up clouds of dust which coated our house from late June through September. The road passed a few yards from our modest front porch, and one driver with an antic sense of humor often would brake to a stop on our doorstep, pick up his megaphone and regale his passengers with the misinformation that, "This here, folks, is the first and only skunk farm in the State of Wyoming. Look over yonder and you can see the little critters in their pens. But better hold your noses. They stink." Smirk, chuckle, followed by nervous laughter. This notoriety mortified Sylvia. But Hal found it amusing. On one occasion he stepped out on the porch, doffed his Stetson and made a sweeping bow, to loud applause. As a matter of fact, his skunks, most of which he surgically sanitized to render them odorless, were not the familiar back-striped variety but a special breed known as "stars," charcoal black with a tiny white forehead blaze, whose pelts were quite valuable, or would be someday.

One minor setback did occur during his first year, a possible portent of future events. Somebody deliberately unfastened the door to one of his pens, part of an ever-expanding complex down the creek, and several young skunks escaped. Hal accepted the loss philosophically, writing a friend that, "I'm pretty sure that I know the party responsible but he's since quit the country accused of slow-elking," a local euphemism for shooting another man's beef, one crime not tolerated anywhere in Wyoming.

City girl Sylvia had another embarrassing lesson to learn. Because our front yard, a barren expanse devoid of brush and trees, was the sunniest spot nearby, she rigged up her first clothesline there and hung out our weekly wash to dry, alongside the road. Practically all valley freight was hauled by teams. In the prevailing west wind the family sheets, petticoats and long johns flapped and snapped like demented ghosts, a frightsome spectacle to mountain-bred horses and mules. After two near-catastrophic runaways and furious teamster protests, Hal selected another drying yard far from the house and carried out the laundry himself.

A frequent year-around visitor was a cowboy named Shorty Kelly, bronc buster and wrangler, who referred to me as "Some Bum Kid," which did not endear him to my mother. "I wish you could see Shorty at the table," Hal wrote. "He has abominable manners. I don't know when he took his last bath. Whenever Sylvia sees him riding toward our house she hurries out and picks a bunch of paint brush or lupin and plops down a vaseful in the middle of the table so she won't have to watch him face to face. He doesn't eat his food. He annihilates it. Slurp, slurp and it's gone. Then he belches and goes to work with a toothpick." Shorty Kelly, or a reasonable facsimile, turned up in *The Settling of the Sage* and several short stories.

Tales of Shorty's horsemanship still survive along the North Fork. According to one old timer, Shorty (his initials were B.C.; no one ever learned his given name), son of a minister in a small Pennsylvania town, broke into his father's store of sacramental wine one night, got roaring drunk and disgraced himself in public, was so ashamed that he fled on the next freight train heading west. Eventually he drifted into Wapiti where he found a permanent job, and home, at the Frost and Richard ranch. It was his boast that he could ride "anything with hair on." He told Ned Frost that the first time a horse, any horse, threw him was the day he would quit for good. Reportedly he kept his vow. Some years later, after our family had moved away, when Shorty was well into his forties he met his nemesis: a bronc pitched him off in the corral. In the best of true-blue western tradition, he picked himself up out of the dust, collected his pay and departed Wyoming, never to sit a saddle again.

During our second summer at Wapiti, in August 1916, Ned Frost had a near brush with tragedy, an episode that I was too young to remember but often heard Hal relate in gory detail. The veteran guide-hunter was camped with several dudes a few miles east of Lake Junction in Yellowstone Park, when a grizzly attacked the party one night and dragged a man out of his sleeping bag by the shoulder. Ned intervened, was bitten in the thigh and nearly bled to death before a doctor arrived from the Lake Hotel. The bear escaped, killed another man three weeks later, before it was finally destroyed, an enormous creature that Hal recreated in his first short story for the *Post*, *The Bald Face*.

Although the North Fork remained largely a domain unto itself, and would until the end of World War II, a number of changes had taken place since Hal's earlier sojourn there. Not only had the road become a thoroughfare to Yellowstone in 1916, albeit a grueling one, but the valley could now boast a schoolhouse, a postal service of sorts and its first telephone. Three times a week, weather permitting, mail was delivered to the imposing home of Dwight Hollister, wealthy gentleman rancher, a *cum laude* graduate of Princeton who often appeared in a black and orange sweater with a "P" emblazoned across his chest, the only Ivy League alumnus for miles around. Hal remembered one New Year's Eve when, after the ladies retired, he and Hollister consumed "a bottle of French brandy, four bottles of champagne and a lot of Havana cigars." There were still no stores, no church, no doctor, but Ned Frost's wife Mary, a licensed nurse, dealt with every emergency from infant colic to gunshot wounds. "Aunt Mary," a formidable figure, scolded Hal about his drinking and urged him to write down some of his endless tales. To her suggestions he turned a deaf ear.

Another friend recalls one occasion when he was entertaining several Frost dudes at the table just before lunch was served. In mid-recital Hal absently reached out and picked up an empty water glass, raised it to his lips, threw back his head, took several swallows of air, returned the glass to the table and resumed his tale with scarcely a break in the narrative flow. The dudes watched this virtuoso performance goggle-eyed, ready to believe almost anything about wondrous Wyoming.

"Your father was a nonstop talker. Most big talkers are bores but he was always entertaining. Two minutes after he came into a room everyone was listening to him. Jokes? No, he didn't tell jokes. What he told were true stories, or what sounded true." This from Ethel Montgomery who at ninety-three could recall her early days in the valley with crystal clarity. Ethel and her husband Oscar were newlyweds, employed at the Frost ranch as cook and foreman respectively in 1915 when Sylvia and Hal moved to Wapiti, and the two young couples became, in her words, "dearest friends. We drove up and down the valley in their new car—Oscar and I couldn't afford one in those days—visiting neighbors and going to all night dances at the schoolhouse. Your mother carried you everywhere because then mothers nursed their babies for a long time. Your parents were very popular and Sylvia was so pretty, so kind to everyone. She was a lady. I loved her. But yes, she did get lonely, though she tried hard not to show it. Once when Hal and Oscar came home after hunting for several days she was so glad to see him she cuddled up in his lap like a kitten. They were real lovey-dovey, those two."

Hal had another ongoing project which, in a curious roundabout fashion, was to affect his future. The Homestead Act of 1862, which afforded citizens the opportunity to buy 160 acres of government land at a giveaway price, did more to tame the American West than the six-gun or the plow; it was still operative in 1916. He filed papers on an abandoned quarter section and a primitive shack several miles higher up on Green Creek. To secure legal title he had to make certain improvements and establish some record of residence. To meet this latter requirement—since he could not be in two places simultaneously—he fell back on a standard tactic: he hired a live-in representative, in this case a former employee from his shoe store.

Wallace Hinkle, a young bachelor, was a western fiction junkie. Evidently he dwelt in a fantasy world of Ned Buntline paperbacks peopled by larger-than-life figures such as Jim Bridger, Sundance Kid and the Hole-in-the-Wall Gang. Writing from Hutchinson, he implored my father to find him some employment in the Wyoming of his dreams. So Hal paid his train fare to Cody and, after a brief indoctrination, installed him and his two suitcases (one containing his clothes, the other a portable library) on upper Green Creek late in the fall. Their working agreement, given the cabin's remote location, was that Wallace might have to spend his first apprentice month in solitude.

Snow, deep snow, fell. There were no means of communication between Wapiti and the headwaters of the Green. Some three weeks later Wallace came tottering down through the drifts looking and feeling, as he said, poorly. To cheer him up with some home cooking, Sylvia, who until her marriage had never cooked anything more demanding than an occasional batch of fudge, burrowed into her canned reserves and baked Hal's favorite dessert, an indigestible concoction she called red raspberry upside down cake. Hal ate a piece or two; Wallace devoured the rest and became violently ill. Next morning Hal made the arduous drive into Cody and a doctor. After a consultation, the doctor called Hal aside and said, "Don't you understand what's wrong with your friend?"

"Sure," Hal said, "he ate a whole cake hot out of the oven. Anybody would be sick."

"Not so," said the doctor. "This man's not sick in the belly, he's sick in the soul. Homesick. He's dying of loneliness up there in the mountains."

"Impossible," Hal said. "Nobody—"

"Listen to me," the doctor told him. "I've seen it happen too many times before in this country. Loneliness. Send that fellow back wherever he came from. Now. I won't have his death on my conscience."

Humbled, Hal put Wallace on the outbound train next day and later sent him his clothes, but kept the other suitcase, the sole return on his investment. The Green Creek homestead faded into limbo.

The winter of 1916-17 was so severe the family decided that I should be taken "outside" to a milder climate. At the expense of Grandma Emma, Sylvia and I joined her for a few months in a Los Angeles hotel, leaving Hal to the snowbound company of himself and his critters. Good neighbor Ned Frost assured my mother that every morning he would look out his window with his binoculars to make sure that smoke was curling up from our chimney. Not to worry.

This is how Hal described his solitary existence. "There are a few joys of ranch life in winter that I don't think I'll ever become addicted to. Crawl out in the gray dawn at zero, build a fire, chop a hole in the ice and get water, kick around in six miles of snow and chop some firewood, put the eggs on to thaw. Then go blow the snow off the can and then I'm ready to settle down for a comfortable day on the dear old farm and listen to our little friend, the west wind, trying to blow the roof off. 'T'will not ever be thus."

He often asserted that he never got lonely and this was probably so. But earlier, chiefly for Sylvia's sake, he had written two of his closest friends urging them to pull up their Kansas stakes, move to Wyoming and invest some venture capital in land and cattle, touting Wapiti's wonders like a real estate huckster. One couple, persuaded by his impassioned prose, did make the journey to investigate the possibilities. When they arrived at our ranch, the lady was so shaken by the drive through Shoshone Canyon she had to be put to bed. Never, she cried, but never, would she go back down *that* road again; she would die first! Untruthfully, Hal informed her that there was no alternative except a rugged horseback ride over Cedar Mountain. The poor woman, sedated with some of Hardy Shull's moonshine, made the return trip to Cody cowering on the floor of our Buick.

During the winter of his discontent, Hal learned that the Cody doctor had been right to a degree: a human being could come close to dying, if not of loneliness, of a kindred affliction—boredom. He cooked for and fed his skunks and foxes, he milked the cow, shoveled snow and cut cords of firewood, week after week *ad nauseam*. He read every scrap of printed matter in the house twice over. And, although he had long since outgrown the shoot-'em-ups of his youth, at last in desperation he turned to Wallace Hinkle's dog-eared magazine collection.

It contained some good stuff, he conceded later, but more bad than good. One novelette in particular offended him. Laid in the Wizard of Oz West, it dealt with a man who was trapping bears, who in turn was trapped by a forest fire. Hal had done both—trapped bears and fought fires. It seemed apparent to him that the author had never seen a bear outside a zoo. By some process of inverted logic, he concluded that the key to writing fiction was to choose an unfamiliar subject; too much knowledge might hobble the imagination. Ergo, to amuse himself and pass the leaden hours, he dreamed up a plot involving lumberjacks in a logging camp, an area in which he qualified as an ignoramus. His conviction, or its equivalent, probably has been voiced by every would-be scribe since Homer: "I can write a better story than that."

True to his word, Ned Frost stared out his window one subzero February morning and decided to check on the health and welfare of his protege. He saddled a horse and went plowing up the road through two feet of snow, where he found our back door wide open with the trunk of a green young tree protruding through it from inside the house out onto the stoop. Puzzled, he peered in and saw Hal, wearing a fur cap and mackinaw, huddled over a table in front of the smoldering kitchen stove.

"Watcha doing?" Ned wanted to know.

Somewhat sheepishly, Hal admitted that he was writing. He got up from his chair, straddled the trunk and hefted its butt a few inches deeper into the stove.

"So why the goddamnhell don't you shut the door?" Ned demanded. "It's twenty below outside."

"Because," Hal told him, "I got so busy on a story I didn't have time to cut any firewood."

Details of this incident, in one form or another, spread up and down the North Fork, adding an extra dimension to his reputation as a comic eccentric. Amoeba-like his original concept grew and subdivided. Hal soon ran out of writing paper and resorted to what came most readily to hand—brown wrapping and shelf paper. Most of this composition took place at night by the light of a kerosene lamp, accompanied by the snapping of frozen trees outside his ice-glazed window and the yowl of coyotes prowling around his pens. Nothing seemed to sidetrack his powers of concentration.

In the process, without conscious volition, he was storing up a reservoir of impressions, images and information about his one field of expertise—wildlife. A few years later, for instance, he was to write the opening of his novel *The Yellow Horde*— considered by no less an authority than the late J. Frank Dobie to be the "definitive" work on the coyote—from the viewpoint of a trapper named Collins, Hal's alter ego.

". . . he listened to the first night sounds of the foothills. A coyote raised his voice, a perfect tenor note that swept up to a wild soprano, then fell again in a whirl of howls which carried amazing shifts of inflection, tearing up and down the coyote scale. One after another added his voice to the chorus until it seemed that the swelling volume could be produced by no less than a full thousand musical prairie wolves scattered through the foothills for a score of miles. Wild music to the ears of most men, the song of limitless horizons freighted with a loneliness which is communicated to man in a positive ache for companionship . . . for those who have lived so long under the open skies that the song of the mountain choir comes to them as a lullaby.

"It moved Collins to quiet mirth. Always it affected him this way, the first clamorous outburst of the night. He read in it a note of deep-seated humor, the jeering laughter of the whole coyote tribe mocking the world of men who had sworn to exterminate their kind. 'The little devils!' Collins chuckled. 'The little yellow devils. Men can't wipe 'em out. There'll be a million coyotes left to howl when the last man dies.'"

Meanwhile, Hal plodded along with his fictional lumberjacks and when the tale was told, more or less to his satisfaction, he stowed the manuscript away in a drawer where it might have succumbed to the inroads of mice and packrats. He had accomplished, by his lights, what he'd set out to do. There were more urgent, pressing demands on his time and energy.

An early spring thaw brought a providential guest, his brother-in-law Ted Fox. Ted had begun his career peddling insurance policies out of a buggy in isolated areas of Kansas and Oklahoma. A jovial homespun man, no mean story teller himself, he was fond of Hal, despite some family disclaimers. On this extended business trip Ted went far out of his way to look in on "Nellie's little brother." During the course of his short Wapiti visit, he happened upon Hal's discarded literary effort.

At this point, a human eternity later, I find it difficult to resist the temptation to reconstruct a dialogue that might, or might not, have taken place. Fact: Ted Fox bundled up Hal's mass of scribbled papers and took it home, his home then a bedroom suburb of New York City in Montclair, New Jersey. The thought was that Nellie, an ever-aspiring poetess, could critique, evaluate and possibly give her brother some guidance. Hal must have shrugged, metaphorically and physically. Why not? What was to lose?

In April, 1917, Sylvia and I returned to Wyoming from sunnier climes, and the United States declared war on the Central Powers. The Western Front, Kaiser Bill and the barbarous Teutonic hordes claimed attention even far up the Shoshone. Hal's target date for his first fur harvest still lay in the future but a new concern crept into his mind, perhaps inspired by his family's extensive military heritage. Granfaddy's voice and Lee Bigger's too may have been whispering to his conscience. "You will be surprised to learn," he wrote a friend, "that I may get into this scrap. I don't have to go, I won't be called up in the draft, but someday I'm going to read about some Hun sticking his bayonet into a baby about Hal Jr.'s age and I'll go marching out of here."

Later that year he received a nudge of sorts from an unexpected source. Some sixty years later, while sorting through his bales of correspondence, I came upon a fancy green envelope addressed in a familiar hand to: His Honor, The Mayor, Cody, Wyoming. It was postmarked Kansas City, Kansas, December 2, 1917. The enclosed missive, written on matching stationery, read: "Dear Sir, It has come to my attention that you are organizing a group of young men from Cody to go to France and fight the Germans. I strongly urge that you take along a rancher named Hal G. Evarts who lives at Wapiti west of your city." Signed, "A Friend."

The anonymous "friend" was my grandmother Cora, who seemed to be laboring under the delusion that His Honor had powers of impressment for the public weal. In short, Hal's mother-in-law was volunteering him for duty in the trenches, the assumption being that Sylvia, left husbandless, would then come to her senses and return to civilization. How the letter fell into his hands I have no notion; no hint of this episode ever reached my ears while the principals were alive. But I can imagine the uproar it provoked. "Cody's Own" Company K did go overseas, served in combat with distinction, but Hal G. Evarts was not on the roster.

What crystallized his puzzling decision to volunteer himself I can only surmise, but it proved to be the crucial one of his life. He was now within months of reaping his first potential profit after years of sweat, sacrifice and ridicule, at age thirty-one his bid for economic independence. Nevertheless, he applied for admission to officers' training school in the U.S. Army. Was it patriotism, a star-spangled poster with a finger-pointing "Uncle Sam Needs You"? The "Make the World Safe For Democracy" frenzy that was then sweeping the nation? In-law pressure? A cumulative sense of failure, a desperate cast of the dice to prove himself in a publicly acceptable role? With an almost frenzied disregard for self-interest, he leased the ranch to a neighbor, turned over total responsibility for the care and disposal of his fur-bearing animals to an alleged expert, and reported to Camp Pike, Arkansas on September 1, 1918.

Historically, camp followers are the handmaidens of war. My family was no exception. Grandma Emma and Sylvia, with me in tow, followed their warrior to Little Rock. From a rented cottage the three of us journeyed by jitney bus every Sunday afternoon out through the autumn countryside to the camp gate where, along with hundreds of other relatives, we shared a two-hour reunion with our man, picnicking under the oaks in an adjacent field. Even that small privilege was curtailed by the onslaught of the worldwide influenza epidemic of 1918. For the last few Sundays our contact with Hal was limited to conversation through the fence, our very voices filtered through gauze face masks, supposed inhibitors of the spread of the dread "flu bug."

By every physical standard he had the makings, endemic from childhood, to become a superb infantry soldier. Compared to his fellow civilians he was a unique specimen, toughened by years of hard outdoor labor at high altitudes. He took in stride a punishing crash program, the entire Army bag of OCS training. On the rifle range he outscored his instructors. On Armistice Day, November 11, his company was assigned, man for man, each to map a different segment of Camp Pike (now Fort Robinson), complete with contours, estimated elevations and features of terrain. Hal—shades of his survey experience in Indian Territory—turned in a map that any topographer might have envied. But one ingredient essential to a military career was lacking. He had a cynical disrespect akin to contempt for discipline. "Stupid" was one of the milder adjectives he employed to describe his ordeal as a ninety-day wonder.

Awarded a commission as a second lieutenant and a pair of shiny gold bars, he was ordered to the New York City port of embarkation area to await further orders for overseas assignment. An unencumbered shavetail, he proceeded to New Jersey where his sister Nellie and brother-in-law Ted Fox welcomed him as a guest. Unbeknownst to Hal, Nellie had been laboring in his behalf during the preceding eighteen months. She had pieced together his manuscript, copied it by hand, had a typescript made and sent it to a literary agent whose advertisement she had read in the New York *Times*. Ever restless and temporarily at liberty, a country bumpkin awed by his first exposure to the Big Apple, Lieutenant Evarts one day wandered the Manhattan waterfront and observed an Army troop transport disembarking hundreds of doughboys returned to America from Over There. What, he speculated, would they do in private life now that the "big show" had ended? Inspired, he hurried back to Montclair and scribbled a story, laid in Wyoming, which he called *What Next* and mailed it off to the agent.

Several thunderbolts then struck him in rapid succession. The first came from the War Department, an embossed certificate of honorable discharge, accompanied by a letter thanking him for devoted service to his country. Peace had brought about a sudden surfeit of infantry lieutenants. So Hal became free once more, but unemployed.

The second, from Wapiti, was devastating. Details are sketchy but the end result was a blueprint of disaster. Following instructions, the "expert" had hired a professional trapper to kill and skin his animals, clean and stretch their pelts and place the furs in storage. What we today know as Murphy's Law— "Everything that can possibly go wrong, does"—seems to have prevailed. The pelts were carelessly scraped; particles of fatty tissue remained. They were improperly stored; rodents and insects penetrated the cache and ravaged every fur. That is one version. Another version I heard much later. It was rumored along the Shoshone that one dark night a certain neighbor, for reasons of personal spite, loosened the catches of Hal's pens and released several hundred skunks and foxes worth thousands of dollars into the Wyoming winter. Still another version has it that a supposed friend, familiar with the layout and hard up for cash, loaded the foxes (which commanded a much higher price) aboard a truck and peddled them to some shady characters in Red Lodge, Montana. For many years thereafter, so this account goes, Wapiti had a vast oversupply of wild star skunks, a virtual plague, progeny of the few Hal had not deodorized or castrated.

The truth? Academic. On whom to lay the blame? Debatable. Hal, with no insurance to cover the loss, was too heartsick to care. He never set foot on the ranch again and sold it for a fraction of its worth to his friends the Montgomerys. His dream of building a larger, more comfortable house in a sheltered location never materialized. All that remains of the pens today are a few scattered chunks of concrete and scraps of wire rusting under the sagebrush. Almost seventy years later the house stands vacant, overgrown by willow trees and cottonwoods, invisible from the new all-weather highway.

Thirteen days later he received some positive news, a totally unexpected windfall. "You will be pleased to know," wrote M. F. Holly the literary agent, "that I have sold *Buddy's Pal* and *Billy Malloy's Specialty* to *Top Notch* Magazine of Street and Smith for $75.00 each." Enclosed was a check minus a ten percent commission and a reading fee of $7.00. Pleased to know? Hal must have been both ecstatic and nonplussed. Money, coin of the realm, for putting words on paper? "About your other manuscript," Miss Holly added, "please be patient. I am trying to find time to read it in your handwriting.... I will read anything of yours without a fee, *after it is typed.*" Her perseverance paid off. Shortly afterward she sold *What Next* to the slick paper magazine *Country Gentleman*, a property of the giant Curtis Publishing Company, home base of George H. Lorimer. In baseball terminology Hal, in his first three rookie tryouts at the plate, had batted 1,000 percent.

5.

"Fiction was getting more attention in periodicals, although it would be some time before it dominated so many magazines. Fiction's progress was impeded, however, by that same public intolerance that relegated acting and magazine writing to a place just above the gutter. All three were in the same class, as far as the new bourgeoisie was concerned, with dancing, gambling, cock-fighting and horse racing."
—John Tebbel, *The American Magazine*, 1969.

I F CURTIS WAS KING of the majors, then Street and Smith was a prince of the minors, the bush leagues, the pulps. Intellectually and aesthetically the two were kissing cousins, but there all resemblance ended. Pulp magazines were the poor relations in terms of pay and prestige. They were printed on coarse deckle-edged paper, packaged with a lurid cover and served up a no-nonsense meat-and-potatoes diet of physical action: formula fiction directed at a male blue-collar audience which, in 1919, comprised much of the population with a disposable income, however small. They sold at an average price of ten cents a copy on newspaper stands and in tobacco shops, had a devoted following in various fields: Western, crime-detective, foreign adventure, horror-science fiction and one new category—air war. The ads in their back pages reflected the readers' concerns about such basic matters as trusses, piles, muscular development, acne and, discreetly worded, sexual virility. The publishers paid their authors by the word, one cent for beginners, up to a dime for established stable hands and proven stars. Many popular and successful American writers won their first spurs and learned their craft in the pulp training ground. To name a few: Dashiell Hammett, Raymond Chandler, Erle Stanley Gardner and John D. MacDonald. In his salad days John Steinbeck tried but couldn't get the hang of it.

The slicks, on the other hand, were printed on smooth paper with a high rag content, sold in the millions—not thousands—in a larger lap-size format, mostly by mail subscription or door-to-door delivery by small fry entrepreneurs in the Horatio Alger mold. Their life blood was revenue from advertising. Radio would not become a serious competitor for years and the little box that someday would project electronic images was not even a dream. The titans of industry extolled their products and services and institutional images in the pages of the slicks for one reason: general circulation magazines provided the only effective means, the only channel by which an advertiser could reach a nation-wide audience. For that one golden, giddy postwar decade the slicks had a monopoly and Lorimer's *Post* was Number One, leading by a wide margin such weekly rivals as *Collier's*, the *Literary Digest* and johnny-come-lately *Liberty*, the monthlies *Red Book, American* and *Cosmopolitan*, as well as the women's magazines and more cerebral periodicals like *Harper's, Atlantic Monthly* and *Scribner's*.

In a speech before the Society of American Newspaper Editors, President Calvin Coolidge keynoted the credo of the 1920s: "America's business is business." Long before then the *Post* had become almost Holy Writ, the voice of big business. Ever since taking over the reins in 1899, Lorimer, a successful businessman and writer himself, had spread that gospel far and wide, in the process building the *Post* from a sickly readership of some 1800 to a mammoth of the print media. Espousing the goals of business paid off and nobody exploited this fact with more zeal and finesse than George H. Lorimer.

At the same time he possessed what might be called the common touch. Someone has observed that "the 20th Century began with World War I." Lorimer had the genius to perceive that and took dead aim on a vast new yeasty audience out there beyond his Philadelphia command post, a society disillusioned by foreign war but not yet bitter or turned off, one looking inward on the total American experience, and tailored his magazine accordingly. Male oriented, of course. Women could now vote, smoke in public, bob their hair, throw away their corsets and wear short skirts; it was the era of the "flapper." But Daddy still controlled the family purse strings. Generally speaking, though, the *Post* had something for everybody, regardless of gender, education or income, not just for the bloated capitalist in the Union League club. Mr. George H. Everyman.

During its heyday the *Post* often ran more than 200 pages per issue, carried two serials, a novelette, four to six short stories, numerous nonfiction articles and features, several cartoons and an opinion—Lorimer's opinion—page. The *Post* (1) supported high tariffs, lower immigration quotas and the trinity of Mom, Old Glory and Apple Pie, (2) opposed the Bolshevik Revolution, the League of Nations and labor unions, (3) ignored racism, religious bigotry and poverty, and (4) refused all tobacco and liquor advertising, out of deference to the sensibilities of the Curtis family, owners of the magazine. Several times a year a Norman Rockwell painting graced the cover, holding up to Mr. and Mrs. America an idealized and sentimental vision of themselves. All of this, a rich smorgasbord of entertainment and enlightenment, pop style, cost the customer one nickel. The advertisers paid more—up to $14,000 a page, depending on location.

Many contributors—Booth Tarkington and Mary Roberts Rinehart, for instance—were household names. But Lorimer bought more than bylines; he instructed his editors to be ever on the alert for promising new talent. Moreover, he outbid his competitors, paying what were then considered outlandish prices to attract and hold the writers he most admired. For some few jaded perennials, writing a story for the *Post* meant churning out another potboiler. For others the *Post* became a stepping-stone to book publication and fame, life-long careers and substantial incomes. Many more, perhaps the majority, fell by the wayside after a sale or two, never able to repeat.

At this point of entry my father was a novice, a pea green tyro, ignorant of the mechanics and economics and human complexities of magazine publishing, as he would be some years later when he blundered into the motion picture industry. Nonetheless he decided to try his hand at full-time writing. I can almost hear his self-justification, his ghostly interior monologue as he wrestled with his future: "What the hell, I sold my first three stories, made more money in a month than I did in four years ranching. What's so hard about that? Why not write a book?" The answer was a composite of his superb ego, his gambler's instinct and 100-proof naiveté: "By God, I'll do it!"

The family reaction to this is unrecorded but guessable. Even Sylvia, loyal and loving, must have had her doubts. Hal's overall track record as a hunter, realtor, merchant and fur rancher was hardly Chamber of Commerce level. A high school dropout, now a star-gazing would-be novelist? To finance this venture he probably borrowed a small stake from either his mother or his brother-in-law or perhaps both, then parked Sylvia and me with her parents in Kansas City and returned to Hutchinson. The Bigger house was occupied by renters so Hal found quarters in a boarding house down the street, prudently shunning the bonhomie and distractions of the Bachelors' Roost. With a folding card table, a ream of yellow paper and a carton of Camels he moved into a ten-dollar-a-week (meals included) third-floor room.

One bit of wisdom he had acquired since his first groping effort two years earlier was to concentrate on subjects about which he was knowledgeable. No more lumberjacks in never-never land. He did know Wyoming, he did know wild animals. "Those who believe in the legend of the Lost Herd are gone," he wrote as his opening sentence, "and few men know the truth."

It was his own personal moment of truth.

Six weeks later he emerged from his self-imposed solitary confinement with a manuscript of some 60,000 words, a story he called *The Cross Pull*, about a creature whelped by a Scotch sheep dog (herself part coyote) and sired by a lobo timber wolf—in genetic terms a mixed bag, a breed of breeds. Introducing this hybrid pup, Hal explained the significance of his title: "... he felt the first stirrings of the inner conflict—the battling for supremacy between the wild blood and the tame. It was as if the different elements of his ancestry had established cross-currents in his veins, exerting a strange cross-pull upon each thought and deed. The wolf and coyote in him revolted at the man scent but the dog strain responded to the friendly voice and thrilled to the touch of exploring fingers that scratched his neck and ears."

Thus was born the character of Flash who, in his cinematic re-creation, would become Hollywood's first canine star, forerunner of Rin Tin Tin, Peter the Great, Dynamite, Lassie and a host of other four-legged thespians.

Hal's next problem was mechanical. By now he realized that one did not submit a handwritten manuscript to even the most tolerant of agents, nor by any stretch of the imagination to an editor. So he resorted to a public stenographer in a bank, a cooperative lady named Edna Thoma who agreed, for a price, to type his book at her home after business hours. That same evening he received a phone call. Neither Edna nor her husband, whom she had conscripted in the cause, could decipher the author's scrawl. Would Mr. Evarts please—? Mr. Evarts, out of necessity, would and did. Night after night, until his voice grew too hoarse to continue, he dictated *The Cross Pull* aloud, word for word, complete with spelling and punctuation. And from Edna he learned another fundamental—to keep at least one carbon copy of the original.

The favorite topic and/or gripe of professional writers, then and now, is the role played by agents, the ten percenters. Much later, in career midstream, Hal would repeat a joke about an agent who, lunching with a friend in a posh Manhattan eatery, pointed out a man across the room and snarled, "Yeah, he's one of my clients. The bastard takes 90 percent of all the money I earn for him." Hal's recital of this hoary chestnut before the Adventurers' Club of Los Angeles brought down the house.

But in 1919 he had only the foggiest notion of marketing techniques. Who could sell what, where and when, to whom and why, and for how much?

Hal's first agent, a woman more or less picked out of a hat by his sister Nellie, fell victim to male chauvinism. Responding to a query about his projected "wild dog" novel, Miss Holly questioned the salability of animal stories. Not much future, she opined. And therewith Hal dumped her. As a replacement he himself picked one out of a hat, an outfit listed as Brandt & Fitzpatrick in some publication he ran across in the Hutchinson public library. Fitzpatrick never surfaced. Three Brandts— Carl, his brother Erd, who later joined the *Post* as an editor, and Carl's wife Zelma—ran the shop. They were the elite of literary agents in that generation, representing a clientele of distinguished authors, foreign as well as domestic. Hal's association with them arrived at so haphazardly, an incredible stroke of fortune in his new line of work, was to last the rest of his life.

Off went the manuscript, cold turkey, over the transom, accompanied by a letter outlining his background and plans for future stories. Shortly he received a form reply—brief, impersonal, noncommittal. Undaunted and unaware that dozens of neophytes like himself besieged the Brandt offices every week, Hal was already at work on new material. The Bigger house became available at last and Sylvia and I joined him there in June. A rambling barn of a place built by Lee Bigger in 1875 for his first wife, it had rooms to spare. Hal appropriated one as his first den and, when not busy at his desk, set about decorating it to his taste with mounted animal heads, fur pelts, stuffed birds and bearskin rugs until in time it came to resemble a taxidermy shop.

I was four by then, too young to understand the emotional currents swirling around my parents, the misgivings and fears that must have assailed them. They were no actors in some theatrical extravaganza. Their pride and self respect, all their hopes and dreams, their marriage itself was riding on the whim of a distant stranger. Meanwhile from New York—silence. Nothing. Day after steamy summer day. During this period

Hal, to the best of my recollection, maintained his outward cool. It is possible that in his own mind he was already an established author; he didn't dare believe otherwise. But I think it likely that he was racked by agonizing doubt, as he had good reason to be.

And then, July 3, 1919, the Evartses' ship, a timely good luck vessel if one ever sailed the seas of chance, came in.

"It has been a bully experience to read *The Cross Pull*," Carl Brandt wrote. "I'm glad to say that I like animals and stories about them. This one in particular. It seems to me that it has more than a good chance of being really popular. The series of stories—without humans—sounds good to me. Please start work on them. I shall be happy to take on your work with the understanding that while our arrangement lasts you will let us have everything new that you write. My feeling is that unless an author is happy working with me, it is better that he didn't work with me at all. I am going ahead with your work with real enthusiasm. I think that if you develop as this story promises, there is a big future ahead of you."

Hal needed no prompting. He completed two animal short stories, *Bald Face* and *Big Bull of the Shoshone*, which he dictated to Edna and fired off to Brandt in what should have been a state of euphoria. Brandt's confidence in him was not misplaced. Two weeks later he wrote Hal: "I am overjoyed at the news which I am able to send you. *The Cross Pull* has been purchased by the *Saturday Evening Post* for $1,600. I cannot tell you how lucky this is. Appearance in the *Post* is a thing which usually makes an author overnight. The usual course is that a writer will work for years before being able to land there. You have done it right off the reel. You ought to be proud of yourself."

Another truth Hal soon would learn was that Lorimer, almost single-handedly, had effected a revolution in popular print culture. There were no rich or royal patrons of literature in populist U.S.A. But Lorimer, according to his biographer John Tebbel, ". . . stayed one jump ahead of his competitors by virtue of the practice that brought him more writers than any other. That practice was his rule, made at the start of his editorship, to return a decision on any manuscript within seventy-two hours, and to pay immediately upon acceptance. Until then it had been virtually impossible for an American writer to earn his living by writing. Aside from a few eminent novelists, men like Mark Twain, no writer depended on his art for his bread: he had independent means or a job. Without one or the other, he was compelled to live on the rim of starvation."

While it will never make the Guinness Book of Records, Hal's output during the last half of 1919 was prodigious. He wrote and sold: four short stories to the *Post* at $400 apiece; a second novel, *The Yellow Horde*, a story and an article to *Red Book*; three articles to *Collier's*; two stories to *Popular Magazine*. Alfred Knopf signed a book contract to publish *The Cross Pull* and an agreement to publish a collection of his short stories the following year; Little Brown, a book contract for *The Yellow Horde*. It was as though a dam had burst and a torrent of words, a flood of ideas and plots and characters spewed forth. The brash bratty kid from Topeka had finally found his calling.

Now the mail poured in. In 1919 a first-class two-cent postage stamp was the best bargain going. People wrote letters: old friends offering congratulations; editors asking for his work; amateur writers seeking help; nature cranks disputing his facts; strangers trying to hustle a loan; and one to be remembered, the disgruntled mother of a former girl friend who threatened to expose Hal as a fake, a plagiarist stealing somebody else's stuff. He could have laughed this off, but didn't. Enraged, he counter-threatened to sue the lady for malicious slander.

And this poignant one from a companion of his down-at-the-heels bachelor days: "When we meet again I hope to start your tongue wagging in the famous old way when we used to stand on the street corner and talk all night."

Hal struggled to keep abreast of this deluge but a log jam of neglected correspondence was piling up, affecting his magazine and book commitments. Stenographer Edna, employed six days a week by the First National Bank and half the nights and Sundays by Hal G. Evarts, at last demurred. Enough became too much. So he came up with a solution that would have given most wives pause, but Sylvia agreed to try. Hal bought her a portable typewriter and an instruction manual. Working at our dining-room table a few steps from his den, available day and night, she taught herself the rudiments of two-finger hunt-and-peck and thereafter copied his every word. She never discussed with him the work in progress before, during or after the fact. Hal wrote, Sylvia typed, a tandem operation that suited them both. Without her contribution, her backup support, his professional life would have been chaos and he knew it.

A firearms expert since his youth, he still kept several in his den—hunting rifles and shotguns of different caliber and one loaded revolver from his Army days—cradled in a wall rack safely above the reach of a four-year-old. Sleeping in a downstairs bedroom one September night, he and Sylvia were wakened by a woman's screams for help outside their open window. Electrified, he peered out and saw two dark figures, one obviously male, grappling on our driveway. Hal shouted but the struggle went on. Stepping into his den, he grabbed the revolver and yelled at the couple to stop. The man broke away then, flung the woman to the ground and ran. Hal fired a warning shot and fired again. The man stumbled, limped off into the night and disappeared. Arrested by police the next day with a bullet wound in his leg, he admitted that he had followed the woman, a waitress working late downtown and walking home along the deserted street, and tried to attack her in our yard. She was unharmed, her name never mentioned, nor was the word "rape," not in the press of 1919, but Hal's growing reputation drew some unwelcome publicity. "Author Shoots Prowler" headlined one local paper. A friend joshed him about carving "another notch in your six gun," much to his chagrin.

From New York Brandt continued to bombard him with encouragement: "Again I'm pleased and it's fine to be pleased so often. I think I've been able to start a real vogue for you and your work. For the Lawd's sake shoot me some more stuff before the wave dies down. If we can ride it all the way in we won't need to look for any more waves. You'd better give some thought to coming on here and meeting some of the editors. Not to mention the pleasure it would give me to see you myself." Hal had yet to lay eyes on a live editor or agent. The temptation was strong. And he lusted for another autumn duck hunt. But he denied himself all indulgences and labored on with a kind of obsessive passion.

His first year as a free-lance writer, which had begun so disastrously, drew to a close on a triumphant note. His prospects seemed brilliant, boundless. Not one rejection slip to paste above his desk. He had sold every word he'd scribbled on his bilious yellow paper, with scant revision, a feat almost unheard of. For the first time he'd earned enough money to file a federal income tax report, that newest hallmark of success. But some few skeptics in the wings undoubtedly were wondering: Is he a distance runner? How long can he keep up that pace?

6.

THE REMNANTS OF the original American inhabitants had been deported to a reservation before Hal arrived on the upper Shoshone around 1904. No student of anthropology, nevertheless he seems to have developed a keen interest in their tribal culture. Either that or he invented his own and attributed it to the Shoshones. Unbelievable? Not really. Almost a century earlier James Fenimore Cooper in his *Leatherstocking Tales* created, largely out of whole cloth, a mythology for the Mohican Indians of upstate New York. So why not Hal for a dwindling people of northwestern Wyoming? In any event it provided him with a splendid majestic background tapestry for his stories. To explain away some improbable fact or hard-to-swallow premise he could always invoke the name of the alleged Shoshone supreme deity—Manitou. Manitou says this; according to Manitou; Manitou's law. A useful device for any writer.

In the opening paragraph of his first short story published in the *Post*, *Bald Face*, he wrote: "The Shoshones had it handed down straight from Manitou, their revered god and ancestor, that Tumwa, the yellowish brown grizzly, Saka-Tumwa, the silvertip, and Logo-Tumwa, the bald face, were three different color phases of the same beast." What reader could challenge that authoritative statement?

And in *The Tawny Menace*: "It may be that when the Great God Manitou gave the name Loupang to the big yellow cat in the beginning, he had temporarily forgotten that inconsistency in nomenclature is the failing of no one race.... even at this early age the three kits were proving Manitou's wisdom in calling them Ne-loupangs—little killers." Surely the author must speak the Shoshonean tongue like a native.

And in *The Black and Cinnamon Twins*, about the bears Wakinoo and Wakinee: "Their lives were governed by the Law the same as all other animals. The law of the endless circle prescribed by the Great God Manitou who had decreed that life as a whole should go on forever, but that the span of each individual life would be short and fleeting. While each one lived he should reproduce life, and when he died his energy and motion should be utilized by those who fed upon him and so give renewed energy to other life that it might go on through death. And Manitou had accorded to each animal his own niche and purpose in the Law and his own relation to the endless circle."

Not only did Manitou give Hal a connective tissue for a series of unrelated animal stories, the all-wise Indian divinity reflected his personal philosophy, and was actually Hal's conduit for his views on the nature of man. As a boy he attended church only under duress, as an adult never. He did not consider himself an agnostic or atheist. He was, if anything, a Manitouan, high priest of his private one-man religion.

About this time Lorimer turned down two of his stories (they sold quickly elsewhere) and Brandt wrote Hal: "He is tremendously interested in your work but his reaction is that you are telling the same basic story in each yarn. That it is the story of the animal's life from birth to death and the difference between the animals is not enough to keep them from being monotonous. What he wants is that there should be some outstanding twist in the story itself which will fill the reader's eye. He made this suggestion..."

What Lorimer wanted specifically and what Hal tried to give him was some injection of the human element, a person, so that the average reader, even one city-bred, could relate more easily to a dumb creature he probably would never see in the wild. In his next story, *Dog Town*, an examination of the teeming life that goes on in and around a colony of prairie dogs, Hal used what might be called the "sandwich technique."

A girl character observing the series of dirt mounds, says to her male companion, "That must be a humdrum existence. What do the inhabitants find to break the monotony?"

A loaded rhetorical question.

To which the man, a naturalist, responds, "A thousand things a day. If they only published a Dog Town daily it would chronicle more tales of tragedy, comedy, crime and love than the biggest metropolitan sheet." Thus the reader is introduced to the hero, Weekin, the bewhiskered dog "patriarch of the village."

Early next morning the couple returns and spies on the colony through binoculars from dawn to dusk, witnessing the trials and tribulations and survival tactics of Weekin and his relatives, including a cast of predators and victims such as jack rabbits, bobcats, rattlesnakes, badgers, burrowing and great horned owls, golden eagles, hawks, skunks, weasels and toads, each depicted in meticulous and loving detail. In essence, an animated lesson in nature study.

As night closes in the girl, surely the most patient female character since Griselda, admits her astonishment. "I'll take it back," she says. "Weekin must be a nervous wreck after a day like this."

"No, that's Weekin's regular lot in life," the man tells her. "It was no more than an average Dog Town day."

The story ends: "From far down in the flats an eerie soprano voice was raised, a pealing shrill staccato ripping up and down the scale. Voice after voice joined till it seemd that the music issued from a thousand throats as the coyote chorus sounded the Dog Town taps."

A minimum of human involvement, but Lorimer loved it. And so did his readers. *Dog Town* drew bundles of mail.

For Hal his most difficult animal short story, written much later after a trip to Australia, was *Koala*, a study of that tree-dwelling marsupial. Here he had no Manitou to fall back on. After observing the creatures in a preserve near Sydney and discussing their habits with a zoologist, he expressed his doubts to me: "I don't know. They're cute and cuddly. Everybody loves the koala. But they don't *do* anything. They just sit there day and night munching eucalyptus leaves." Overcoming several false starts, he found a way to dramatize the sedentary life of this mis-called "native bear." It became the most popular short story of his career.

During the early months of 1920 Hal continued at a breakneck pace, selling to the *Post* and *Red Book* at ever higher prices. A sprinter out of the starting blocks, he never looked back at any demons that might have been pursuing him. They would overtake him later, but for now he was unbeatable. Looking back myself over a vista of years, I find it difficult if not impossible to analyze his supreme self-confidence, his absolute belief in himself. An overnight wonder, instant celebrity, big frog in a small town puddle? A phenomenon, one-of-a-kind, uniquely gifted? He never perceived himself in any such gaudy terms. He was, in fact, hideously embarrassed when an eastern book reviewer referred to him as "the man who put Hutchinson, Kansas, on the map." My theory is that throughout his formative years his one unqualified success had been entertaining people with his tales, true or contrived. At thirty-two he was simply doing what he did best, having discovered how to channel his talent into the literary mart.

My mother who, if anyone, should have known, could not explain him either. As she grew older her memory of him blurred almost to extinction. "No, he was not a modest man," she told me. "Not modest at all. But neither was he conceited. Never. I think he was put on this earth to tell stories. Hal was—just Hal."

The inscription in my personal copy of *The Cross Pull* offers a glimpse of how he saw himself and his work: "To my Son, this first edition of my first book is lovingly presented. You'll be able to read it someday, Son, so don't deal too harshly with it. Dad." Hardly the reflection of a man burdened with vanity.

To a fan he responded: "I don't know that I can throw any light on the requisites of becoming a writer. I hear much of inspiration but have never found any of that commodity descending in my neighborhood. I simply pick a topic I know a little about and set forth what I know of it. If it's satisfactory I send it in; if not, I tear it up. In regard to your request for an autographed photograph I would certainly accede if possible but I have had but one picture taken in ten years and Mrs. E refuses to part with it."

And then, inevitably, he stumbled—sort of. His third book-length serial presented problems. His first two, written at fever heat, *The Cross Pull* (wolves) and *The Yellow Horde* (coyotes) had—as most of his short stories and articles did—revolved around animals. *Settling of the Sage*, about the confrontation between homesteader and cattle baron, was a people book and Hal, as Brandt pointed out, soon ran into "girl trouble." In a diary he kept sporadically he made this entry: "Today started *Settling of the Sage* but gave it up. Idea not ripe yet and could not start it off with any snap."

A few weeks after Christmas he wrote Brandt: "I have completed about two thirds of the new serial which I am sending on for your verdict before completing it. This strikes me as the poorest story I have yet written and I need your advice. I have known several ex-cow thieves and some that were not ex, putting in one winter with a man who had just finished a sentence for rustling. And from what I saw of him he seemed soon due to serve another. . . . In reading over what I have written it seems to me there is too much detail; not enough continuity of action and succession of incident. Also that I have failed to bring out any very strong characters. If you can suggest any way I can reshape it, please outline it for me; if not I will ditch it and start something else."

As usual, Brandt had some suggestions and encouragement. To establish his boy-girl conflict Hal had borrowed from that master plotter, William Shakespeare, a variation on the *Romeo and Juliet* theme, which led him into a quagmire of implausibility. The subject of romantic love in the abstract bored him; consequently his early heroines came across as two-dimensional goody-goody gumdrops, although they satisfied the fictional conventions of the day. The "female stuff," as he called it, was to bother him throughout his career. But after two revisions he sold the serial rights to Karl Harriman at *Red Book* for $2,500 and contracted with Little Brown for book publication.

Eighteen desk-bound months after he had first declared himself a novelist, Hal decided he needed a break, a change of scene, a renewal of his sources. Brandt was trying to sell the screen rights to *The Cross Pull* but there seemed no dog available in Hollywood to carry the role of Flash; actors and actresses abounded but no wolf-like canine emerged. Lorimer queried him about some nebulous Yellowstone Park project. Hal himself was sketching an outline for a boys' book. But Wyoming beckoned.

To my five-year-old mind the entire state was a sea of mud that July of 1920. In our new Buick sedan, tires chained, we churned and slithered our way west to Cody and the Frost and Richard ranch. And there coincidence reared its head. Horace M. Albright, superintendent of Yellowstone, had written Hal several letters commending him on the authenticity of his wildlife stories; the two had never met but were by way of becoming pen pals. It so happened that the Albrights had as summer house guests Mr. and Mrs. Emerson Hough. Hough, newspaperman turned novelist, a favorite of *Post* readers, was in Yellowstone at the request of his editor, Lorimer. The name of this game was "writer's block" and Hough had it bad; even in the sylvan surroundings of America's first and finest national park he could not complete his new serial, *The Covered Wagon*, for which Lorimer was chafing with impatience. Lorimer, on vacation with his wife, decided to look in on his becalmed author and get him under sail again.

"Away from the *Post*," wrote John Tebbel, Lorimer's biographer, "his abiding love was for the outdoors. He was always minding the national parks. He knew their custodians well and they would not have thought of planning a major project without asking his advice. On his travels they passed him freely through the chain of Western parks and he accepted their homage as though he owned the system.... His feeling about the parks amounted to the pride of personal ownership.

No one ever questioned that attitude, because no citizen did more for these public domains."

Host Albright met the Lorimers at Cody's end-of-the-line depot in the Park's official VIP limousine as if they were touring royalty. Unknown to Hal, all the players were now assembled on the stage to act out another drama in his career.

The gist of a conversation, reconstructed for me years later by Horace Albright, went as follows:

LORIMER: How's Hough coming with my serial?
ALBRIGHT: You'd better ask him.
LORIMER: I intend to. Do you know a writer named Evarts?
ALBRIGHT: Not personally. I like his stuff though.
LORIMER: So do I. That's why I buy it. I understand he's in the area.
ALBRIGHT: Yes, he is. As a matter of fact we'll pass right by where he's staying.
LORIMER: Do they have a telephone?
ALBRIGHT: I think so.
LORIMER: Then call ahead. I want to meet the man. I have a job for him.

One hour later a nervous and apprehensive Hal was waiting at Ned Frost's front gateposts alongside the road when the limousine pulled up and a stranger stepped out. That conversation was unrecorded but at last Hal met the Boss Man face to face and shook hands, half a mile from the old ranch house where, some three years earlier, he had scratched out his first story to pass the lonely nights away.

The following day Hal and Sylvia joined the Lorimers, Albrights and Houghs for lunch in the cavernous dining room of the Lake Hotel in Yellowstone. Lorimer's "job," offered across the table, was to write in fiction form the history of Yellowstone Park from earliest days, emphasis on conservation. That scene is one to tickle the imagination: Lorimer, presiding over coffee and cigars with four wives looking on, exhorting two authors—one to undertake a new book, the other to finish a book half done, both destined for best sellerdom. Flattered but inwardly dismayed, Hal promised to think it over. The historical concept struck him as impossible.

As the luncheon was breaking up Hough took Hal aside and said in a hoarse whisper that came through distinctly to the assembled guests: "Listen, Evarts, you're new to the game so I'll tell you this: When George H. Lorimer asks a writer to do something, you don't say 'no' or 'maybe.' You say, 'Yes, sir' and you do it, goddamnit!"

Upon reflection Hal heeded his advice.

Emerson Hough soon broke out of his writer's block. The film version of his *The Covered Wagon* became one of the smash hits of the silent movie era. As for Hal, ten days after he'd set out on an overdue vacation, he was holed up with Sylvia and me in a one-room log cabin on isolated Jim Creek above Wapiti, hard at work again.

Lorimer, a prescriptive Republican, a political moderate with a highly sensitive finger on the public pulse, was in one respect far ahead of his time, a dedicated advocate of what today we know as the environmental protection movement. He recognized and deplored the rapid depletion of America's natural resources. On the *Post's* editorial page and in a special outdoor section, he hammered away at what he saw as the rape of the national heritage in the name of development. One situation had captured his attention and outraged him to the flash point.

The once immense herds of elk in western Wyoming, now critically diminished, had found a temporary haven within the federally protected boundaries of Yellowstone. They bred and birthed their calves there, grazed through the lush high country spring and summer; then with the onset of autumn snow drifted north along age-old migration routes across the line into lower terrain, the state of Montana, beyond Uncle Sam's sanctuary. Near the town of Gardiner hundreds, sometimes thousands, of trigger-happy meat-hungry hunters awaited them in shooting gallery array. The annual slaughter of magnificent antlered elk had become, in Lorimer's eyes, a sickening abattoir, a national disgrace. To expose this scandal, to stir up protest on the broadest possible scale, he had chosen Hal.

"Once Manitou looked down upon plains made dark with buffalo; now his nostrils are poisoned with the reek of a million carcasses stripped of their pelts and left to rot under the sun. As the otter and beaver are gone from the plains, the deer from the valleys and the bull elk from the hills, even the last bighorn among the highest peaks have been sacrificed to the greedy God, Development!"

With those words Hal bugled the battle call of his fourth novel, whose title underwent a sea change from *The Good Old Days* to *The Old Timer* and finally to *The Passing of the Old West*. It was a curious hybrid, part fiction, part polemic, a socio-economic tract attacking not only game hogs but such hitherto sacred cows as the lumber, mining and grazing interests who leased government land. For that time it had a definite anti-establishment slant. If "female stuff" had given him minor problems in earlier work, the writing of *Old West* gave him fits. His assignment, the substance of it, was to sugar-coat propaganda as an outdoor adventure yarn. He started over and over again, stuffing our pot-bellied stove with wads of discarded yellow paper. From time to time, confronted by a block of his own, he would switch to his other current novel, *Fur Sign*. Throughout that summer and fall he worked on the two books in alternating streaks.

Our cabin, built by Oscar and Ethel Montgomery on their honeymoon to establish homestead rights, far from the nearest neighbor, was confining. To protect Hal from domestic interruptions, Sylvia allowed me to play up and down Jim Creek by myself most of every day. Until one morning I bellied down for a drink of water beside a coiled rattler. (With Hal's retelling it grew longer each time, to monstrous proportions). My startled yowl brought Hal and Sylvia running. That afternoon we packed up and moved out, farther west, to another cabin near Moran under the Tetons, presumably a less snake-infested locale. Ten summers later my parents returned to the same spot with a motion picture production crew on location to shoot the then most expensive film ever undertaken outside of Hollywood.

Hal bought his first camera, a cumbersome Graflex, with

which to keep a photographic record and illustrate his articles. On many an afternoon our family hiked to the pristine mountain gem, Jenny Lake, where Hal, instructing himself in the mysteries of shutter speeds and lens openings, would fashion a blind and lie in wait for whatever wildlife came his way. Sylvia and I would wait at a discrete distance out of sight in some glen or meadow, while she read aloud to me until the light failed and the three of us filed back through the silent timber to our cabin for a late supper. This pattern repeated itself countless times over the years, from Kansas to Alaska, from the Florida Keys to the South Pacific, wherever Hal stalked his quarry, be it an osprey nest, fox den, beaver dam or mongoose lair. At an early age I learned to carry some reading material when I traveled with him.

In September the H.O. Davis Corporation bought the screen rights to *The Cross Pull* for $2,500 at the behest of producer-director Laurence Trimble, who had found a suitable dog, a foreigner at that, which he would import from Germany and train himself. It was perhaps ironic that Trimble's co-producer happened to be a woman, one of a handful in early Hollywood, Jane Murfin, who would adapt the novel into a screenplay. Brandt assured a dubious Hal that she was "awfully good on animal stuff."

Brandt also kept pressing for a progress report on *Old West*; Lorimer wanted to see some manuscript immediately, if not sooner. But Hal was still struggling. He never thought of himself as a perfectionist but he sensed the importance of this one, as much as its construction frustrated him. *Old West* was Lorimer's pet, his baby, and it had to be right. Sylvia returned to Hutchinson to enroll me in school but Hal stayed on in Moran. For one cobweb-clearing week he played hooky and went trapping, then returned to the story recharged. With a late November blizzard shrieking over the Tetons, he brought it to a close at last, exhausted, moderately pleased and a good deal wiser about the pitfalls and perils of his chosen trade. Inspiration did not always come easily, on demand.

The story line is deceptively simple—his only novel without a romantic interest—told through the viewpoint of Mart

Woodson who first sees the Yellowstone country in 1874 as a youth of seventeen. The country itself becomes Mart's passion and to it he gives a lifetime of dedication, first as an Army scout, then as a ranger, protecting his beloved Park from every kind of human predator. At the end of an often thankless career, now an old man, he thinks to himself: "What nobler monument could be bequeathed to future Americans than this one spot where they might come and with their own eyes look upon a miniature of the greatest day of their country's history, one last bit of the Great West left intact?"

But in the finale a disillusioned Mart, sickened by witnessing one day's slaughter of elk on Gardiner's main street, is gazing off into the sunset and talking to his spavined horse, Teton, a convention honored by the likes of Owen Wister and Zane Grey: " 'Here we are, Teton. All the old he-ones of yesterday gathered for a final rally. It's sunset for us old-timers. We're just a whisper of the past, fossils of the old days that are gone. It's time to kneel and say our prayers.' For in the sunset old Mart had seen the symbol of the Mad God—Overdevelopment."

Sentimental? Absolutely. But it had a bite, a sting. Hal had delivered his—and Lorimer's—message.

On acceptance Lorimer wired him: "You have really done a wonderful piece of work in the new serial and a genuine service to the American people. It is a conservation classic."

Three days before Christmas he received his check from the *Post* and this praise from Brandt: "It is tremendously gratifying to realize how consistently your work has kept up and improved. You should be a very proud man to have come along so fast in the short time you have been writing. I am immensely proud of you and of such share as we have had in that success."

Publication of *The Passing of the Old West*, illustrated by the incomparable wildlife artist Charles Livingston Bull, marked a professional turning point for Hal, a new dimension, although he did not immediately recognize this. Heretofore he had been a spinner of tales, a figurative yarner around the campfire, an entertainer. Suddenly he caught the interest of small determined groups involved with the serious issues of conservation, members of such organizations as the Sierra Club and Audubon Society, who in future decades would grow in number and national influence. Inadvertently he had become a spokesman and champion of their causes, a popular writer, now a respected one, with an audience of millions. He had acquired, without seeking it, some of that precious commodity called clout.

From his Yellowstone office Horace Albright, soon to become director of the entire National Park system, released this public endorsement: "I consider this book one of the most powerful outdoor stories ever written, and I do not see how it can fail to attract the attention of everybody in America that is interested in the preservation of wildlife and in the protection of our heritage of distinctive world famous scenic resources." One immediate result: both Montana and Wyoming passed tighter game laws in their next legislative sessions.

7.

AT THIRTY—THREE Hal was a slim and wiry 5'9", a handsome man with thinning brown hair. He had the hazel "Evarts eyes," a ready smile and he laughed a lot, sometimes uproariously. To my adoring gaze he was the ideal parent—warm and caring but strict on occasion when I "acted up." Some time would pass before I saw him in the round, warts and all.

He did well so many things that I could not—hammer a nail straight, whistle between two fingers, recite from memory all the heavyweight boxing champions from John L. Sullivan on. He was never too busy to play catch in the back yard or help wax my sled runners at the first snowfall of winter. One example: Approaching my seventh Easter, I yearned to possess a live rabbit. "Why don't you catch one yourself?" Hal suggested, and built for me a cunningly constructed wooden box trap with a sliding door and a trip release mechanism consisting of a length of cord and a dangling carrot. We sited the trap under some bushes behind what had been Lee Bigger's carriage house, over which I maintained a more or less constant vigil. Nothing happened until early Easter morn when I found—surprise, surprise—a white fluffy red-eyed bunny with long pinkish ears nibbling on the carrot inside my box. Hot spit! Diggety dog! I rushed off to inform the neighborhood of my prowess as a trapper.

A blabbermouth kid down the block punctured my balloon. "You never caught no rabbit," he sneered. "Your old man bought it in a pet shop."

I knew, instantly, that he was right. Crushed, I could never bring myself to tell Hal that his hoax had been unmasked. But Hal knew that I knew. Several days later my first and last Easter bunny unaccountably disappeared from its pen, followed by an airy explanation that: "It must have jumped out and gone back to the wild where it belongs."

Hal never read to me at bedtime nor any other time. He left that to Sylvia or various visiting female relatives. He never told me stories of make-believe from the lode of children's literature—about fairies, elves, gnomes, adorable monsters, anthropomorphic animals and the like. The stories he did tell were *real*, supposedly based on fact or history, often during trips about the countryside while I sat entranced beside him on the front seat of our car. One I remember in particular: a full scale account of the Johnson County War around Buffalo, Wyoming, in 1892, a struggle between ranchers and rustlers. I became familiar with the derring-do deeds of the Purple Sash Gang long before I heard of King Arthur and The Round Table or Robin Hood and his Merrie Men.

Another tale, related with vivid hair-raising detail, concerned one of Lee Bigger's alleged Civil War exploits. Grandpa Lee, trapped in a Confederate ambush, was the sole survivor of a band of Union raiders. It ended with Grandpa racing across an open field toward the forest, while the Rebel sharpshooters frantically tamped bullets down their single-shot muzzle-loading rifles and screamed "Kill the Yankee som' bitch!"

What was a som'bitch? I wanted to know. Never mind, Hal told me. It's not a nice word and don't you use it. No one else in the family ever heard of this event, expurgated or otherwise.

Curiously, he never talked to me about his childhood or peripatetic youth or years on the ranch. For an articulate, even voluble man, he was reticent about himself, a very private person. His early life, inner life, he kept in a separate sealed compartment except for one public relations disclosure—his sketchy and truncated memoir *On Inspiration's Trail*. I should have sought out the young Hal while he was alive but, regrettably, didn't.

In the spring of 1921 he completed *Fur Sign*, described on Little Brown's dust jacket as: ". . . adventures of two sixteen-year-old lads of the city slums, living in squalid quarters and toiling for mere existence, when a welfare society sent them into the country for a trial month." The plot grew out of a talk he'd given to a group of youthful inmates at the State Reformatory in Hutchinson, the background from a boyhood trapping venture along the Arkansas in 1903. It ran as a serial in *The Country Gentleman* and drew queries from several youth oriented magazines, but it was the only juvenile fiction he ever wrote. Sales of foreign rights—the first to the British *Royal Magazine* for "fifteen guineas"—began to swell his income. Eventually, he would be translated into several foreign languages.

He corresponded with Ned Frost about a joint hunt in Alaska but this was not to be. Lorimer, impressed by the volume of mail drawn by *Old West* and seeing Hal as a kind of roving environmental journalist as well as novelist, asked him to investigate reports of a new oil strike in Arctic Canada that he thought would interest American readers. Details of this undertaking, replete with photographs of Hal and Sylvia, were featured on the front pages of Hutchinson's newspapers. "Exotic journey," "adventure into the last frontier," "noted author seeks fresh material," were some of the comments. Plus this bottom line: "The Evarts will leave their six-year-old son with his grandparents in Kansas City."

The early stages of this trip, which covered some 5,000 miles in the summer of 1921, gave Hal his first taste of name recognition. He had become newsworthy not only in his home town but to a larger audience. Interviewed enroute by the press in Kansas City, Minneapolis, Winnipeg, and Edmonton, he proved to be affable as well as quotable: " 'Nothing important, really,' Evarts said and grinned modestly. 'I'm just going along for the boat ride to get some rest.' "

Hal and Sylvia departed Edmonton aboard the Alberta & Great Waterways "Muskeg Limited—limited to five miles per hour." The roadbed, subject to thaws and other vagaries of weather, was notoriously unstable. Twice during the 250-mile journey the coal burning locomotive derailed and had to be muscled back on the tracks. The passengers detrained and camped overnight in tents provided by the railroad, fighting swarms of ferocious mosquitoes. An adaptable traveler, Hal was so intrigued by the operation that he titled his report *End of Steel*, which designated the railhead at Fort McMurray on the Athabasca River. Here he and Sylvia boarded the Northern Trading Company steamer S.S. *Mackenzie*, which made an annual midsummer round trip down the Mackenzie River deep into Canada's Yukon Territory, above the Arctic Circle. "In this part of the world," Hal wrote, "you travel 'down north' and 'up south.'" This steamer, before the era of bush pilots, was the only once-a-year link to the outside for a few scattered trading posts and a small native population that lived along the banks. Ordinarily the passenger list might have included a few government officials, fur traders and company bigwigs but this year, because of the oil excitement, it was packed to the gunwales. Sylvia shared one of the few cabins with an Indian woman; Hal slept outside on deck.

His "boat ride" took them via the Great Slave Lake to the distant end of the line, Fort McPherson, almost to the Beaufort Sea. He had planned to cross into Alaska by horse and canoe but was warned against it: "Too rugged for a white woman; your wife's no squaw." So my parents retraced their route up the Mackenzie, a voyage that took twice as long as the down run, but gave Hal a double opportunity to photograph and interview the locals.

His account of this journey, which he wrote in ten nonstop days, appeared serially in the *Post* that fall, a potpourri of travelogue, historical commentary and wildlife observations. His assessment of the oil field potential was negative: "Too remote and too costly to develop," which did not delight the promoters of Imperial Oil Company, half a century ahead of their time. Hal brought back an assortment of pelts, Indian bead work and weaponry which he added to the collection in his den. His most important trophy, though, was the idea for another novel, *Moccasin Telegraph*.

Meanwhile in Hollywood, scriptwriter Jane Murfin was

converting *The Cross Pull* into a screenplay retitled *The Silent Call*. Dogs had been used before as bit players in movies but this was the first time that a dog was to be given the leading role in a major production and top billing in all advertising and publicity. The dog that director Larry Trimble finally selected bore the aristocratic kennel name of Etzel von Oerengen with a blue blooded pedigree to match. This was a bit much for the American public to accept so soon after World War I, so Trimble made another switch: He coined the name "Strongheart" in place of the original "Flash."

Hal had no interest in these developments but my mother did. Through a Hutchinson friend who had moved to Hollywood and gone to work as a film industry publicist, she followed Strongheart's screen career.

"And so to Hollywood to try his luck in the movies came this big German shepherd, a famous champion in his own country but practically unknown on this side of the Atlantic." So wrote J. Allen Boone, who later became Strongheart's keeper. "Strongheart crossed the United States from New York to Los Angeles as just another dog in the baggage car. Without ceremony he was driven to a Hollywood studio for screen tests. ... A little over a year later Strongheart was again placed on a train but this time he did not ride in the baggage car. Instead, he was escorted through lanes of excited admirers and placed in a special suite. He was attended by a manager, a valet, a press agent and a representative of the railroad to see that he got the best of everything."

In Los Angeles *The Silent Call* ran for sixteen weeks in a downtown theater, a record for that time. Strongheart went on to score one success after another, starring in such movies as *Brawn of the North* and Jack London's *White Fang*, creating a vogue in dog pictures.

Here is how Boone described a Strongheart cross-country promotional tour: "At every stop crowds of people were on hand to acclaim the new celebrity where he was to make a theater appearance, special citizens formally welcomed him, hung a 'key to the city' around his neck and paraded him to the nearest hotel where the best suite of rooms would be ready for him and his staff.... With his fame reaching into every part of the world where motion pictures were shown, Strongheart became the Number One attraction in the world of entertainment, most glittering of all the Hollywood stars, the monarch of all he surveyed."

None of this early Hollywood hype and hoopla rubbed off on Hal, isolated as he was in the hinterlands of Kansas. But when at length *The Silent Call* was booked into Hutchinson, the management of the leading theater staged a "Hal Evarts Night," a sort of "local boy makes good" theme presentation in the lobby. Hal, Sylvia and I were ushered into seats front row and center, my first ever attendance at a movie. The huge curtain covered with the ads of local merchants parted, the house lights dimmed, credits flashed on the screen and a woman pianist in the orchestra pit pounded out some pulse-stirring mood music. I remember only one scene—the opener, a sure fire attention grabber: A bearded character in buckskins, identified by the caption as "Dad Kinney, hunter and wolf trapper," was peering into the mouth of a small cave. He then pulled a stick of dynamite from his pack, lit it and tossed it into the opening, whereupon the camera panned in for a closeup of the horrid, writhing sputtering fuse.

I held my breath. This part of the story I knew: the newborn puppy Flash was denned up in there with his brothers and sisters and parents. But this was no story now; this was real, unfolding before my terror-stricken eyes. The pianist banged a chord fortissimo. The screen exploded in a cloud of smoke and flying debris. I gulped and burst into tears.

Poor Flash! What have they done to you?

Sylvia had to lead me up the aisle in public ignominy. The author's son—a cry baby. Almost two years went by before I was allowed to attend another movie.

In November that year Hal wrote Brandt: "I seem to be rather short of short story material but have two book length stories sort of half formed in my mind. I want to base one of them on the big rush into the Cherokee Strip which was the most spectacular rush in the West and has never been written up, and the other I thought to lay in Wyoming when they struck oil in the cow country. I can't be much more definite than that but I am starting out tomorrow to pitch a tent on the Arkansas River and trap until December 15th. I am going to be on the ranch of a man who made the Cherokee Run and expect to get a great many first hand items from him."

Hal's Wyoming oil boom novel aborted but his first idea became the genesis of *Tumbleweeds*, taken from his experiences in Indian Territory as a surveyor's transit toter.

This is how he described the trapping trip to pal Ned Frost: "I was getting sort of fat and useless so Sylvia and I stuck a tent out in the sandhills forty miles west of town November 30th. I strung out fifty-five traps and the next day a blizzard nailed us. Wind blew for two days and drifted clear to the tops of the willows along the river and snowed my muskrat traps under so deep that it took me a good many days to dig them out from under the ice and snow. The tent was perfectly comfortable and I went ahead trapping the best I could and managed to catch twenty-nine pelts of rats, badger and skunk in the two weeks. I walked off some of my surplus by bucking the drifts and the river with hip boots about ten miles a day. Like to killed me off at first but I kept at it."

To Hal this was an ideal vacation and his account of it, *Prairie Blizzard*, later sold to the *Post* for $1,000. Sylvia, so far as I know, never went trapping again, on the Arkansas or elsewhere.

Oddly enough, his previous serial, *Fur Sign*, intended for teenage readers, had proved one of his most difficult efforts. He had underestimated his audience, Hal realized belatedly. "Too much talk and too little story," he commented, tore up the first draft and rewrote it from start to finish. But *Tumbleweeds* gave him no such problems. He promised Brandt he could complete it within three months and did, with two weeks to spare. Lorimer bought the serial rights for $5,000 and urged him to consider future novels with historical themes. Brandt quickly sold the screen rights for an additional $5,000. With the proceeds Hal made a non-typical conservative investment—a quarter section of wheat land fourteen miles west of Hutchinson. It still remains in the family, known to his descendants as "Tumbleweeds Farm."

The lowly ubiquitous tumbleweed symbolized in his mind the wandering footloose rider of the open range, and his story was more than somewhat autobiographical. In an early scene a key character, a cowpoke who has squandered his pay in town, promotes a scheme of selling cheap whiskey to some thirsty Cherokees at a 400 percent profit (a federal offense at any price), then embarks upon a night of booze and bucking the roulette wheel, wakes up next morning with a single silver dollar and a thunderous hangover. Hal never punched cattle, never sold whiskey to anyone, although he bought and consumed more than his share, but I can hear his voice in this doggerel he composed long before the song *Tumblin' Tumbleweed* emerged from Tin Pan Alley:

> 'Our size and shape is similar'
> Said the tumbleweed to the pumpkin,
> 'I'll run you a race from here to there
> And all the way back again.
>
> I'm a wild free blade of the open,
> The spirit of all unrest.
> I may end up in some worse place
> But I'm going to make the test.
>
> I'd rather be a travellin' weed
> Than a stationary squash.'

The girl, one of his more sympathetic and believable heroines, has certain overtones of Sylvia: practical, sensible, seeking security in a turbulent world, a pumpkin who longs to put down roots and go to seed. She refuses to marry the hero until he forswears his wastrel ways, settles down and acquires some land of his own. I have often wondered if Hal's purchase of the farm, where he never intended to live, was not a subliminal response, a fleeting impulse that he regretted afterward, for he and Sylvia argued bitterly about the disposition of it the rest of his life.

The federal government opened the Cherokee Strip to

homestead settlement at twelve o'clock noon on April 22, 1889. An estimated 20,000 land-hungry Americans, some of whom had been waiting for weeks, were lined up on their horses, in wagons, buggies, buckboards, even on bicycles, held back by U.S. Cavalry partols, until the signal. The best, the most desirable land would go to the swiftest, or luckiest.

Here is how Hal depicted the scene: "The troopers had ceased patrolling the line and now sat their saddles at half-mile intervals and faced the eager horde they had held in check for so long a time. The strains of a bugle sounded faintly from afar, penetrating the buzz of conversation and silencing it. A second note, far to the westward, joined the first, and in a space of two seconds the clear ringing strains of the bugles pealed the same message along a front of two hundred miles. There was a sudden tense hush, the troopers sitting rigidly in their saddles. As the last notes died away each soldier fired a single shot, and with a tremendous sullen roar the most spectacular run of all time was off to a running start."

Tumbleweeds, like *Old West* before it, was a lament, a salute to the end of an era and a way of life, the plow replacing the pony, the fence the open prairie. Progress had overcome and tamed Indian Territory for all time. The film version of Hal's story, starring a famous western actor of the day, Wiliam S. Hart, in his final Hollywood role, appeared some four years later. Hal, Sylvia and I saw this one together too. By then, having sat through many a magic Saturday matinee, transported by the heroics of Tom Mix, Hoot Gibson, Buck Jones, *et al*, I was a seasoned movie addict. When relentless, steely-eyed Bill Hart gunned down the villain in the final reel, I shed no tears; I clapped and cheered.

"*Tumbleweeds*," said George N. Fenin and William K. Everson in their authoritative book, *The Western*, "was one of the best of the Western epics, staged on a truly lavish scale." In many ways they rated it as superior to the more popular *The Covered Wagon*. The authors singled out one scene "when Hart and his riders, on the crest of a hill, watch the great trail herds being driven from the land that is soon to be made available to all settlers. As the herds drift by, Hart removes his hat sadly and remarks: 'Boys, it's the last of the West.' And the others remove their hats reverently, and watch as an era passes into history."

After Hal's death Hart bought the sound rights to *Tumbleweeds* from my mother and in 1939 reissued the film with music and an eight-minute prologue delivered by Hart himself, "... unquestionably one of the most moving reels of film ever made. Hart, dressed in his beloved Western costume, walks slowly up to the camera to address the audience. He is old, but still a fine figure of a man. He stands there more as a representative of the old West itself than as a silent picture star. In a firm, beautifully modulated voice Hart explains what the opening of the Cherokee Strip meant to both the white man and the Indian. Then he goes on to discuss Western pictures, tells how sorry he is that he is too old to make more of them, a magnificent, superbly touching speech, his farewell to the screen." Both of these scenes were replayed on national network TV in October 1986 in the series *The West of the Imagination*.

In the spring of 1922 Lorimer gave Hal another assignment, one that would solidify his reputation in the forefront of the national conservation movement. This plan, enthusiastically endorsed by Horace Albright and his boss, Stephen T. Mather, director of the National Park Service, called for him to visit, inspect and report in depth on wildlife conditions in several major western parks. Delighted at the prospect of physical action, Hal caught up on his current commitments and ever-tardy correspondence, and when school let out in June he and Sylvia deposited me for the summer with my Grandma Emma in Berkeley and took off for the High Sierra.

With a string of 14 horses and a retinue of two packers, a cook and ranger-guide they packed into the Kings Canyon watershed and the northern reaches of Sequoia Park, an area then so remote that in a trip of 30 days they encountered only one other party. Moving on to Montana, they packed through Glacier in much the same fashion, under Park Service auspices. In September Sylvia shepherded me back to Hutchinson and school, while Hal continued his horseback travels for another two months, this time in the Southwest—Zion, Kaibab Forest and the North Rim of the Grand Canyon—where he hunted mountain lions behind a pack of hounds and took part in a wild horse roundup. This last provided material for a subsequent novel, *The Painted Stallion*, also destined for Hollywood.

Returning to his desk after nearly half a year's absence, he plunged into another of his nonstop workaholic binges. Fiction had been his forte but he now discovered that writing non-fiction, while less lucrative, was easier and less demanding. Above all, it afforded a reprieve from the "love stuff" he found so burdensome. Week after week his articles appeared in the *Post*, an outpouring of his observations, opinions and recommendations. In that regard Lorimer had imposed no restrictions; fortunately their views coincided in most instances. But not everyone was happy. Then, as now, conservation came in different guises. Knowingly, almost gleefully, Hal jumped into the midst of an ongoing power struggle between the Department of Interior's National Park Service and the Department of Agriculture's National Forest Service.

In one of his earlier articles proposing limited grazing rights on government land by stockmen, he had offended ranchers in Wyoming's Jackson Hole, several of his friends among them. Now he drew fire from militant bureaucrats in the nation's capital. "Amateur," one critic labeled him. "Self-claimed naturalist with no academic credentials to support his position." Hal would have agreed. He had no professional qualifications, no scientific background, no degrees. As he stated often publicly, without apology: "I only write about things I know from personal experience." But the barbs must have stung. His spotty ninth-grade education left him vulnerable to attack.

The programs he advocated in the 1920s—some of them compromises between opposing factions—have become more or less standard practice in public land management: soil erosion control, controlled burning, controlled game harvesting, controls on timber cutting and mining, establishment of wilderness areas, increased tourist facilities within an overall framework of nature preservation for future generations. None of these proposals were new; he never considered himself an innovator. But for the first time he presented them as a unified entity, a comprehensive long range conservation policy, to a wide cross section of Americans.

The most controversial issue was his recommendation that Yellowstone and General Grant be extended in specified areas, that those two national parks be enlarged. In governmentese the ugly word was "relinquishment," a term which in plain English meant that the Forest Service would turn over some of its lands to the Park Service, such lands to be permanently closed to lease or any form of private enterprise, a radical idea for any popular magazine to espouse in 1922. Eventually, after many a lengthy hard-fought battle, both of Hal's recommendations bore magnificent fruit, accomplishments he did not live to see. General Grant, enlarged and renamed Kings Canyon, became a separate national park in 1940; part of Jackson Hole was added to the Grand Teton National Park in 1950.

In the spring of 1923 he received this letter from Albright: "I am so pleased with your article regarding Yellowstone game conditions I can scarcely express my happiness. In your series of articles you have done a great thing for the American people and have made things easier for us. We are all grateful to you and appreciate your fine public-spirited stand on our policies and principles."

In an earlier letter Albright had written him about plans to build the Park system's first natural history museum at Mammoth Hot Springs in Yellowstone. In response Hal shipped to him a crate containing a splendidly mounted whooping crane—"The grandest bird of all America," widely believed to be extinct at that time—a gift to be put on display there. How this particular "whooper" came into his possession, illegally, he recounted to a park official years later:

"In the fall of 1920 I drove out to the salt marsh alone and went to a blind. Just across a stretch of shallow water a mud flat stretched away. Just at sundown I heard whoopers. Eight of them sifted down and made a majestic landing on the flat within a hundred yards of me. Half an hour later, when it was growing dark, I heard others. Those on the flat answered. Several of them spread their great white wings and waved them slowly, as if signalling a safe landing for the newcomers. Three others came down out of the dusk and joined them. I believe that every surviving whooper in America was in that flock, a sight that may never fall to the lot of man to see again.

"I had written a short story, *The Vanished Squadrons*, ringing in the legend of the 'golden cranes,' sending a young bird on his first southward journey with the clanging hosts of which Audubon wrote. In the end he set forth alone on the last long journey into the south in search of the golden plumes of his youth. In view of that yarn, it seemed a unique coincidence that when a lone whooper came winging his solitary way down the flyway in the fall of 1922 two years later he should fall into my hands.

"A hunter shot the bird from a fringe of rushes. It fell far out in thigh-deep mud. He didn't care to navigate that mud so he departed. From far across the marsh an old market hunter had recognized the bird, had seen it fall and, to his amazement had watched the hunter walk off without even going out to inspect his prey. That night he telephoned a friend of mine. The latter drove to the marsh and at sunup was floundering through the mud before the hawks would have a chance to tear up the dead crane. He found it, had it mounted and gave it to me.

"But the end was not yet. The crane arrived in its crate one evening in March 1923. We left it in the kitchen to be uncrated in the morning. That night our house burned and most of my collections were destroyed, but the kitchen and the whooping crane were untouched. Next morning a federal game warden arrived to confiscate the bird for the national museum in Washington. I declined to part with it. I had lived in the Yellowstone country so long that I felt it was my home neighborhood. So I sent the last whooping crane as the first bird in the new Yellowstone Museum."

Thus Hal thwarted the Feds. Washington's loss became Wyoming's gain. His whooper, miraculous survivor of our fire, still on exhibit today, was *not* the last of its kind. A small flock of whooping cranes and its precious gene pool, rigorously protected and on the endangered species list, does exist, winging down the flyway every spring from its nesting grounds in northern Alberta to a sanctuary on the Texas Gulf coast. The vanished squadrons of yesteryear have made a comeback of sorts.

Hal received his ultimate reward when Albright and Director Mather offered him the job as first resident naturalist at the new museum, to supervise exhibits and lecture during the summer tourist season. For practical financial reasons he had to decline but no tribute or recognition in his lifetime pleased him more. Hal Evarts, a certified naturalist—college degrees be damned! Thereafter he could thumb his nose at his more learned detractors.

8.

Hutchinson, Kansas, July 9, 1923:
"President Harding in white flannel trousers, white doe-skin shoes, blue coat and straw hat, shocked sheaves of wheat after the approved Kansas method. The President then drove a tractor binder around a 90-acre field while the cameras clicked."
Time magazine.

THE FIRE THAT SWEPT through our house in the early hours of March 8, 1923, marked a change in my perception of my parents and their relationship to each other. For the first time I came to realize, to fully comprehend, that all was not serene in my boyhood paradise. Far from it.

Here is how Hal described the event in a letter to his mother: "It started about 2:30 A.M. and must undoubtedly have come from the wiring of a table lamp beside the davenport. Sylvia waked and smelled smoke, roused me and I meandered casually down to the foot of the stairs. As soon as I opened the door I could see that the whole back end of the living room was a mass of flames. I called to Sylvia to grab Son and make a run for it. The heat was so intense that two minutes later would have been too late for us to get out except by jumping through the windows. I was cut by flying glass and nearly put under by smoke, trying to reach the telephone. We huddled out front waiting for the fire department, and poor little Sylvia flinched every time some vase or lamp exploded with a crash inside.

We do feel it was exceptionally important that it started on a night when we were home instead of when we were gone with Son sleeping alone upstairs."

If Hal's den was a taxidermist's delight, our living room was a miniature Oriental bazaar, repository for all the curios, knicknacks and trinkets that my grandmother Emma, a compulsive shopper, had accumulated on her travels with Lee Bigger: Japanese bronzes, Chinese porcelains, Indian brocades, Egyptian scarabs, Arab daggers, tablets from the Holy Land, ivory fans and camel bells. The showpiece, from my point of view, was a tiger skin on which I loved to lie before the fireplace, fingering its fangs and dreaming of adventure in some far-off jungle. All of these treasures went up in flames, along with many of my illusions.

The question, impossible to ignore, was how the fire had originated. Hal clung to his contention of a short circuit. Sylvia countered with the accusation that he'd been drunk and left a smoldering cigarette. Drunk? A new word in my vocabulary. The argument raged on, repetitive and cruel and corrosive, never in my presence but agonizingly audible in the small apartment we rented for several weeks while our house was being repaired and refurbished. For a long while clues had been abundant: angry voices in the night, slammed doors, tears, Hal's frequent unexplained absences. Now, I was able to string them together like random beads into a single strand, my eight-year-old version of reality: My father was a problem drinker. "Alcoholic" was another word I soon would learn, not only the definition, but how to live with one.

Colonel Houston Whiteside, a retired West Pointer and one of Hal's oldest friends, saw him as ". . . a fine likeable man but a very heavy drinker by the time he returned to Hutchinson. Hal was a fascinating story teller before and after he began to write. Everyone was awed by his tremendous talent. But sometimes he went on benders, would go off for days. It was very hard on Sylvia; the whole town knew and sympathized. My mother, who liked Hal especially, was one person who could talk to him like a Dutch Uncle and try to straighten him up.

"He had a variety of friends from all classes of society, some not welcome in the better homes. One was Koon Beck, who managed an amusement park and collected rare birds. Hal and Koon would get together and down glasses of straight alcohol in a competition to see who could drink the other under the table. There was another, an Irish tailor named Pat, a goodhearted fellow who often tried to help Hal taper off, but would end up in worse shape than Hal, and both would have to be carted home. More than once Sylvia locked Hal out of the house."

Kansas was a dry state long before national Prohibition and remained so long after the eighteenth amendment was repealed. Even the public sale of cigarettes was illegal, at least in Reno County. From time to time officials descended on Hutchinson to conduct token raids and confiscate a few cartons. Liquor in one form or another was always available, if not from a bootlegger then from a friendly neighborhood druggist who would cheerfully sell a quart of whiskey from his licensed stock with a bogus medical prescription for "heart disease" or "nervous disorders."

Hal's favorite haunt was Big Em's, a speakeasy-roadhouse in an isolated section of the sandhills north of town. I never saw the place but I had a lurid picture of a landlocked pirates' den, presided over by an enormous bosomy female with gold earrings and a pistol in her sash. Em also provided games of chance—craps, blackjack, poker—in which Hal indulged at all-night, high stake sessions.

Despite his lapses and dissipations he, in some four years as a free-lance writer, had racked up a remarkable record: six serial-novels, one anthology, dozens of short stories and articles in the leading slicks. As an apostle of conservation he had reached a wider congregation than he knew, including politicians in high places. Now he had an opportunity to plead his cause in person to Number One.

That June he received an invitation from Mather to join the presidential (Warren G. Harding) party at Yosemite later in the summer to discuss with the President various national park projects. In a follow-up letter Albright urged Hal to promote the Teton extension idea with the President "as he and Mrs. Harding are very much interested in it." Flattered, Hal of course agreed.

Harding, regarded by many historians as one of the less illustrious occupants of the Oval Office, had seen his administration rocked by the recent Teapot Dome oil scandals and set out on an image-mending tour across the country. During his brief Hutchinson stopover he not only posed for photographs but met a few local dignitaries. Unfortunately Hal was not among them; two days earlier he had left town with Sylvia and me on one of his "working vacations." Meanwhile, the President proceeded to Yellowstone, visited Alaska and arrived in San Francisco where he fell ill with pneumonia.

The Evarts family spent most of that summer in a rented beach front apartment at Ocean Park near Los Angeles. A few days before Hal's Yosemite commitment he stepped on a rusty nail. He ingored it until his foot became infected. A hastily summoned doctor swabbed out the puncture and gave him an anti-tetanus injection, to which Hal had a severe reaction with alternating fever and chills. He almost cancelled out but decided that the meeting was too important, regardless of his health. Not only that, he felt obligated to the National Park Service. Weak and shaky, he arrived on schedule but President Harding was by then under intensive medical care. A show, planned weeks in advance to entertain the Harding party, had to go on. To his consternation my father learned that he had been programmed as a star performer. "Famous outdoor author Hal G. Evarts" would demonstrate his skills as a mountain climber. The climb, a precipitous 3,200-foot ascent from the floor of Yosemite Valley up Ledge Trail to Glacier Point, timed by stop watches, left him in a state of extreme exhaustion.

The next day, August 2, President Harding died. With the nation in mourning, a saddened Hal returned to Ocean Park to recuperate, depressed by the meeting that never took place, by his two missed chances to lobby for park expansion at the highest level, and discouraged about his own physical conditon. "I feel like I died with Harding," he said. "That climb killed me." Thereafter he referred to his heart as "my bum ticker."

On our return trip to Kansas, we turned aside to attend the annual Snake Dance ceremony at the mesa top village of Walpi on the Hopi Indian Reservation. The Hopi prayers for rain produced immediate results, a night-long downpour that mired us in northern Arizona for three days. From this experience he wrote *Rattle and Drum*, memorable only for the fact that it was his first rejection. Brandt could not sell it anywhere. In his sixteen-year career Hal would have only two more rejections—a novelette and another article.

That fall he received a letter from Will H. Dilg, founder of the Izaak Walton League and publisher of that organization's monthly journal *Outdoor America*: "I am earnestly hoping that you will send us a story or an article for the magazine. It is obvious that each great American who declares himself for us now adds to our national prestige and our convert-drawing ability. You, of course, know what a splendid thing an editorial by you would be for the magazine and the cause it espouses." So, from time to time Hal contributed pieces to *Outdoor America*, along with such conservation-minded authors as Theodore Dreiser, David Starr Jordan, Zane Grey, Irvin S. Cobb and Mary Roberts Rinehart. For free.

In the early 1920s Hutchinson was lily white WASP, largely of northern European stock. The public grammar school I attended had only one black child out of an enrollment of some 400. Our family had a black gardener, Old George, born a slave in Louisiana who somehow had found his way to central Kansas. There were two Jewish boys in my class, a few mercantile families; anti-Semitic jokes were standard fare at dinner parties and sevice club luncheons. There was a small Catholic community. Another colony at the nearby hamlet of Yoder—Amish—provided a note of variety; their menfolk delivered fresh milk, butter and eggs door to door from their one-of-a-kind buggies, garbed in austere, homemade black suits. I never met an Asian of any ethnic strain until we moved to California.

There was still a sizeable immigration of Scandinavians, whose first generation males found employment as farm hands and sent their daughters into town to work as live-in domestics at a wage of one dollar a day. Monday was "washday." Our Danish laundress received two dollars for her ten-hour stint. For the affluent, life was comfortable. I never saw my father mow a lawn, wash a dish or rinse out a pair of socks. My mother ordered our groceries by telephone, free delivery.

On the surface, Hutchinson had been affected very little by World War I. The American Legion became a voice in local politics, the *News* editorialized against foreign-born anarchists, a short-lived Ku Klux Klan klavern burned a cross or two. Farm prices were depressed but a flurry of exploration for oil and natural gas took up the economic slack. On sultry summer nights Hal would drive the family out to various well sites where he had a royalty interest, often as small as 1/64th, to watch the drillers at work under the lights. But about this time he concluded that the New York Stock Exchange was heading for a fall and switched his interest to the Coolidge bull market, the biggest crap shoot of all time.

At school I demonstrated no promise as a future writer, although I did develop an insatiable appetite for books. In the other basic disciplines I was adequate, in the fine arts—deficient. In deportment I often brought home a report card marked: "mischievous, needs improvement." Despite this mediocre record the powers-that-were saw fit to "skip" me ahead by semester increments, so that I entered the sixth grade two years in advance of my peers, smaller than all of the boys and most of the girls. Two results have been my lifelong difficulty with fractions and a conditioned awe of the opposite sex.

That winter I fell in love for the first time, with a bright pretty girl named Barbara who was several inches taller than I and seemed unaware of my existence. On Valentine's Day I made my move. I squandered ten cents on a frilly card, signed my name and slipped it in the classroom box, which our teacher had decorated for the occasion. Barbara continued to ignore me.

An older more worldly boy whom I considered a friend, Richie, came up with a daring, direct action scheme. If I would turn over to him my weekly candy allowance of six cents, which I received in a lump sum every Tuesday, he offered to negotiate with my darling and persuade her to meet me after school at some secluded spot for a kiss. One kiss.

Not to be satisfied with a sisterly peck on the cheek, I insisted, "On the mouth."

"Sure, on the mouth," Richie said. "Where else?"

"Do you think she'll do it? Maybe she's not that kind of a girl."

"I guarantee it," said my intermediary. "No girl's gonna turn down six cents for one measly kiss."

Unaware that I was embarking upon Step One of the world's oldest profession, I handed over my money.

Barbara did not appear at our rendezvous for the assignation. Nor did Richie. But on hand was a gang of my sniggering, leering classmates eager to watch. For weeks I remained the butt of the Winans School sixth grade pubescent humor.

At some midpoint in elementary school, the realization had percolated through my layers of awareness that my father was, for lack of a more precise classification, someone special, different, apart from mainstream Hutchinson. The fathers of my friends took their vacations in summertime, two or at most three weeks. My old man took off for months, anytime he chose. He often went to work in his bathrobe, strolling from the dining room into his den. No office, no boss, no confining hours, free as a bird, or so it appeared to me; an altogether ideal life style for adult or child. He wrote stories; why shouldn't I?

My early efforts were verbal, my first audience a dedicated teacher of junior high school English, Miss Mattie Kent, who lived across the street. I spun out my fantasies for her several afternoons a week, encouraged by her interest and home-baked cookies. My first material success came at the age of ten when I won second place and a check for three dollars in a county-wide essay contest on the topic *The Evils of Nicotine*.

By then Hal was a four-pack-a-day consumer, his "bum

ticker" notwithstanding. One morning I returned from Sunday School at the Presbyterian Church and relayed a warning from the minister, who occasionally visited our class to deliver brief sermons, that cigarette smokers would burn forever in hellfire and brimstone.

Hal exploded. "I won't have Son stuffed with that kind of claptrap!" he thundered at Sylvia. Consequently my formal religious training suffered a permanent eclipse.

By 1924, five years after Hal's self-introduction to the Brandt brothers, his relationship with them had ripened from one of perfunctory exchanges into friendship, progressed from the standard salutation of "Dear Mr. Evarts" to "Friend Hal" and "Old Top," with a signoff, no longer "Sincerely yours," but "As ever thine." He met with them several times in Chicago, halfway point between Hutchinson and Manhattan, to confer on long-range prospects for his career. They had become his counselors and father confessors, attuned to his moods and fluctuations of the marketplace.

In May that year Secretary of Agriculture Henry C. Wallace invited him to serve on a committee to study the Kaibab deer situation in Arizona. And from Philadelphia Lorimer wired that the Izaak Walton League, conservation bellwether of its day, was "anxious to have you attend conference at Washington and to become member of advisory board to President Coolidge." No eager public speaker, Hal felt this was another command performance, not unlike his Glacier Point climb, although less strenuous—a civic duty he could not refuse. Accompanied by Sylvia, he delivered the keynote address on the touchy topic of *Grazing Control*, was entertained at the Lorimer Wyncote estate, and made his first tour of the HQ and nerve center of the Curtis publishing empire, the font of his good fortune.

Of the *Saturday Evening Post* "everything I saw seemed symbolic of the magazine's awesome age and solemnity." So wrote Otto Friedrich, one of the *Post*'s last editors, recalling years later his impressions of his first day in the Curtis employ. "The building itself was symbolic. An eleven-story structure of white marble that had been shipped from Maine by Cyrus

H.K. Curtis (who had bought the periodical for $1,000 in 1898), it overlooked the gardens of Independence Square and the brick tower that contained the Liberty Bell. The lobby was also symbolic. Stained-glass windows darkened the interior, and, at the rear, fountains splashed softly before a gigantic mosaic mural entitled *The Groves of Academe*, created from designs by Maxfield Parrish. The elevators were symbolic, lined with dark wooden paneling, and gently maneuvered upward and downward by Negroes in gray livery and white gloves. Even the towels in the lavatories were symbolic. There were no paper towels because there had never been paper towels. After washing one's hands, one took a clean towel from a large pile of folded linen; one dried one's hands and dropped the towel into a wicker hamper. At the end of every day Negroes came to carry away the towels, launder them, and return them to service."

Much of this symbolism may have been lost on Hal, no respecter of hallowed tradition, but he must have been impressed. He and Lorimer agreed on an idea for his next serial, based on the history of the Maxwell land grant in New Mexico's Territorial days, and Hal returned to his Hutchinson den.

That summer Sylvia and I spent with her parents in San Diego, where they had retired after leaving Kansas City. Sylvia, I am sure, was debating whether to leave Hal permanently, but in the fall we rejoined him. Next spring, 1925, he completed *Spanish Acres* and, three days after Lorimer's acceptance at a price of $10,000, departed on a trip to Alaska by himself, the dream of his life, one that was to last seven months. Although convinced that he had suffered major heart damage, he never went near a doctor for an examination, another of his idiosyncrasies under the banner of self-sufficiency.

In Anchorage he chartered a launch and chugged around the eastern arc of the Aleutian chain photographing marine life. Following a successful sheep count in the Alaskan Range, he set out on foot across rugged Kodiak and bagged a specimen of that island's huge brown bears, a giant whose pelt measured eleven feet from snout to tip—his last big game hunt. Earl Crouch, a friend from Wapiti who joined him for this portion of the trip, recalled it this way: "We were on this island covered with real dense willows. Hal got off a shot into a big old boar bear but didn't kill the s.o.b. That bear started hunting us. I got lost from Hal after he charged between us. It was the worst half hour of my life. I never came so close to cashing in my chips. That bear was hunting us just like a coyote hunts mice in an alfalfa field by jumping up and down where he thinks you are, only this brute was smashing willows ten feet high. We knew what would happen if he found either of us. Hal finally dropped him with a second shot. That bear was a monster; measured over thirty inches between the ears."

Hal's next project, a survey of the Kenai Peninsula's moose population, began inauspiciously in bad weather. Accompanied by a guide and two U.S. Army officers, he rope-lined a small boat up the Kusilof River with great difficulty and made camp on Tustemena Lake. After a week the officers had to return to duty. Hal elected to stay behind alone with a tent, one blanket, an axe and his ancient .33 caliber rifle. The guide would return to pick him up "as soon as possible." This is how he described the experience in *Outdoor Life*, a popular Denver-based magazine:

"One night a terrific storm caught me afoot several miles back in high country, the rain driving in torrents. It seemed probable that I would have to sit up against a tree all night, as it was pitch black and tough traveling. But I kept plugging along until I could hear the pounding of breakers on the lake shore above the roar of the storm, which guided me into camp. It was certainly one large relief to crawl into that little tent and strip off my wet clothing. The storm increased hourly until one could not even hear the breaking of trees close at hand. Morning found my apprehensions lively when I saw a number of birches and big cottonwoods that had been snapped off by the wind. Instead of abating the storm grew worse and that second night a birch did hit the tent and knocked one corner down. I was assailed by unpleasant visions of being pinned down myself but toward nightfall of the third day the wind moderated.

"By the eighth day I began to fear that Judd (the guide) had come to a smash in the storm. I had only meat, flour, corn meal and baking powder for food, not even such camp staples as coffee and sugar, and worse—no tobacco. There is so much food in that country—fish, berries, grouse, ptarmigan, porcupines, sheep, moose, bears, rabbits and other provender for the taking—that one could not starve if he tried. But six more days on a straight meat and cornbread diet was growing monotonous. Perhaps, too, I am not as good company for myself as I was a dozen years ago. My own society was boring me. All told, this Robinson Crusoe business for two weeks was beginning to wear thin. My natural indolence recoiled at the thought of packing my equipment on my back and bucking the brush to salt water. Nevertheless it had to be done, so I set forth with a pack of some sixty pounds, the axe and my rifle.

"Traveling the lake shore with its deeply indented swamps and overhanging thickets proved too arduous after the first few miles, so I cut back into the hills. Anyone who has bucked the alder growth of Alaska can testify to the fact that it is the world's worst. In midafternoon I had a trying experience with a bull moose. He moved very slowly toward me across a clearing and when he had approached to within forty yards it seemed high time to apprise him of the fact that I was not another moose, so I called out and whistled a shrill blast. Still he moved toward me. I was inclined to think it was curiosity on his part but that pair of little eyes up close to his big antlers seeemd to hold a malignant flare. Suddenly I was acutely alarmed and brought up my rifle. He broke and ran then, passing me with a rush not over twenty-five feet distant. I have always heard of moose attacks with mental reservations, but I was conscious of considerable weakness in the knees all the same.

"At dark I made a halt, having been on the trail about fourteen hours. I ate some cold cornbread and rolled up in the timber a few yards back from the lake. In ten seconds sleep claimed my weary frame. Round midnight I waked with the notion I had heard the stutter of an outboard motor. I had. It was Judd, delayed by the storm, returning to pick me up.... A cigarette will never taste so good again."

During this period when he was beyond the reach of communication, Sylvia, acting as his representative with power of attorney, conducted negotiations for two motion picture deals. Totally innocent of business experience, she held out for and got $10,000 for screen rights to *Spanish Acres* from Famous Players. And refused $7,500 for rights to *The Painted Stallion*, which turned out less successfully. Eleven years later, in the depth of the Depression, they sold for a mere $600.

Hal was proud of her acumen nonetheless, when he learned the news. To friends he jokingly praised her: "Now I have two agents. The one in New York keeps ten per cent, the one at home spends the rest."

That July Sylvia and I met him in Seward and the three of us passed the balance of the summer hiking and horse packing into the scenic wilderness of McKinley National Park. Our final stop was Fairbanks where a government official and his charming wife drove us on a picnic to a nearby river. With his relish for ferreting out facts, Hal soon learned the lady's background: she had come north as a prostitute in the Klondike gold rush of 1898, risen to the top of her profession and married into respectability. Back home in Kansas he delighted in shocking dinner guests: "Sylvia spent the whole day hobnobbing with the most famous red-light madam in Alaska. And liked her. Never guessed her business."

For that time and place I was a child of privilege. The 1925 dollar when factored for inflation had the purchasing power of approximately six dollars today. My first dog, Flash, was no mutt from the pound but a thoroughbred collie shipped from the Ohio kennels of Albert Payson Terhune, one of Hal's pen pals and a fellow contributor to the *Post*. I had my own horse, a fat nag stabled at the county fairgrounds, which I dutifully rode every Saturday morning around the track into stupefying boredom. I had a Lionel electric train layout mounted on a platform. I had an Erector set (a mechanical booby trap in my clumsy hands), a Chemcraft, a motion picture projector with reels of Charlie Chaplin twirling his cane, and book shelves full of the *Motor Boys*, the *Rover Boys* and *Tom Swift*. In our backyard Hal set up a horizontal bar and high jump standards and helped me dig a cave, a far cry from his "Evarts Cave" of the Kaw River woodlands.

One afternoon two schoolmates, whose father operated a dry cleaning shop, came to play. "Gee!" they said in awe. "You sure must be rich."

Rich? The idea had never occurred to me.

I had one brief exposure to the realm of commerce. Under pressure from Hal I took on a route for the *Literary Digest*, a respected magazine of the day that was more political than literary. One afternoon each week I tramped up and down the neighborhood with a heavy canvas bag slung over my shoulder, ringing doorbells, mumbling, "You wanta buy a *Digest*?" then slouching away in defeat to the next house. At the end of six weeks I had only one regular customer, my benefactress, dear Mattie Kent across the street, whose ten cent purchase was an act of mercy.

Hal relented. "I guess you're not cut out to be a salesman," he said. "Like your old man."

At an early age he began instructing me in the use of firearms. A safety fanatic, he rehearsed me over and over, then bought me a .22 rifle and a 20-gauge shotgun. From the outset I proved to be a failure, both with fixed targets and afield. For some reason I could not hit a bird on the wing or a tin can on a post. Hal was patient. "You'll get the hang of it, Son," he reassured me. "Just takes a little time and practice."

Many a frosty autumn night after dinner, we would drive out to the salt marsh to sleep at his gun club and be ready on the spot for the early morning hunt. The first part of this ritual I liked, lying snug and warm in a bunk listening to man talk about other hunts and laments for the good old days when millions of mallards and canvas backs darkened the skies. But the mornings I detested. I hated to crawl out in the dark and cold, slosh through mud and reeds, only to shiver for hours in some sinkhole of a blind, waiting for ducks that never flew within my range. I did at last shoot one, a teal that was unwary enough to swim directly at me.

You did not shoot sitting birds, I was informed. It was not considered "sporting."

That winter my parents kept me out of school and we spent several months in Miami Beach, the first of Florida's boom-to-bust real estate psychodramas. Sylvia finally surrendered her waist-length hair to the new styles and came home in tears from the barber shop—women's beauty salons did not yet exist—with her shorn tresses in a paper bag. For consolation Hal took her dancing to the music of Paul Whiteman's band in Coral Gables. He ordered a trunkful of foreign liqueurs smuggled in from Cuba and, when not preoccupied with the last chapters of *Moccasin Telegraph*, took us deep sea fishing in a chartered cruiser off Long Key.

Despite his professed scorn for the military, he shipped me off to summer camp at Culver, Indiana, where I learned the rudiments of close order drill and a cadet's discipline. The results pleased Sylvia, at least. Back home, I overheard her tell members of her bridge club: "Hal Jr. doesn't just drop his dirty clothes on the floor any more. Now he picks them up."

But my cozy, secure small-town world in which everybody seemed to know me or my parents or my grandparents was about to shatter. Two days after Christmas Sylvia, without a word of explanation, bundled me up and the two of us boarded the westbound Santa Fe Limited. I was eleven years old. More than half a century passed before I saw Hutchinson again.

9.

BY THE MID-1920s Los Angeles had become the favorite whipping boy and target of national ridicule, some good-humored, some waspish, perhaps much of it inspired by a form of perverse jealousy. Knocking L.A. and its sprawling environs was a popular sport of eastern visitors. They came, they saw, they sneered—but they returned, often to stay. "Seven suburbs in search of a city," "Iowa West," "Tinsel Town," "Cuckoo Country" and "Nut Hatchery" were a few of the derisive labels. Scandals involving such film stars as Roscoe "Fatty" Arbuckle and Wallace Reid and Mabel Normand had tarnished the Hollywood legend. Prophets and priestesses, gospel spielers and swamis flourished from San Bernadino to the sea. The L.A. *Times,* fiefdom of the powerful Chandler family, embraced all the area's eccentricities and excesses, its tackiness and infinite variety under the journalistic tent of "The Southland." An unwitting refugee from midwestern winters and conformity, I was easily seduced. I liked it.

On New Year's Eve, my parents' fourteenth anniversary, Sylvia and I rode up and down Wilshire Boulevard on an open double decker bus admiring the sights and lights, which included a restaurant that resembled a derby hat and a palm tree festooned with winking Stars of David. We smelled orange blossoms and the asphalt stench of the La Brea Tar Pits. Next morning from our hotel window, I could see a chain of snow-tipped peaks and the splendors of the world's most opulent movie palace, Grauman's Chinese, then nearing completion. Kansas had never been like this, winter or summer, fall or spring.

Sylvia's intention, although she did not confide in me, was to start a new life apart from Hal. With the ingenuous faith of childhood, I took for granted that our family soon would be reunited, and it was. Within the month he drove west, never to return. They patched up their differences, out of my earshot, and we rented an apartment on the mainline of America's dream factory, Hollywood Boulevard. I was enrolled in a new school and Hal installed himself in his new den, a cubicle off the kitchen formerly designated as the "maid's room." Life went on much as before, superficially, as if we had moved across town, not halfway across the country. But their truce was only that, an effort to provide some kind of harmonious home life for me, to paper over their acrimonies and bitterness in a strange unfamiliar land.

A connoisseur of the paradoxical, Hal would have chortled had he known (he never learned) that his new home base had been founded in 1887, the year of his birth, by a Prohibitionist couple from his native state of Kansas. They dreamed of creating a Christian utopia when they bought 120 acres of chaparral in what was then called Cahuenga Canyon and offered free lots to any church community. Gambling halls, billiard dens and saloons were strictly forbidden.

That March he finished *Moccasin Telegraph*. Some six years earlier, on his trip into Arctic Canada, he had written a friend: "At Fort Simpson, about 1100 miles from the end of the railroad, I met a chap who had come down the Liard River to the Mackenzie. He had spent a number of years in that country; in fact it was according to his reports that the course of the Nahanni River was put on the maps last year. The next two rivers running into the Liard are not yet mapped. The point is that he told me of a tremendous falls of which he could hear the roar for some twenty miles."

This mysterious waterfall, soon to be discovered "officially," became the setting of *Moccasin Telegraph*, Hal's one venture into the field of semi-fantasy. His heroine, an innocent nature girl of highborn Anglo-Saxon lineage, abandoned in the wilderness, not unlike Tarzan's Lady Jane, dominates the story. In rapport with Indian culture and her environment, this delectable lass falls in love with a roving Yankee trapper. (Here Hal permitted himself the sexiest scene he ever wrote—"She yielded to him with fierce unrestraint and answered with a little crooning moan of delight.") In the finale she rejects inherited wealth and a role in society to return to the wilds with her lover.

Hal closed the novel with this paean to the native Americans he so much admired: "Now the North is a land of odd rumors, any of which may prove to be true, for there are vast areas that have never known the tread of a white man and it is from these unknown regions that most of the strange tales emanate. It may be that these things are true. In any event, those who have lived long in the North do not turn a deaf ear when the Moccasin Telegraph is rumbling."

Midway through the book he digressed into a prolix rambling essay on his views of natural selection—Evolution versus Creation and Christian theology. He sold the serial rights to Lorimer for $10,000 and book rights to Little Brown for a $3,000 advance. Some of his mail accused him of advocating paganism, free love and worse, all of which he answered with straight-faced solemnity, but no retractions.

In many respects 1927 was a notable year:

1. Charles Lindbergh flew across the Atlantic.
2. Calvin Coolidge declared, "I do not choose to run."
3. Babe Ruth hit 60 home runs.
4. Henry Ford introduced his new Model A.
5. Al Jolson starred in the first real "talkie," *The Jazz Singer.*
6. *Wings,* starring Buddy Rogers and Clara Bow, won the first Academy Award for best picture.

It was a banner year for Hal as well. Here is his log for sales to the *Post*, exclusive of his income from other magazines, foreign rights and book royalties:

February 16	$ 1,250	*Red Raccoon*
February 25	1,250	*Blue Bear of Yukatat*
March 11	10,000	*Moccasin Telegraph*
March 23	1,250	*Disciples of Solomon*
March 30	1,250	*Kobi of the Sea*
April 13	2,250	*Seeing Is Believing*
June 10	1,250	*Chaparral*
July 15	7,000	*Border Jumpers*
August 10	1,000	*Restocking the Coverts*
August 18	1,000	*Deer Tracks in the Snow*
August 24	1,250	*Sage*
September 28	1,000	*Elk Steaks*
November 17	1,000	*Prairie Blizzard*

That fall he tailed off somewhat, having started a new novel.

In Hollywood he continued his practice of bringing home what Sylvia referred to as "Hal's strays." By now he had become caught up in what he perceived as Wall Street's pell-mell hell-bent course of disaster and, reversing his regular work habits, spent the morning hours at E.F. Hutton's local board room watching his short call margin investments melt like snow in the bull market sunburst. After the market's close, licking his wounds, he walked back the dozen blocks to our apartment and wrote nonstop into the early evening.

The sole recompense from this frustrating exercise was that E.F. Hutton's clientele, winners or losers, offered an assortment of personalities, some of whom Hal found he could empathize with and draw upon for background story material. Invariably these individuals would turn up at our door by dark and, after the most cursory introductions—"This is Jim, he's a stunt rider in the rodeo business"—follow Hal into the den and there, behind a closed door, spend much of the night yarning and smoking and sharing Hal's bootleg bourbon, to the accompaniment of raucous laughter and the clink of glasses.

If Sylvia was something of a snob—and certainly her rearing had not prepared her for such encounters—she struggled to accept Hal's "friends" as a necessary adjunct to his career. Still, she correctly saw this routine as another milepost on his descent into alcoholism.

One of our visitors claimed to have been a U.S. marshal who had killed the nefarious outlaw Jefferson "Soapy" Smith in a gun battle on the Skagway waterfront during the Klondike gold rush of 1898 (untrue, as I learned later) and produced Soapy's gold collar button to "prove" it. Another was a former Texas Ranger who parked his cowboy boots on the furniture and sprinkled cigar ash on the carpet. But the most memorable figure from this period was a small brown-faced man with a conspicuous scar across one cheek who Hal introduced to Sylvia and me as "De Preyto"—Hal's pronunciation—"he rode with Pancho Villa." "De Preyto" reappeared several times, arriving mysteriously and unannounced at the kitchen door for all-night sessions in the den, then vanished from our lives.

When I questioned Hal he told me: "De Preyto was a *pistolero*, one of Villa's bodyguards, a professional killer, the most dangerous man I ever met. There's a price on his head right now. That's why he's so secretive. But he gave me all the stuff I need for my next yarn."

Not quite all, as it turned out. That Easter vacation Hal drove us south to San Diego, spent several days interviewing agents of the U.S. Border Patrol and rode with them on a border sweep. Back in Hollywood he spent a month writing a serial with a contemporary setting about smuggling aliens, *Border Jumpers*, which sold to the *Post* for $7,000.

At first Sylvia felt somewhat lost in the cultural melting pot that was Los Angeles but quickly acquired her own group of friends, mostly the wives of business men who had Kansas roots or relatives, emigres from the nation's heartland like ourselves. The majority of these Hal found dull and diligently avoided. "We don't speak the same language; all they talk about is money," he complained, ignoring the fact that his own obsession had become the Dow Jones Industrial Averages. On one occasion, badgered into attending a formal dinner party, he pushed the host, fully dressed, into the man's swimming pool. I was not present at this event but was to overhear for years about Sylvia's monumental embarrassment and the shock to her "dear friend."

"Jesus Christ, Sylvia," Hal retorted, "I apologized, didn't I. What more do you want?"

"You were drunk," she declared. "Disgustingly drunk!"

"So maybe I'd had a few drinks. Do I have to stand around all night listening to some hot shot salesman brag about his deals?" Then a pause, an unrepentant chuckle. "But, my God, it was funny! Tuxedo and all."

The swimming pool episode was uncharacteristic. Although Hal wrote much about physical violence, he himself was the gentlest of men. During my childhood he spanked me only once, a punishment I richly deserved, and even then he was contrite. He went long periods without touching a drink, then suddenly, unpredictably, would fall off the wagon, an expression I came to dread. These intervals of abstinence became shorter after we moved to California, his behavior and appearance more noticeable—slurred speech, uneven step, bloodshot eyes. Now and then he'd forget where he had parked his car, return home at dawn by taxi and pass out on the couch.

Drunkenness was regarded, if not a mortal sin, then as a character flaw or weakness, a lack of will power or a social peccadillo; but never as a medical problem requiring treatment. Alcoholics Anonymous lay far on the horizon. The attitude of the public, associated with widespread scorn for Prohibition, was one of amused tolerance. Comedians like rubber-limbed Leon Errol carved out entire careers impersonating inebriates. Rum runners, bathtub gin and speakeasy souses stamped their indelible imprint on the era, along with the Charleston. The most popular fictional character of the day, created by author Guy Gilpatric in the pages of the *Post*, was a whiskey swilling engineer on a tramp freighter. America took Colin Glencannon, the wily bibulous rogue, to its heart.

My feelings toward Hal became increasingly complex, perhaps in part because of the Lotus Land nonchalance into which our family had plunged so abruptly. This was no small town of established values, mores and customs. Los Angeles was a vast tidepool of ceaseless ebb and flow. Nothing seemed permanent. I had one advantage over my parents—immaturity; I could adapt more easily to change. Sylvia understood this to a degree and encouraged my first wobbly steps in America's most maligned and publicized city.

For Hal I experienced surges of anger and resentment, voids of shame, moments of pity and compassion. I loved the man. He was the star and sparkle of my universe. But why did he have to make such a spectacle, a mockery of his real self? At the age of twelve I was too insecure and confused to confront him, to ask for answers. Probably he had none to give. But the rows between him and Sylvia—about his drinking, his stock market folly, his uncollectable "loans" to deadbeat friends, his mother-in-law, an endless litany—grew steadily more intense, often to the point where I turned up my triple-dial Atwater Kent radio full volume to drown out the sound and fury. The interminable no-win arguments had their elements of black humor which I would not be able to recognize as such until half a lifetime later.

Hollywood, as often noted, was not so much a geographical entity as a state of mind. 1927 was the twilight of its golden age, the last pre-talkie year, when actors and actresses could emote before the cameras without the bothersome restraint of dialogue. It was also a company town, if not numerically, then in terms of visibility. A large percentage of its residents labored in the studios, on the sets behind guarded gates, the technicians and craftsmen without whose skills the industry could not have cranked out one fast take. World famous celebrities often strolled or drove along the Boulevard, largely ignored by blase natives, this before the business moved west and north, far out of physical Hollywood, before Sid Grauman conceived the notion of immortalizing their foot and handprints in wet cement in the forecourt of his theater. In my own small world I could look out my window every evening and watch the great German actor Emil Jannings pace up and down his colonnaded porch across the way, no doubt rehearsing his lines for the next day's shooting schedule.

Later we moved into the heart of the Hollywood hills,

directly under the HOLLYWOODLAND sign, the symbolic and most famous civic logo in the Western Hemisphere. Across that street from us lived baritone John Boles, who entertained us daily practicing songs for his upcoming musical *The Desert Song*. Tyrone Power Sr., the fiendish arch villain of *The Covered Wagon*, wheeled past our house every morning on his way to work and more make-believe skulduggery. In time I met my idol, Charlie Chaplin, and attended a birthday party at the home of Jackie Coogan. At the private academy for ballroom dancing, which Sylvia compelled me to attend with the direst of threats, I rubbed sweaty shoulders with the sons and daughters of Hollywood's near great, including Hal Roach, Jr. and Eric von Stroheim, Jr. Blasé? Not I. But neither was I awed into tongue-tied veneration.

That summer, at Catalina Island Boys' Camp across the channel, where Hal sent me for six weeks, I gained my own measure of celebrity-hood. Every night around the campfire a counselor read aloud one chapter of *Fur Sign* to some 120 spellbound kids, while I squirmed with embarrassment and secret pleasure. Maybe my old man couldn't act or sing or direct a movie but he could write one helluva book.

That same summer I discovered, at long last, why I would never become a member of the U.S. Olympic rifle team, another Sergeant York in my country's future wars, or even Hal's pride and joy in a duck blind. The camp had one single-shot .22-caliber rifle and a make-do range consisting of a standard target thumb-tacked to a crate set against a bluff forty yards distant. This solo performance facility was in great demand and I awaited my first turn somewhat apprehensively. After a demonstration of safety procedures—old stuff to me—I was handed the piece and assumed the prone position on the firing line.

"Not that way, Evarts," the instructor chided me, with a wise-guy crowd of my co-campers looking on, ready to cheer or jeer. "You weren't listening."

"But I always shoot this way," I protested. "I can see better."

"That's not how we do it at CIBC," my man said. "We shoot

from the right side, Evarts, not the left. You've got it basackawards."

Obediently but with misgivings I shifted the .22 from my left side to my right, snuggled the butt plate against my shoulder, squinted through the rear-sight vee and lined up the front bead on my target which, unaccountably, had diminished to microscopic size.

"Fire when ready!" came the command.

I slipped off the safety catch, sucked in a long breath and let half of it out slowly, following Hal's instructions to the letter, then squeezed the trigger. Splinters flew up from the crate.

"You're aiming high, boy. Way high. Settle down."

I ejected the empty casing, reloaded and with total, almost fanatical concentration, fired again. A ricochet went zinging off toward the beach. Somebody behind me snickered.

We were allowed five rounds each. After my fifth, engulfed in a merciful silence, I slunk forward with the range officer to inspect my handiwork. My first shot had been my best, at least I'd nicked the crate. The other four were clean misses. The author's son, child of the Great White Hunter, couldn't hit his own backside with a fly swatter.

"Something's wrong with my eye," I tried to explain. "Everything just sort of shrinks—so little—"

"Sure, sure," the instructor muttered, not unsympathetically. "Better go see the nurse."

And so it passed at the end of summer, back on the mainland, that Sylvia took me to one of the city's leading oculists. After a thorough examination he peppered me with questions. Any chilhood head injuries? Measles? What about my reading habits? He conferred privately with Sylvia, then delivered his diagnosis: I had a condition doctors call amblyopia, "lazy eye," possibly a birth defect, with only one-fifth normal vision in my right eye, non-correctable by surgery or medication. My overworked left eye, in its effort to compensate, had developed acute astigmatism to the minus degree of 20/200 on the chart. This pronouncement brought tears of self-pity welling into both my malfunctioning eyes. Thereafter I wore glasses, as seldom as possible in public out of unadulterated male vanity. Who wanted to look like a bug-eyed bookworm?

That autumn and the next Hal hauled me out of school intermittently to share in his hunting trips. I went along for the ride and the pleasure of his company, for ducks in the marshes of San Joaquin Valley, for doves in the stubble fields of Imperial County, for quail along the Colorado River and below the border in Baja. Now an accepted non-hunter, I became a glorified gun bearer and one-man audience for his endless tales afield and on the road. We never mentioned my failure as a Nimrod.

10.

SHORTLY AFTER WE MOVED to California I had my first experience, in an abstract sense, with death. Sylvia's father, Charles Abraham, who had been ailing for some while, died of a heart attack in his sleep in Hollywood. I remember no pangs of grief, no acute awareness of loss. In the simplest of terms he was no longer "here," a presence that had ceased to exist. I thought of him as a kindly, mild and reserved man who shot marbles with me on the living room floor and took me to the corner drug store for chocolate ice cream sodas, but never once told me of his life in South Africa.

My grandmother Cora, out of some misbegotten notion of gentility, had insisted that I address her as "Mater" and Charles as "Pater," rather than "Grandma" and "Grandpa." I did, but only among family and never in my mind. I would sooner have walked naked down Hollywood Boulevard than refer to my grandfather in public as "Pater." And so he remains in my consciousness, Grandfather Charles, a shadowy pilgrim from Zululand who, in his will, left me the two small diamonds he had brought to America as a young man to make his start in the New World.

Hal turned forty that August of 1927. His hairline had receded and his waist was no longer trim. Since his Alaskan trip two years earlier, he had gained considerable weight, due to his alcohol consumption and sedentary city life. In response to Lorimer's urging he now launched into his "early American" trilogy, three novels spanning a century from about 1775 to 1875.

His first, *Fur Brigade*, covered the period 1815-1835, the era of the Mountain Men, trappers who roamed the West in search of beaver, fighting Indians and blazing trails across the wilderness. Always an avid reader, he began to assemble a library of first edition Western Americana, such basic works as the journals of Lewis and Clark, Thwaite's *Early Western Travels*, Chittenden's *History of the American Fur Trade*, Coues' *Expeditions of Zebulon M. Pike*, The *U.S.-Mexican Boundary Survey*, and collections of various state historical society publications. He went on buying sprees along L.A.'s downtown Bookstore Row and ordered widely from the catalogues of dealers in New York and Boston, until his current den, a small converted bedroom with little shelf space, became a bibliophilic jungle.

"I know the room's a mess," he told Sylvia, "but please don't try to tidy it up. I'll never be able to find the right book when I need it."

So Sylvia, a model of orderliness, confined herself to emptying his ashtrays and an occasional dusting. And continued to type his manuscripts.

"The singing river crooned its seductive song to Hunter Breckenridge as he leaned upon his long rifle and gazed out across its swirling waters. Its gurgling current chanted a refrain of far places and battles unrecorded. It whispered to him invitingly, the Missouri. 'She's done laid her spell on me,' he said. 'She's got me. I reckon—the river has.'"

With this evocation of a sixteen-year-old youth lured by the mystery of the great river, Hal opened *Fur Brigade*, recapturing some of his own restless spirit at that age. The book developed into something of a tableau, an elaborate folk tale almost epic in scope and theme, its three principal characters symbols rather than recognizable humans: the superman hero, Big Mandan; the stately Junoesque heroine, Hair-that-shines; and the black-hearted villain, Wolf Strike. And Hal, as he frequently did, introduced a bewhiskered old party who offers sage commentary on events, a kind of one-man Greek chorus—in effect, himself. He did not fall into the sentimental trap of deifying the Noble Savage, neither did he crucify: he portrayed both "bad" Indians and "good" Indians along with their white adversaries. The strongest element was the author's obvious love and intimate knowledge of the country about which he wrote so vividly. His descriptions of wildlife—birds, mammals, plants—and the weather are superb by any modern comparison, the sum total of a lifetime's observation. Overall, *Fur Brigade* might be classified as a history-text-cum-entertainment with patriotic overtones, a form that George Lorimer favored as a means to inform Americans about their land and their recent past. For the serial rights he upped Hal's fee to $12,000.

Southern California had entered the climactic phase of still another real estate frenzy and Hal stubbornly resisted Sylvia's determination to buy, rather than rent, a house. Inflated prices, he cited; owning a house was a luxury, not an investment. He had long since sold the Wyoming ranch and would have sold the Kansas farm except for Sylvia's adamant opposition. "I want a home of our own," she said. "I'm sick and tired of living in other people's houses."

Hal temporized, coining one excuse after another to justify pumping much of his income into Wall Street's bottomless pit. "One of these days," he promised her, "when the time is right."

One afternoon we drove out to Harry Carey's ranch for a picnic with the actor and his family. Harry, the original purchaser of screen rights to *Tumbleweeds* who became a friend, invited us to meet him next day to inspect some bay front property near a resort called Balboa on the coast south of L.A. Anticipating golden beaches and creamy surf, I was dismayed by a wasteland vista of mud flats, ugly tidal inlets, one rickety wharf and a couple of dilapidated sheds.

"You know, Hal," said Harry Carey, "this place has a future as a boat anchorage. You could buy every parcel around here for chicken feed."

Hal gazed about, unimpressed. "Well, thanks, Harry," he said. "But I don't invest in land. I wouldn't buy the whole state of California for one cent on the dollar."

"The only investment Hal believes in," Sylvia spoke up tartly, "is the stock market. On the downside."

Harry winked at Hal and changed the subject.

Some fifty years later I happened to read that the last remaining forty-foot lot on that same island had sold in the pricey neighborhood of $750,000. When I reminded Sylvia of our long ago visit she said, "I don't remember. But that sounds exactly like Hal."

From time to time he would temporarily lay aside his *chef d'oeuvre* and turn out shorter pieces to—as he expressed it—"get something off my chest" or have "a change of pace." One of these was *The False Status of Bruin*, an essay castigating various state legislatures for failing to enact laws to protect the dwindling wild bear population. Too controversial for even the *Post*, it appeared in *Outdoor Life* at a twentieth of his customary price. Editor John McGuire commented: "It is a delight to read an article such as the foregoing from one of America's greatest sportsmen and conservationists. Mr. Evarts is a Western man who recognizes the fate of the grizzly and big brown if we don't protect them."

Another was a novelette, *Renegade*, an attack on owners of domestic cats who let their pets go "wild," multiply and become feral hunters of birds and small mammals. This, as Hal saw it, posed a deadly threat to the delicate balance of nature. But the *Post* and other slicks did not care to risk offending thousands, perhaps millions, of readers who might be kitty lovers and buyers of cat food products advertised in their pages—an editorial leper. So this piece also appeared in *Outdoor Life*. Hal's reward: another enthusiastic endorsement from John McGuire.

During this period he sandwiched in three more short stories for the *Post*: *Sage*, *Trout Meadow* and *Postoffice at Dry Fork* at $1,500 apiece. In the latter he resurrected his earlier homespun philosopher character as "Pop" Saunders, who dispensed bunkhouse wisdom to innocent young cowpokes, spinning a tale within a tale with a dollop of folksy humor. Pop proved so popular that Hal re-introduced him in several stories.

For the second novel of his trilogy, he turned back to the late 18th Century and one of his forebears. Details of the life and death of his great-great grandfather, John White, the Revolutionary War veteran scalped by Indians on Kentucky's "Dark and Bloody Ground," were few and contradictory but nevertheless had been woven into family legend by succeeding generations. Hal first heard it as a boy from his mother, who had heard it as a child from *her* grandmother and so eventually I heard it too. An undisputed fact is that shortly after John White's murder, the long sanguinary struggle for control of the Ohio River Valley ended with a smashing victory by General "Mad" Anthony Wayne at the battle of the Fallen Timbers near present day Toledo in 1794. Out of these disparate strands Hal fashioned his own legend, *Tomahawk Rights*, his only piece of work laid east of the Mississippi.

The title derived from an early-day frontier custom whereby a would-be settler, in lieu of a licensed surveyor, asserted his "rights" to a chosen piece of land by hacking a blaze mark with tomahawk or axe on the four corner trees, thus declaring his intention to defend the site unto death against any and all encroachment. Not surprisingly the Indians interpreted this practice as an act of war and responded in kind. Hal's protagonist, Rodney Buckner, born into a prosperous, slave-owning Virginia family like John White, was—in the plot synopsis provided by the publisher— ". . . captured by the Indians as a boy, grew to young manhood in a Shawnee village before his relatives could ransom him. Skilled in all Indian craft and tactics, though he became the leader of a band of frontiersmen who fought the Indian allies of the British, he was mindful of his Indian loyalties."

This spokesman hero reflected Hal's sympathy for the dispossessed Indians as well as his disdain for the mass settler mentality, which he perceived as greedy, petty and mean-spirited, a lust for land often clothed in pious cant. But out of his own family history he understood what underlay it:

"And suddenly it was given to Rod Buckner to lift for a moment the veil of the future. The meaning of that growing desperate hatred between the red men and the white was clear to him. It was in the basic difference in which they viewed the land and the uses to which it should be put. So long as that difference existed there would be war until one race or the other was conquered. The two could not possess the land together. Why did white men sell themselves into bondage for a period of years in return for their passage to this new country? So that when their tenure of labor was ended they could stand where they had but to tomahawk the trees and say, 'This land is mine.' Then they would be free men and landowners, never again to be near-serfs and mere workers on the soil.... It was the true motivating force—the irresistible magnet of free land."

In the final scene Rod Buckner is evicted from his tomahawk claim by a conniving land grabber and sets out with his woman into an unspoiled West beyond the Mississippi. As a footnote Hal points out that the real heroes of the Kentucky-Ohio wilderness—Daniel Boone, Simon Kenton and Anthony Wayne himself—were fleeced out of their property and hounded into ruinous lawsuits and poverty. Quite possibly Hal's negative views on owning real estate had their roots in such historic flimflams.

His limitations included a tin ear for music, popular or classical. He danced beautifully, according to Sylvia, but could not hum a single tune on key. "I go most everywhere/ I don't pay no fare/ I can ride those freight trains/ Most any old where"—a souvenir of his young hobo days—is the only ditty of his that I recall. But he did have one related accomplishment, the imitation of bird and animal calls, and with this he endowed Rod Buckner. Hal acquired his skill in the hardwood hills above the Kaw, Rod as an eight-year-old captive of the Shawnee along the Ohio.

"The boy started off with the call of the crow, then the liquid whistle of the cardinal. From the extreme back of his throat came the quavering falsetto of the screech owl, then the querulous yelping of a hen turkey. He gave a perfect imitation of the quail, then the bobwhite note and the more difficult muster call by which scattered coveys reassemble. From the seductive cooing of a dove he broke suddenly into the shrilling chorus of young frogs on a spring night, the metallic whir of cicadas on a July afternoon, the chattering bark of a red squirrel; the plaintive cry of the phoebe, the hoarse rasp of the bull bat, the thunder-pumping notes of a bittern far out in the marshes, the silvery notes of migrating plover and the surprised cry of the killdeer."

Hal could do any of these on request. He once told me laughingly, "Maybe I should have gone into vaudeville."

That spring one of his E.F. Hutton chums introduced us to the southern California desert. Our male trio camped in a remote corner of the Mojave east of Randsburg (now a sealed-off military reservation) and the first night a violent sandstorm blew up, virtually imprisoning us inside our tent for the next forty-eight hours. Accustomed to mountains, timber and running streams, Hal was unprepared for this initial exposure but, after the wind subsided and the sun emerged, we crawled out into a wonderland of wild flowers and pastel-tinted buttes—he was enchanted on the spot. During the next few years the two of us returned to the Mojave many times, hiking, rock-hounding, locating historical sites but more often just siting against a boulder to observe wildlife through binoculars—his first and enduring love.

That summer, still struggling with *Tomahawk Rights*, he proposed a family motor trip around the West "just for fun." There was, however, a hitch: Hal was broke. Not stony broke but close enough so that he could not afford any extended travel.

Many parents of that day did not believe in discussing money matters in the presence of their children. It was considered, well, vulgar. My parents did not discuss; they shouted. So I became privy to all household financial problems. A goodly share of Hal's earnings since our arrival in Hollywood had gone the way of the wind to cover margin calls at the House of Hutton. Could he borrow, say $1,500, from the small sum Sylvia had inherited from Grandfather Charles the year before? He would pay her back from the next sale.

Sylvia refused. That money, she declared, was set aside for Hal Jr.'s education. The argument seemed endless but eventually Hal prevailed, after a fashion. Sylvia agreed, with one iron-clad stipulation: If, during our vacation, he took a single drink or so much as looked in the window of a brokerage firm, she swore, Heaven help her, to leave him for good and take me with her. Under an ominous cloud we loaded up our Buick with enough luggage for a safari to darkest Africa and went forth.

By 1928 cars and roads and travel conditions throughout the nation had improved considerably since our junkets of the early 20s, but the risk of breakdowns and misadventures still ran high. Our seven-passenger sedan, which I thought rather stylish, boasted folding "jump" seats, a crystal bud vase, pull-down curtains at the rear windows and, mounted on the radiator cap, a thermometer that seemed to register in the red "Danger" zone much of the time. Crossing the desert our first August afternoon on the dusty road to Las Vegas, we boiled over twice and suffered a blowout. Water, we discoverd at the few wayside stops, sold for ten cents a glass and two dollars for a radiator refill. Early on, Hal bought two large canteens, a backup fan belt and a second spare tire.

In Utah we detoured a washed-out bridge and got stuck in a creek; an accomodating rancher pulled us out with his team for a five dollar bill. In Idaho we broke a spring and limped into the next hamlet; there was no garage but the local blacksmith bellowed up his forge and welded the crack. In spite of such setbacks the journey resides in my memory as a serene, tension-free, even joyous occasion for my parents. Hal and Sylvia, on their best behavior for my benefit, skirted any confrontations. We climbed in snow on Mount Rainier, trolled for salmon off Vancouver Island, swam in Lake Tahoe. Hal drove all the way and often during the tedious miles entertained us with a running account of Western history and lore.

Perhaps Sylvia naively hoped she could reform him. For her I like to think this was a golden interlude, a lull before the storms and heartbreak reefs ahead.

11.

Hal's difficulties with *Tomahawk Rights* stemmed in part from his attempt to compress thirty years of history into the format of a popular magazine serial—the entertainment blockbuster of the big slicks. Too often his story line bogged down into passages of information masquerading as fiction, while the actors stood waiting in the wings. In the effort to satisfy himself, Lorimer and his ever-growing audience, he came perilously close to writing a thesis instead of a novel. When the *Post* bought it for $12,000 that December it was as though a boulder had been rolled off his back.

I have no evidence that he repaid Sylvia her $1,500; perhaps she wrote it off as a gesture of confidence. She had long since had her fill of camping, of roughing it, and for Christmas week he took us to Furnace Creek Inn at Death Valley to explore old mining sites and ghost towns. Then, back in Hollywood, he plunged into the fateful year of 1929 with renewed energy. His *Post* log for the period:

March 21	$ 1,500	*Dethroned Monarch*
March 27	1,500	*Ride and Tie*
April 4	1,500	*The River Bottom*
May 9	1,500	*Snowhide*
August 12	15,000	*The Shaggy Legion*
September 14	1,500	*Tide Flats*
October 30	1,500	*Phantom of the Aspens*
November 23	1,000	*Early Game Trails*

He also wrote the second failure of his career, *Long Trail of the*

Tortoise, a novelette that grew out of our first encounter with desert tortoises in the Mojave. Hal was so entranced by these remarkable creatures—some of the battle-scarred old bulls measured fifteen inches across and weighed as many pounds—that he rounded up a dozen or so and brought them home to our fenced back yard for closer observation and study.

Once plentiful, like the beaver and buffalo before them, the tortoise population is sadly depleted today, on the threatened species list, surviving only on special preserves. Cuddly and lovable pets they were not. Harmless, they withdrew hastily into their shells with an emphatic hiss when approached. They decimated Sylvia's rose garden, fouled the paths with droppings and drove my dog, an excitable terrier, into paroxysms of rage. Hal greatly admired their distinctive markings, around which he devised a legend dating back to a tribe of pre-Columbian Indians in Central America. But Brandt could not sell this far-fetched tale anywhere, much to Hal's puzzlement and chagrin. Even his friend and ardent fan, John McGuire, declined to publish it in the pages of *Outdoor Life*.

The Shaggy Legion, concluding volume of his trilogy, ribboned off the Hal-Sylvia production line without a hitch. Using a technique scorned by professional historians, he avoided the problems that had beset him in *Tomahawk Rights* by attributing imaginary dialogue to non-imaginary characters like Buffalo Bill Cody, "Wild Bill" Hickok and Sheriff Bat Masterson, and let them tell their versions of history within his fictional framework.

His hero, Breck Coleman, great-grandson of the protagonist of *Tomahawk Rights*, was what Hal called a "plainsman," a hunter, adept with knife and gun, a nonpareil tracker, knowledgeable about Indians and ways of the wild. For all that, Coleman was not a stereotype but, rather, a composite of several old timers Hal had quizzed as a teenager in the high plains country. The story dealt with the destruction of the last great buffalo herd, culminating in the battle of Adobe Walls in the Texas Panhandle, a three-day fight between twenty-six besieged white hunters and 700 Commanche-Kiowa warriors. Except for the disparity in numbers the whites had every advantage: .50-caliber 17-shot repeating rifles, unlimited ammunition and stout walls for defense. The Indians, fighting on horseback in the open, had some ancient single-shot rifles, bows and arrows, lances and buffalo hide shields. This mismatch came to be glorified as an epic victory for the forces of progress and profit. Without a reliable supply of buffalo, on which the tribes depended for food, clothing and shelter, they could not survive. Within months they were streaming onto reservations, hungry wards of the government, their free roving life gone forever.

With a factual dispassionate viewpoint Hal recreated the horrendous buffalo slaughter through the eyes of Breck Coleman, in three stages: first, for meat to feed the U.S. Army and on-pressing railroad crews; second, for the sale of robes and hides to eastern markets; and third, for bones to be pulverized into fertilizer. In 1874 alone, the climactic year, some 3,500,000 buffalo bulls, cows and calves fell to hunters' guns, according to Hal's estimate. As a testament of national greed it has rarely been surpassed. Only the buffalo wallows remain today as reminders, a few depressions on the prairies some four feet deep and ten feet across—one on our Kansas farm.

Riding away from Dodge City, capital of the cowboy empire that supplanted the buffalo, Coleman made this final observation: "After crossing the Arkansas River he stole one backward glance at the great white blot of bones along the railroad tracks, a ghostly monument to the shaggy legion that had passed."

That June I graduated from junior high school where my one distinction had been the editorship of the monthly news magazine, the *Le Conte Life*, for which I wrote ponderous essays on such topics as "Honesty," "Truth" and "Industry." At this point Sylvia stepped up her campaign to pressure Hal into buying a house. From her mother she had acquired the conviction that people in the entertainment industry, particularly actors, were less acceptable socially than merchants or lawyers; consequently she was determined that her only child should not attend that pit of depravity,

Hollywood High. Their team name—the "Sheiks"—(of which she was unaware) also happened to be the name of a popular condom available, even to minors, in most local drugstores. At the grassroots level I had been assured by my more sophisticated classmates that all girls who went to Hollywood High "did it" with great frequency, a prospect that whetted my prurient interest.

In that era a strange educational anomaly existed in southern California. The well-to-do sent their daughters to private schools, but generally not their sons. The belief persisted, at least among my peers, that only dummies or behavioral basket cases were sent to private schools for boys, boys too stupid or unruly to make it in the public school system. Therefore Sylvia set her sights on Los Angeles High, located just south of Wilshire Boulevard, which in that section formed the southern border of one of the city's most exclusive, prestigious residential neighborhoods, Windsor Square. Grumbling and protesting and not committing himself, Hal at last agreed to "take a look."

In *The Shaggy Legion* he had written this about the male-female relationship: "Coleman could cope with any situation among men. But he knew less than nothing of the ways of women, not having learned that no normal woman is ever logical."

Hal *had* learned, or so he told himself. All three women in his real life—his wife, mother and mother-in-law—he considered illogical, flighty, unreasonable and emotionally unstable as quicksand. No man born of woman, he contended, could ever hope to understand one. He could not comprehend why Sylvia wanted him to withdraw his money from the stock market, borrow from the bank, assume a mortgage, go into debt, to buy a house. We had a roof over our heads, didn't we? We had two cars now, a maid, a gardener (not to mention a yardful of tortoises), membership in the Hollywood Athletic Club. Who needed more? That was the *status quo ante* when I departed for my second summer camp on Catalina Island.

During my absence he capitulated. When I returned at the end of August, it was to a new house, much larger and more imposing than any we had occupied during my fourteen years. (In the midst of Hollywood notables, we soon learned. Actor Warner Baxter lived around the corner and, down the street, such studio nabobs as B.P. Schulberg of Paramount, Harry Rapf of MGM and Sol Lesser, producer of the Jackie Coogan and Tarzan movies). The final inducement, an irresistible lure that corrupted Hal's better judgment, was a separate library room, one with shelf space for all his book collection. There was also a cunningly concealed "secret" room for storing cases of liquor and wine in those Prohibition times but which, during our tenure, remained empty. Hal didn't store his liquor; he drank it.

"The first day the real estate agent brought us here," Sylvia confided to me, "I had to drag your father through the door. But he fell in love with the library."

It was Sylvia's dream house, which she proceeded to decorate and furnish from bottom to top. Hal, established in a permanent den of his own, seemed reasonably content although he complained about expenses. One afternoon a tour bus, one of a fleet that cruised the area with loads of rubberneckers to see the "homes of the movie stars," stopped at our front door. Through his open upstairs window he could hear the amplified voice of the guide: "And this is the home of the famous Western author, Hal G. Evarts."

"They must have been hard up for stars that day," Hal joked about the incident later. "But it sure beats raising skunks."

The irony of our situation came to light the day I tried to enroll at L.A. High. It seemed that Sylvia had neglected to check out school district boundaries. When I submitted my application to the registrar he frowned and said, "This address—you must live north of Third Street."

I admitted that I did, one whole block north.

"Well," he informed me, "you live in the Hollywood High district. You can't register here."

When I bore this bombshell news home to Sylvia, she reacted with a slyness of which I had not suspected her capable. She arranged with a former Kansas sorority sister who lived one block *south* of the boundary, on the right side of the tracks, for me to substitute her address for our tainted one and so to falsify our residence. Which I did, for the next three years, an impostor, segregated from the hussies of Hollywood High.

Probably I was more conversant with the operation of the stock market than most school boys for the reason that Hal delivered bulletins at our dinner table six evenings a week. "My God, XYZ went through the roof this morning!" he would announce. Or, "PDQ closed ten points higher—hog wild." The momentum was always up, up, UP. On the sidelines now, completely "out" of the market for the first time in years, he watched the seemingly inexorable rise in stock prices with a morbid fascination through the months of September and October. "This can't keep on, Sylvia; it's gotta go bust someday!" At times I almost felt as if E.F. Hutton were a member of the family, a rich and crochety old uncle who somehow controlled our destiny.

On several occasions I accompanied Hal to the Hollywood office, his home away from home, to observe and listen, mesmerized by the chatter of the ticker tape machines, the incessant clamor of telephones, the boy runners not much older than myself chalking up their cabalistic symbols and quotations on the big green boards, the grim and feverish concentration of the habitues. We all were spectators and players alike in some deadly numbers game. The atmosphere crackled with excitement and high pressure tension. Or did I only imagine this after the fact?

I cannot recall Hal's reaction on October 29, 1929, when the Dow Jones plummeted thirty-eight points, 13 percent of its total value, and the world fell apart. Probably he tied one on, along with millions of investor-speculator-gamblers who believed the bubble never would burst. The few non-believers, a comparative handful, who had bought stock shares on the short, or down side, made fortunes out of disaster overnight. Hal missed his rendezvous with wealth by a margin of two months. He bought a house instead. He had predicted Wall Street's decline and fall with a vengeance. Only his timing had been off. To his credit he never blamed anyone but himself, thankful that he hadn't run with the herd, that other shaggy legion, whose multitudes soon would be unemployed, destitute and devoid of hope.

The word "depression," spelled with a capital "D," had not seeped into public consciousness by the opening of the new decade, the 1930s. Neither the pundits of Washington and Manhattan nor Main Street America could yet envision the shape of things to come. Hal himself was not pessimistic or optimistic; by his own definition he was a fatalist: "If it happens, it happens." At the peak of his popularity and earning power, he had several new projects under way. Twice Lorimer wrote from Philadelphia urging him to consider a serial about the Pony Express. He demurred, wary of fictionalizing another historic event.

"The Pony Express is overrated," he told me. "Only lasted a few months, till the telegraph line was finished. How can I write a yarn about a bunch of jockeys delivering mail from one relay station to the next for 2,000 miles? I'd have my characters strung out from hell to breakfast."

During January he sold four articles: one to the *Post*, one to *World's Work* and two to *Country Gentleman*. If he couldn't make a killing in the market, he could still earn a living at his desk. In February he signed with Fox Studio for $1,000 a week, an open-ended contract that, he was assured, might be renewed indefinitely with periodic raises. The proverbial wolf had never seemed farther from our door. The wolf, in fact, was Hal's good luck talisman. He designed his own personal *Ex Libris* bookplate featuring that villified animal, the hero of *Cross Pull*, and had 5,000 copies printed. So much for hard times.

Hal and Sylvia, Hutchinson, Kansas, 1913.

Sylvia, ca. 1920.

Hal Jr., 1929.

Ranch house, Wapiti, Wyoming.

Kitchen, Wapiti, where Hal wrote his first stories in 1917.

Sylvia, Hal Jr. and pet cow, Wapiti, 1916.

Illustration from *Fur Sign* in "The Country Gentleman," 1921.

Hal and friend, Mackenzie River, Arctic Canada, 1921.

Hal and his trophy bear, Kodiak, Alaska, 1925.

Sylvia, Hal Jr., Hal and guide, Mt. Rainer, Washington, 1928.

Hal and director Raoul Walsh confer on *The Big Trail*, 1930.

12.

"Despite the trainloads of literature appearing annually about the movies there is one side, the most gripping story of them all, that has never been written—the vast drama of a great picture in the making. So it occurred to us to keep a log, somewhat of a day-to-day chronicle of the building of *The Big Trail* from its inception to the opening night, portraying the tremendous amount of planning, labor and generalship required to give birth to, and rear to maturity, a really great production."

So WROTE HAL IN THE opening paragraph of a curious house organ reportage that, if nothing else, unintentionally laid bare a movie *modus operandi* that was as doomed as Westbrook Pegler's "era of wonderful nonsense."

His transition from the ranks of the self-employed to salaried working stiff was comparatively smooth for the first few days. He met the production chiefs, Winfield Sheehan and Sol Wurtzel. He settled into an office in the Writers' Building and was assigned a typist from the stenographers' pool. He prowled the 150-acre Fox Hills back lot off Santa Monica Boulevard, as intrigued as any tourist by the beehive of activity, the false front sets, the actors in costume and makeup.

At a press conference he and numerous reporters were informed that *The Shaggy Legion*, retitled *The Big Trail*, with a budget of two million dollars, a mind-boggling sum for that time, would be filmed not only in standard 35 millimeter but in an experimental new process called "Grandeur," a quantum leap to 70mm, requiring special wide-lens cameras and, for projection in theaters across the country, super-size screens. It would be the most costly, colossal, record-breaking classic since D.W. Griffith's 1915 *Birth of a Nation*, with a cast of thousands. A skeptic by nature, Hal recognized this studio flackery for what it was: a public relations promotion to pre-sell the product. He was gratified, though, that any movie moguls would gamble such big bucks to transfer his story from printed page to the screen.

But whose story was it? In fact, what story? Answers to these questions were to plague him for the next seven months, to embitter him for the rest of his life.

"How did things go at the studio today, dear?" Sylvia would ask at our dinner table.

"Okay," Hal might say. "The technical stuff, it's pretty interesting. I just might get to like this business."

"Are you working on the screenplay yet?"

"As a matter of fact, no. I called in my steno and dictated a batch of letters. I'm catching up on my back mail."

"That's nice," Sylvia said. "But why did they change the name to *The Big Trail*?"

"Beats me," Hal told us. "They're waiting for Walsh to get back from Paris. He seems to be top dog on the lot."

"They" were were the hierarchy of studio executives, several layers deep, the upstairs "moneymen," as distinct from the creative or "artistic" level. Hal met the head man, Sheehan, only once again. With Raoul Walsh, the director, he was to work cheek by jowl seven days a week on almost every aspect of the picture, from script to tiniest historical minutiae.

Walsh, then forty-two, Hal's age, already a Hollywood legend, was perhaps better known to the public than most of Fox's contract players. Like Hal, he had quit school at fifteen and left home to "seek adventure," according to his autobiography. He had been a sailor, a minor participant in the Mexican Revolution, a Texas cowboy, a semi-professional boxer, a two-fisted boozer and womanizer, who drifted into the movies in the days when directors wore puttees and shouted through megaphones and cameramen cranked their machines by hand. One of the most successful directors of outdoor-action films, he had made such hits as *What Price Glory* and *The Thief of Bagdad*.

While on location in Arizona for his previous picture, in which he was both to direct and play the lead role, he had lost his right eye in a freak automobile accident involving a jackrabbit and now wore a black patch, which added a dashing piratical air to his Irish charm. When asked about his missing eye he would say, "A buzzard pecked it out."

Returning from surgery and a recuperative vacation, Walsh recalled his first news of *The Big Trail*: "Sheehan and Wurtzel were there to meet me when the Chief pulled into Los Angeles. Neither, rather obviously, mentioned the loss of my eye. On the drive to Malibu Sheehan said he had a story for me to look at, 'As soon as you feel up to it, of course.'" And later: "I thought the story rambled and would have been better suited as a travelogue."

This differed 180 degrees from Hal's version, delivered to Sylvia and me in daily takes at dinner.

"You won't believe this," he said. "It's crazy!"

"What's crazy?" Sylvia wanted to know. "I thought you liked Mr. Walsh."

"I like Raoul fine. He's my kind of folks. But he's already cooked up some half-baked plot before I've written a word. It sounds like a rehash of Emerson Hough's *Covered Wagon*."

Hal had never seen that movie, but I had—three times.

"It's about a wagon train," Hal went on, speaking slowly under stress. "Sort of a celebration of the Westward movement. A bunch of pioneers start out from Missouri and go all the way to Oregon. Fighting Indians and each other. My God, it's impossible!"

"How can they do that?" Sylvia asked. Having typed and retyped the manuscript of *The Shaggy Legion*, she knew every twist and turn as well as the author did. "Your story's about killing buffalo in Kansas."

"That's how these people work—I guess. I told Raoul it would be a disaster." Hal shook his head. "You know what he did? He laughed and slapped me on the back and said, 'Don't worry, Hal. We'll shoot from the hip.' Shoot from the hip! Two million dollars riding on this and all they've got is the damned Oregon Trail."

"It's their money," Sylvia pointed out. "Mr. Walsh must know what he's doing."

Raoul Walsh had proved himself a master of improvisation. While based in New York on one of his early pictures in 1918, he had a script, *Siren of Seville*, set for filming against a jerry-built backdrop across the river at Fort Lee, New Jersey. A violent early storm swooped down the Hudson, burying the mid-Atlantic seacoast under two feet of snow, with more of the same forecast. Faced with a delivery deadline (in those days the exhibitors, not the producers, put their cash up front), Walsh churned out a new story line overnight, hired some carpenters to alter the facade of his Iberian church and transferred the action from sunny Spain to the frozen steppes of Czarist Russia. Renamed *The Serpent* (Rasputin), it starred Theda Bara as the grand duchess Anastasia and Walsh's brother George as her lover, a boyar colonel of hussars who dashed about in a wagon that had been "converted" into a droshky.

"It wasn't too bad a picture," Walsh commented later. "Made some money too."

Hal knew nothing of this background, the birth pangs of the movie industry. His learning process progressed from initial enthusiasm through acceptance to disillusionment and frustrated resignation to outright rebellion. Most major members of the cast, he discovered, already had been signed: a beauteous leading lady, Marguerite Churchill; two villains; a comedian, El Brendel, in the role of a dimwit Swedish immigrant; and a darling dimpled six-year-old, Honey Girl, to be played by Walsh's daughter Marilyn. Only two of Hal's original characters survived: Breck Coleman, heroic plainsman, and the heavy, bullwhacker Red Flack, who had the unhygienic habit of chewing up willow stalks and spitting them out at the scenes of his dastardly crimes. Flack's role went to our former neighbor, Tyrone Power Sr., a distinguished New York stage actor before he was lured to Hollywood.

"But how," Sylvia wanted to know, "can they hire actors to play a part when they don't know who's going to do what?"

"Maybe God knows," Hal said. "I sure don't. And we're supposed to start shooting in a month."

"So tell me this: Who's going to be the lead, the star—Breck Coleman?"

"That's another thing. Straight out of the loony bin—"

Evening after evening I listened to these over-the-table exchanges between Hal and Sylvia less than attentively, my interest focused on such pressing concerns as homework, girls, cars and spring football practice. But some few facts did filter through my membrane of self-absorption: Fox had made strenuous efforts to borrow Gary Cooper from Paramount for the Coleman role. Failing this, Walsh decided to find a fresh new face, unknown to the movie-going millions, to carry *The Big Trail*. He, Walsh, would play his own role of star-maker.

One day when Hal and Walsh were swapping story ideas on the set, the director called over a tall gangling young man who was moving scenery and introduced him as Duke Morrison—"he played some football for USC." A football fan ever since his teenage days as "Tack" Evarts, Hal fell into conversation, learning that Duke too had played the position of tackle, third string varsity, on Coach Howard Jones' great "Thundering Herd" teams of the late 20s. His career cut short by injury, Duke had quit college, landed a job as prop handler and occasional stunt man at Fox Studio. After he returned to his props Walsh turned to Hal and said, "You heard his voice. What do you think?"

"Nice kid," Hal said. "And he does talk English, with a midwestern drawl. Kansas, maybe, my home state."

"Iowa, actually," Walsh said. "Out of Glendale High. I've just about made up my mind to test him for the Coleman role."

Even at this early stage Hal had become inured to shock and surprise in what seemed to him the chaotic topsy-turvy realm of show biz. "Oh," he said, "but can he act?"

"I don't want an actor," Walsh said. "I want someone to get

out there and act natural, be himself, who'll project on the screen. I can hire professional actors a dime a dozen. Also, this kid can ride a horse."

"A plow horse?" Hal laughed. "Hell, Raoul, you've already hired twenty of the world's top trick riders for the battle scenes. Have you ever seen Duke in a saddle?"

"He can learn," Walsh insisted, "if I have to teach him myself. Hal, this is my 80th picture and I guarantee you that he has real potential. Personality. I think Duke's our boy."

There exist three published versions of the next development: one by Duke Morrison in several as-told-to biographies; one by Walsh written in his mid-eighties; and one by the author, Hal's official 40,000-word *Log of the Big Trail*, written for the Fox publicity department, a gushy P.R. document notable for its omissions. Hal provided a fourth version, a contemporary one for family consumption only—verbal, unofficial, uninhibited and undoubtedly self-serving. Table talk:

"We've got a problem here, Hal," Walsh said. "The boss upstairs doesn't like our boy's name."

"What's that got to do with anything?" Hal said.

"Everything. Box office. His real name, you know, is Morrison. Marion Morrison. *Marion*. Get that? Morrison sounds like some kind of preacher. And *Marion*, Christ almighty, that's a girl's name, a sissy name!"

"You never told me that before. So what's wrong with his nickname—Duke?"

"Duke's too English," Walsh said. "Sounds like royalty. What we need is a real all-American, rugged he-man name. Socko at the ticket window."

"How American can you get?" Hal said. "How about John Smith?"

"Aw, quit kidding, Hal. This is serious. The publicity people are on my ass to come up with a name. And fast. For pre-release to the press. I've got my staff working on it."

"Ummm. Well, there was a character in my last book I always liked. A real character. 'Mad' Anthony Wayne."

"A lunatic?" Walsh said. "*Anthony*? That's a sissy name if I ever heard one."

"Not this one, Raoul. An honest-to-God general. No crazy, no sissy. An authentic hero of the Indian wars, who got screwed by politicians. All-American as baseball."

"But *Anthony*? And *Tony*, that's wop—"

"Forget his first name," Hal suggested. "Try it this way: Robert Wayne, Bill Wayne, Bucky Wayne, John Wayne—"

"Hey, John Wayne!" Walsh exclaimed. "That's not bad. Has a zing, a dignity, some class. Maybe I'll take it upstairs."

And so John Wayne, nee Marion Morrison, a.k.a. Duke, emerged on the all-American, macho scene. According to Hal.

While the newly minted John Wayne took his first elocution lessons and practiced throwing knives at a target to prepare himself for the Coleman role, Hal and Walsh "talked" story line in marathon bull sessions. In late February they set out to scout the site Hal recommended for the picture's major location. From the railhead at Victor, Idaho, they crossed 8,400-foot Teton Pass in a sleigh during a blizzard into Jackson Hole, which Hal knew intimately from his Wyoming years. Walsh was delighted by the scenery, the photographic possibilities. Hal also knew many of the residents on a first name basis and through them made preliminary arrangements to accommodate the Hollywood mob that would descend on the tiny hamlet of Moran four months later. Throughout this journey and others he and Walsh often worked on the script late into the night, then Hal would stay up still later scribbling lines of dialogue and last minute plot changes, adding to and subtracting from what he referred to gloomily in private as "this patchwork quilt."

On the spring morning that Walsh and Hal, heading a retinue of 400 Fox employees, departed Los Angeles by train for the first location scene, Sylvia kept me out of school, insisting that I dress in my "spiffiest" clothes: plus-four knickers, Argyle knee-length socks, blue blazer, white shirt and tie. Despite her ingrained prejudice against actors, she harbored the secret hope that I might catch Raoul Walsh's eye and be signed on for a role in his picture. The Great Man gave me a preoccupied nod, shook my hand and swung aboard the train. My first and last chance at cinematic immortality dwindled down the tracks.

Some 36 years later in an article called *They Don't Make 'em Like That Any More*, Bill Brent, a sound technician for Fox who recorded *The Big Trail* from start to finish, described that first location at Yuma, Arizona: "The Fox Special, hauling eight Pullmans of actors, extras and crews, with two dining cars, pulled into the S.P. yards in April 1930. This was preceded by twenty-one cars of baggage, props, wardrobe, horses, Conestoga wagons, bull train equipment, oxen and all other paraphenalia needed to film an epic like *The Big Trail*. A hundred construction men had been in Yuma for weeks building the Independence, Missouri, set on the Colorado River. Yuma, hurting from hard times, welcomed the troupe with open arms, since we were a free-wheeling high-spending outfit and that money would certainly hype up the economy. It turned into one big wingding.

"The pace of shooting was leisurely, as we had no fixed schedule, no set budget, and with constant rewriting of the script by Hal G. Evarts, a noted *Saturday Evening Post* writer, we rarely got a shot before eleven in the morning. Today you'd better have a script, a set shooting schedule and a tight budget or, brother, you don't roll. Raoul Walsh, the director, cut something of a figure as he strode about in his English riding boots, whipcord breeches, western hat and black eye patch, issuing orders. He confined his direction mostly to the principals, leaving the crowd stuff and background action to his numerous assistants.

"Hal Evarts was galled and appalled at this 'on the cuff' writing to order and threatened to walk off the picture several times. But Walsh would talk him out of it, pointing out that since material for *The Big Trail* came from two of Hal's published books he could not easily be replaced. Hal was appeased somewhat but still didn't like it.

"John Wayne, the star, was a big, rugged, good-looking guy with a wide open infectious grin—and he couldn't act a lick. Understandable, since just a few weeks before he'd been an assistant prop boy on the Fox lot. Producers today would consider such arbitrary casting as sheer folly, but not in those days. They took the big gamble then. The scenes between nonactor Wayne, Tully Marshall, Ty Power Sr., Ian Keith and other old pros were sheer murder. These old boys knew every trick in the book—a lifted eyebrow, exaggerated facial expressions, little mannerisms and bits of business with their hands, anything to steal the scene. And there was nothing John could do to fight back, except talk louder in that Polly-wants-a-crackerish way he read his lines when he wanted to emphasize a point which, of course, only emphasized his immaturity and lack of experience.

"On the phone to the boss man back in Hollywood Walsh swore that Wayne would be okay. From here on this was the line that Walsh chose to follow—big spectacular scenes, relegating the actors to secondary importance.

"The troupe left Yuma about a month later. After that it was Sacramento, for more river scenes, then on to Jackson Hole, Wyoming, for the summer. By then the picture was so bollixed that nobody knew what it was all about, the story line had been changed so many times. Hal Evarts finally blew his stack and quit the picture."

The reason for Hal's displeasure was not only the story, but the credit. In New York Carl Brandt, his agent, received a copy of a Fox press release giving solo credit for original story and screenplay to Raoul Walsh. No mention of his client Hal. Novice that Hal was, he might not have recognized the significance of this slight, but Brandt did. In Hollywood a writer's credits were his bread and butter, his union card. Furious, Brandt phoned Fox's corporate headquarters and threatened to file an immediate lawsuit. The Fox brass, already nervous about their two million investment and daily "rushes" from location they were screening in Hollywood, hastily backed down and gave Hal sole credit as author.

After a thirty-six hour walkout he returned to work, still seething. He'd had his day in court. Interestingly, neither Walsh nor Wayne mentioned his existence in their memoirs. Perhaps for good and obvious cause.

No hint of story problems emerged in Hal's innocuous *Big*

Trail Log: "It had been decided that, instead of merely writing the incidents of a story to be scenarized later, I was to collaborate with Walsh and that between us the story, scenario, dialogue and continuity were to be carried along at one and the same time."

And this glimpse of a script in progress: "After dinner Walsh asked me to join him while he and Dave Hartford (a drama coach) rehearsed various groups of characters in their parts for the morrow. If the dialogue did not sound right when spoken, the parts were rewritten on the spot. Walsh asked suggestions from all present and eventually just the right lines, every word in place, would be worked out."

In the first week of July an army of actors and extras and staff detrained at Victor and, accompanied by 1,700 head of livestock and twenty covered wagons, crossed the Tetons in a mighty caravan, a sixty-mile trek through deep mud and snowy slush. Jackson Hole had not known such a human invasion since a Mountain Man rendezvous one hundred years earlier. A tent city had been thrown up near Moran. Carpenters were frantically constructing a replica of old Fort Hall, the historic military post of Oregon Trail days. Shortly several hundred Indians from four different Northwest tribes—Crows, Cheyennes, Arapahoes and Shoshones—arrived, set up their tepees and began slaughtering the cattle that Fox had provided as their walking commissary; they shared no common tongue but conversed in sign language. The overall complexity of the operation would have challenged any generalissimo, even one of Walsh's caliber.

Struthers Burt, an author and friend of Hal's, owner of a local ranch who had rented out a number of his horses to Fox, wrote this account: "The script called for a scene in which four braves, one a chief dressed in full war paint, out scouting, discovered a wagon train and galloping back to the village alarmed it for attack. At the entrance to the village sat four women grinding corn. One spoke English, the other three didn't. As the four warriors came shouting and galloping back from the hills, the four women were supposed to rise and express interest and concern. Six times the warriors came shouting and galloping back from the hills, and each time only the woman who spoke English showed interest. The others knew it was merely a play. The director finally decided to put that scene off for another day.

"Meanwhile the village had been awakened six times to life and six times a couple of hundred warriors had ridden past within ten feet of me at a full gallop, shouting and shaking their spears. Leading them was a naked and fierce young Crow. Each time they passed my heart jumped with the color of it and the thunder of the ponies' hoofs. A hundred of these ponies were mine incidentally, and—white men's ponies—they had a baffled look in their eyes due to days of Indian riders, and the red and yellow paint that had been smeared upon them, and the strips of red flannel that had been tied to their manes and tails.

"With the order 'to cut' the Indians got off their ponies, and the fierce young Crow saw me and strode over to me. 'Why, old man,' he said, 'hello! I haven't seen you for years!' and slapped me on the shoulder. 'Where have you been?' He still had his guttural voice and it had lost none of the inhuman, ventriloqual effect of the Indian voice speaking English. I told him where I had been and I asked him where he had been.

"'Oh, I've been in Paris. With the pictures. You know Paris? Cognac?... That French cognac!'"

Alas and alack, I was not allowed to witness any of this glittery hippodrome. While in Yuma Hal had come to the conclusion that after-hours life on location with Hollywood troupers was too "rowdy" for a susceptible fifteen-year-old boy, so I was banished to yet another wholesome, character-building summer camp, this one in Blue River, Oregon, far from the action. I never quite forgave him, inasmuch as he *did* take along my mother—shy and sheltered Sylvia—as a backup typist.

There was, however, another boy on the premises that summer, fourteen-year-old Robert Parrish, who had been hired as a mule skinner because his little sister Helen, a child actress, was on the payroll as an understudy for the part of Honey Girl. In his memoir *Growing Up In Hollywood* Parrish recalled: "Late one night Helen and I were awakened by sounds of a fight outside our cabin. Cheyenne Flynn, one of the cowboys, was drunk and accusing Charlie Stevens, an actor playing a halfbreed in the picture, of cheating at cards. Helen and I watched through the window until my mother hustled us back to bed. The fight went on and I heard Cheyenne say, 'I'm going to bite your ear off, you goddam half breed.' Poor Charlie was a gentle Irishman with straight black hair who only *looked* like a halfbreed. I heard him make a weak protest, then scream in pain. There was a scuffle, running footsteps, and then a diminishing whine as Charlie made his way to the first aid tent.

"The next morning I found a neat mouthful of Charlie's ear covered with ants outside our cabin. I cleaned it up and took it to my boss. He said it was too late to sew it back on Charlie, so I put a piece of rawhide through the lobe and hung it on our cabin door until my mother made me take it off."

Hal was playing poker with Charlie and Cheyenne and several others when the fight broke out and he described it to me later. "I've seen some nasty fights in my time," he said, "but this was a bearcat. People busting whiskey bottles over heads, people stomping people with their boots. I got out fast."

Since Charlie had appeared in several scenes with both ears intact, this called for another script revision. Hal and Walsh whipped out a sequence in which a squaw bit Charlie's ear off during an Indian raid.

The script change that disgusted Hal the most dealt with some low comedy relief. Walsh wrote an episode in which El Brendel, the buffoon, is helping two ladies bypass an ominous looking mudhole in a village street, said mudhole bridged by one narrow plank. Seen in the background is the ample rear end of his virago of a mother-in-law, played by actress Louise Carver. When her turn comes Carver haughtily disdains El Brendel's proffered arm and steps forward. Plank breaks. Kerplunk! "Mama" sinks up to her chin in goo. (In the original version he was to have booted her behind, but Hal strenuously objected.) Walsh thought it was hilarious, "a surefire belly laugh."

Hal disagreed. He told Sylvia, "I'll be mortified if any of my friends see the show and think I'm responsible for that kind of slapstick hokum." When the scene played to an opening night audience months later the crowd roared.

In the *Log* Hal wrote: "The Wyoming hills are full of both moose and moonshiners. Many moose were seen around the location. The moonshiners had made up their quota for the year and put it down in charred barrels, expecting to cater to the usual summer tourist trade. They had no idea that such a crew of conscientious drinkers would invade their country, but the suppply never seemed to run short. 'Moose Milk' became a brand name on the set. In Moran we were dependent upon ourselves for amusement, and after many a fourteen-hour work day the strain was beginning to tell. Little rivalries and enmities cropped up and tempers flared. At least half a dozen mass fights erupted when two factions begged to differ."

There was another form of "amusement," one which Hal did not mention in his *Log*. But sharp-eyed Robert Parrish had no such inhibitions: "As a boy just turned fourteen I was aware that a lot was going on between people who were not married. I had to start getting my mules organized while it was still dark, so I often saw cowboys scurrying from the stock girls' tent to the bunkhouse (and vice versa) just before dawn. I never could figure out which actors were married to which actresses. It seemed that everyone was in on it except the makeup man and me and my mules."

According to Parrish "everyone" connected with *The Big Trail* knew that Walsh's redheaded wife was having at least a dalliance with the number-two villain, suave sinister Ian Keith, while the director was away on location, sometimes all night. The burning question was: How much did Walsh know and when did he know it?

"On the last day of shooting, Walsh staged the fight scene in which John Wayne finally catches up with Ian Keith and thrashes him for the scoundrel that he is. The last shot was to be a closeup of Keith. Wayne was to throw a final punch from behind the camera, and Keith was to react like a man with a broken jaw.

"Walsh said, 'I'll throw Duke's punch, Ian. You put up your hand to ward off the blow. I'll feint with my left, then throw the right between you and the camera, and if you jerk your head back it will look like the blow connected.'

"Keith said, 'Look, Raoul, I've been taking punches on the stage and in movies for years. You just throw your punch when you want. I'll get out of the way.'

"Walsh said, 'Okay. Camera' The assistant cameraman said, 'Running.' Then a few seconds later he said, 'Speed.' Walsh said, 'Okay, Ian. Action. Here it comes.' Ian braced himself. Walsh feinted with his right, then threw his left. Ian was too slow. Walsh's left fist crashed into his jaw and fractured it in three places."

13.

IN ADDITION TO HIS CHORES as co-author, historian and official recorder, Hal performed a function as door-opener to U.S. government facilities that otherwise would have been closed to the Fox Corporation. Walsh, acting on one of his impulsive hunches, wanted to shoot a few extra scenes in Yellowstone Park that involved trapping some live bear cubs, to appeal to lovers of wild animals. Hal wired his friend Horace Albright, now director of the National Park Service, for permission. Permission granted.

And then Walsh decided he must have some shots of his pioneer survivors reaching their hard-won goal in trackless Oregon Territory, circa 1840. A location team that had been sent ahead reported back that the state of Oregon was no longer wilderness. The new long-range Grandeur-size lenses would pick up every farm, factory and telephone wire like the Mount Wilson telescope scanning the heavens. So once again Hal wired an old friend, Colonel John R. White, superintendent of Sequoia National Park, for help. White obliged, turning himself and his rangers out in force to facilitate this much ballyhooed movie. Thus *The Big Trail* limped to a close, not on the banks of the Willamette River but in the Giant Forest of California's High Sierra.

In his innocence Hal may have logged the following comment in sincerity, but more likely with a tincture of acid: "Hollywood is a queer camp. It lives, thinks, breathes and talks pictures. While various troupes are out on location, news leaks back as to how pictures are going. We had not been long in

Wyoming when the news poured in that our picture was 'In the air and how!' Naturally these advance predictions that *The Big Trail* was destined to be the biggest hit in years added to the enthusiasm of those in our troupe."

To the end he retained his admiration for the actors, the technicians, the stunt men and stock handlers, for Raoul Walsh himself. It was the "system," the Olympus-like producers who dictated policy that Hal railed against. Old pro Bill Brent, sound engineer and veteran of many a movie, delivered this verdict: "In Hollywood, Jack Dennis, head cutter, was quietly going insane. Walsh had dumped 400,000 feet of film, both wide and standard, in his lap, which he was supposed to cut to 12,000 in both versions. The continuity was full of big holes, sequences which didn't match or make sense, and the plot was too involved to follow with any coherency. *The Big Trail* wound up one big turkey, which in studio lingo meant a king-sized stinker."

The world première, Hollywood's gala event of the tumultuous year 1930, took place November 14 at Grauman's Chinese Theater, gift-wrapped in all the traditional symbols: batteries of klieg lights raking the sky; bleacher seats for hordes of fans; the Boulevard roped off for traffic control; movie queens gorgeously gowned, coiffed and jewel-bedecked; red carpet rolled out from foyer to curbing. It was, in retrospect, a swan song, a spectacular the likes of which Tinsel Town would never see again on the same grandiose scale.

For the occasion Sylvia rented a tuxedo from Western Costume and shoe-horned me into a boiler-plate shirt and cummerbund. Hal refused to rent a limousine, hiring two taxicabs instead. He, Sylvia and I rode in the first. My grandmothers Emma and Cora and my Aunt Lala followed in the second. Fox had trucked in a covered wagon, two mules and several bales of hay for atmosphere. In a brief ceremony in the forecourt, Walsh, the first director invited by impresario Sid Grauman to leave his prints for posterity, signed his name in wet cement with a stick. Not far away lay the prints of William S. Hart, who had starred in Hal's earlier picture *Tumbleweeds*.

To his signature Hart had added the imprints of two Colt .45s. Not to be outdone, Walsh doubled up his left fist, pressed that too into the wet cement and added two words: HIS MARK.

Of the movie itself I remember only a single scene—Louise Carver's mudhole immersion.

Of the principals involved in *The Big Trail*:

RAOUL WALSH went on to direct a number of other pictures, most more successful artistically and financially.

JOHN WAYNE, who received a salary of $75 a week for his role, made a series of low budget "B" Westerns until his 1939 breakthrough into stardom in John Ford's *Stagecoach*.

WILLIAM FOX, founder of Fox Film Corporation and an entertainment empire worth an estimated $300 million, was wiped out by the market crash and by 1936 had lost his studio.

BILL BRENT, sound technician, encouraged by his friend Hal, became a fiction writer for the *Post* and other big slicks.

HAL EVARTS, in a farcical epilogue, became briefly entangled in a plagiarism lawsuit. One Florinda Gardner filed a claim in a federal district court charging Fox Film Corporation, Hal Evarts and Raoul Walsh with using material from her book, *The Trail and Trials of the Mormon Pioneers*. Hal responded with typical exaggeration: "I have in my library—I collect that sort of thing—perhaps 25 or 30 books on the early Mormons. They are chiefly books written prior to 1860. I don't recall this name. I might have some book that I don't recall, there are so many on the Mormon situation, and I have got the whole Mormon history, everything they ever did."

Hal denied that he and Walsh had "borrowed" anything from anybody in writing *The Big Trail* screenplay. He could have added, truthfully: "Except from each other." The suit was dropped.

As a final footnote, in reply to the question, "Approximately how many published works have you written?" Hal responded:

"I couldn't tell you. However, I can state that in thirty months I wrote five serials, one two-part story, and thirty-one short stories and articles for the *Saturday Evening Post* alone. I wouldn't care to go on record as stating that is the exact number. I have had hundreds of articles and short stories in various works, chiefly the *Post*. I have also written twelve or fourteen published books."

One evening at the dinner table, Hal announced to Sylvia and me, "Fox offered me a new contract today."

"That's interesting," Sylvia said. "Doing what?"

"More of the same," Hal said. "They must be gluttons for punishment. At $1,500 a week."

"Why, that's a big raise! What did you tell them?"

"I told them, 'I want $2,000 a week.' They said '$2,000, that's too much.'"

"Hal, you didn't really say that!"

"I did. I said, 'Even $2,000 isn't enough. Thank you, gentlemen, and good day.' And walked out the door." Hal laughed. "And now I'm going to write my next book, which I should've been doing all this time."

The Big Trail did establish a few firsts. On the use of "Grandeur," which would not be tried again for another twenty-five years, one critic said: "It wasn't a bad picture but it was too far ahead of its time. To show the film, theaters had to buy bigger screens and 'squeeze' lenses to fit onto their normal projectors. The lenses would throw out bigger images. It was a practical idea, certainly, but during the Depression the theaters couldn't afford the extra expense. Audiences could barely afford to go to the movies at all in those times."

Commented another critic: "Scenes of the vast wagon train winding across the desert, fording a flooded river, and literally being hauled over mountains were especially effective because they were suited to the wide screen treatment, and no film since, even in the period of Cinemascope, has ever approached the effectiveness of this footage. By now, too, Walsh had developed more constructive ideas concerning the use of music. The grand scale of the Indian battle was made doubly effective by the sudden introduction of a furious agitato with Indian themes."

Although *The Big Trail* flopped at the American box office, it proved a great success overseas, especially in non-English speaking countries. "All of the big action scenes could be used intact with occasional cut-in close-ups of the foreign (American) players. The German version, for example, was especially well put together, dialogue taking second place to action. Although German audiences were deprived of John Wayne except in the long shots, Germany's exhibitors had a much more profitable product."

Hal's next book, which he had projected so blithely early in 1931, became an emotional nightmare, an albatross that haunted him. He brooded about *The Big Trail* and took its failure to heart as a reflection on his professional and personal integrity. He began to drink more heavily. Sylvia would hide his bottles or empty them down the drain, but he always came up with more. On several occasions he vanished for two or three days at a time, holing up alone in seedy Hollywood hotels. Sylvia tracked him down through the E.F. Hutton old-boy network, avoiding the public humiliation of a police search. He refused to seek medical help; psychiatry or mental therapy he regarded as a black art, akin to phrenology or the reading of tarot cards. But at Sylvia's insistence he finally agreed to undergo a drying-out process, a withdrawal regimen of orange juice and vitamin pills administered by a retired nurse who specialized in movie business casualties. When he returned from his first such treatment—ashen and shaky—I mustered up enough gumption to confront him.

"Dad," I said, "Why? Why do you drink so much?"

"I don't really know," he told me. "But by the time you reach my age maybe you'll find out."

During this period he completed only one short story, *Pilot of Sentinel Nob*, which after nine rejections sold to a pulp magazine for $250, a painful comedown. Two articles on Indians that he had promised Lorimer died aborning. For the first time he squabbled with his agent, complaining about the pickiness of editors. His problem was more complex than the familiar writer's block. He was suffering a crisis of confidence. His discipline, which had been so rigorous throughout his career even in the fog of countless hangovers, began to fail him. Days passed when he could not bring himself to face his desk; he sat in his den reading and smoking or took long aimless walks up and down the streets. And now, along with the rest of the nation, he worried about money.

By mid-1931 happy days were not here again, nor would be soon. Magazine editors were slashing their prices and buying less, as advertising revenue dwindled. Book publishers were offering smaller advances and lower royalty rates on a take-it-or-leave-it basis. He did sell the sound rights (as distinct from the old silent screen rights) to *Spanish Acres* to Paramount for $5,000, a sum well above the average citizen's annual median income, but that did not dispel his gloom. That was the past, out of the golden '20s "Prosperity," Herbert Hoover assured the country, "is just around the corner." But nobody believed him, including loyalist Republican Hal.

He still followed the stock market but only as a spectator, not speculator. He cancelled his life insurance policies, although Sylvia begged him not to. He gave up city driving, not as an economy measure but, I think, because he no longer trusted himself behind the wheel in traffic. Sylvia and I and Yellow Cab became his chauffeurs.

"This new serial is driving me nuts," he told us. "I can't afford to take a trip now, but I have to go away somewhere, anywhere and get a new slant on things." And so that summer he did not ask Sylvia for another "loan" from her small inheritance, but indulged himself in the extravagance of renting a beachfront apartment at Ocean Park, among the amusement piers and hurdy-gurdies, and went into virtual seclusion. In his mind there must have been the memory of that long ago time when he had locked himself in a boarding house room and written his first novel, a best seller, in six weeks. Maybe the magic would work again.

Remembering how much he had enjoyed deep-sea fishing in the Florida Gulf Stream, I persuaded him to take me on an outing aboard a public fishing barge anchored a mile or so out in Santa Monica Bay. The day turned into a fiasco. For millions of Americans fishing was no longer a sport but an inexpensive way, if one were lucky and skillful enough, to put some food on the family table. Packed shoulder-to-shoulder with a crowd of grim anglers, we did not catch or even hook a single fish. Hal remained glum and withdrawn, then became violently seasick over the rail in the gentle on-shore swell. I too was sick, not from the sea, but from the agonizing spectacle of my father's rapid and seemingly irreversible disintegration as a writer and human being.

The seaside change of scene wrought no miracles. In September he returned to our Los Angeles house, depressed and still mired in the early chapters of his book. From New York Erd Brandt wrote him: "It has your usual good stuff but the opening is too slow, too talky. You need some action to get the story moving."

With that Hal laid aside his manuscript and charged off on a new tangent, what he called his "one-man crusade, Don Quixote tilting at the windmill." The windmill in this instance was an agency of the federal government, the Bureau of Biological Survey, whose wildlife control practices he had consistently supported in many *Post* articles. But now, urged by a group of concerned professors at several universities, he switched to the attack. Specifically, he opposed a new Bureau policy sponsored by the powerful Stockgrowers Association lobby in Washington: a campaign to poison off so-called predators, mainly coyotes, and such "nuisance elements" as ground squirrels, who dug their burrows all across the Western landscape.

Week after week Hal drove by himself, on what were then meandering country roads, to Antelope Valley on the edge of the Mojave where, across vast areas, Bureau agents had set out "baits" of grain treated with strychnine near waterholes and in natural animal runways. For hours on end he would observe one or another of these sites through his binoculars from some vantage point, then tramp across the desert with pencil and notebook, recording the body count. It became an obsession; he could talk of nothing else at the dinner table.

"Disgraceful!" he would storm. "A national outrage. A slaughter, that's what it is."

"You mustn't get so worked up, dear," Sylvia said, trying to calm him. "It isn't good for you."

"You know how many dead quail I found yesterday?" he said. "Over a hundred. And doves. Some game birds. Song birds. Red-tail hawks. Rabbits by the bushel. My God, it's like a war zone out there! Throwing nature completely out of kilter."

"It sounds dreadful. But, Hal, you can't take on the whole U.S. government by yourself."

"Predators, hell! Those Bureau lunkheads have killed off everything for miles. Everything *but* coyotes and ground squirrels. Too smart to eat poison grain. How's that for crazy?"

In a burst of energy he hadn't displayed for over a year, under the title *Perfection by Poison*, he hammered out a 20,000 word article—four times the *Post's* optimum length—in which he lambasted the Bureau's philosophy and challenged their statistics, calling the director and his staff a pack of liars in all but name. Lorimer promptly rejected it as "too long and too controversial."

To one of his supporters, Dr. E. Raymond Hall, University of California, Berkeley, Hal described the situation: "Bad luck, I'm afraid. The *Post*, who was not very keen about the article to begin with, until I egged them on, turned it down because it was too viciously opposed to the Bureau. I kidded their alleged tabulations from hell to breakfast. I'm sorry I let you down. Keep it quiet from government circles that I flopped, because I'm dead hostile about this poison business and will arrange a program against it so that I can follow up with other articles."

Fearing the worst, Sylvia and I ached for him with unspoken commiseration, acutely aware of how much he had counted on this project. How would he react?

Hal withdrew the article from circulation, refusing to revise or shorten it, and never wrote another word on the subject. The *Post* had been his platform for conservation matters for so long that he decided, evidently, that he'd backed a lost cause.

He had written that particular venom out of his system, a kind of literary therapy, if nothing else.

Surprisingly, at this low, pit-bottom point in his career, he did not dwell on past failures. It was as though this latest setback somehow primed his creative juices, galvanized his sagging morale. Within three months he thrashed out his story line and finished *Shortgrass*, his fourteenth novel. Lorimer was delighted to have him back on track and bought the serial rights for $15,000, his previous pre-Depression price. The demons of the disastrous *The Big Trail* had been exorcised, temporarily at least.

14.

SHORTGRASS WAS AN extension of Hal's trilogy, a fourth volume that covered the decade of 1880s, from the decimation of the buffalo to the great blizzard of 1888 that brought to an end the era of unfenced cattle range. Laid in the plains of north Texas, the story pitted rustler against rancher, outlaw against law and order, including some characters from *The Shaggy Legion*—the Breck Coleman role played by John Wayne, and an "idiot female" who, until the final chapter, could not distinguish the good guys from the bad. What elevated it above the level of pulp magazine cowboy grist was the historical framework, an abortive attempt to create a new state of the Union—"Cimarron"—for cattlemen only. That, and Hal's extensive knowledge of workaday cow business detail, which most writers in the genre lacked and too often faked. He concluded with an hilarious spoof of that indestructible legend of the romantic Old West, the lost treasure—in this case some "buried Spanish gold bullion," which had nothing whatsoever to do with his plot but alone was worth the price of admission.

He had dedicated *The Shaggy Legion* to his mother, and now this one to me: "To my son, who was born in the Shortgrass country, and with whom I have roamed afield from Arctic to tropical clime, this book is affectionately dedicated."

Neither Hal nor Sylvia ever pressured me to become an achiever, to bring home straight-A report cards, nor helped me with homework. They allowed me to journey at my own erratic pace through the public school systems of Kansas and

California. Socially, I graduated from Boy Scouthood into dancing academy and then into a cotillion called the Fortnightly, held at the Wilshire Country Club. Here a tuxedo was obligatory and a young gentleman was expected to present his young lady of the evening with a corsage of at least two gardenias and fill her program card with suitable partners. During those pimply gawky years of adolescence I "fell in love," or so I fantasized, with a series of blue-eyed blondes. Under the hawk-eyed supervision of chaperones, we managed at the most a few hasty kisses or some awkward experimental grappling in dark corners—prim and timid rites of spring.

At sixteen when I entered the eleventh grade at L.A. High (The Ramblin' Romans—"any old team/ can get up steam/ but you can't beat L.A. High"), college began to loom somewhat menacingly. But which college? Sylvia had vague leanings toward Yale or possibly Williams, one of the eastern Ivies. Hal's attitude was lukewarm, based on his own educational vicissitudes. Who needed four more years of expensive schooling to earn a living? But if I really wanted a college degree, so be it. If, he added darkly, he could afford the tuition.

A friend happened to describe to me a prank in which his older brother and three classmates had been involved while students at Stanford University. One night this fearless foursome had dismantled a Model T, carried the parts up to the fourth floor of Encina Hall (the freshman dormitory), reassembled them and driven the vehicle up and down the corridor until cooler heads intervened. I had never seen the Stanford campus—any campus for that matter—nor glanced at a catalogue of courses, but to my sophomoric mentality Stanford sounded like a fun place to go.

On inquiry I learned that one did not arrive at the portals, suitcase in hand, and say, "Here I am. Where do I sign up?" Stanford, in fact, had some stringent, rather intimidating entrance requirements such as a high grade point average, an outstanding score on a special Aptitude Test and several letters of recommendation, preferably from alumni. Plus a fourth category of intangibles loosely classified as "activities." The director of admissions looked with favor on applicants who had demonstrated promise in such areas as drama, art, debate, music, science, ROTC, leadership and, of course, sports. What did I have to offer? Aside from a large Victorian vocabulary acquired by reading the corpus of Charles Dickens with a dictionary at my elbow, not much. As an athlete I was a marginal case, a 155-pound pulling guard on the junior varsity. Leadership? I'd been leader of the Beaver Patrol, Troop 79, Hollywood District, in the Scouts. That appeared to be my only avenue of hope. Contemplating this dim assessment, I ran for every elective school office in reach—a back-slapping glad-handing politician—including student body president. And, not to be immodest, I won a couple. All in the cause of Leland Stanford, Jr., University.

In the half century and more since then, I have never run for another office. For anything.

L.A. High was one of the few high schools in the country that enjoyed the luxury of publishing a four-page newspaper five days a week through the academic year. The Journalism Department consisted of one teacher, Katharine Carr, to whom we referred behind her back as "Kiddy Carr," and a fully equipped student-operated print shop across the hall in the basement. Carr, sister of Harry Carr, the acerbic author of *The Lancer* column in the Los Angeles *Times*, was a sprightly diminutive spinster who presided over her classes perched atop a high stool, and ran her domain as though it were a metropolitan city room. Only a few hand-picked students were accepted; they performed up to her exacting standards or were summarily dismissed.

"I am going to teach you boys and girls," she announced on my first day, "how to write a simple declarative sentence in the English language. Would anybody care to define that?"

Cowed by this tiny but commanding presence, the class sat mute.

"So," Miss Carr continued, "I shall read you a few pertinent examples and then assign each of you a news beat, for which you will be responsible during the next semester."

My "beat" was the Stamp Club, one unlikely to generate

many scoops, but it was my very own. I attended the first meeting, at which the young philatelists elected their officers; then raced back to the basement, hastily scribbled my copy and presented it like an offering to Miss Carr on her throne, anticipating her warm praise—an embryonic Lowell Thomas or Richard Harding Davis. She read it at a glance, pursed her lips and slashed away with her blue pencil. "Sloppy, too many words," she said. "Write it over."

Crestfallen, I returned to my desk, gnawed on my own pencil a while, then cut, trimmed and rearranged my precious prose. On my second submission Miss Carr nodded and handed it back. "Better," she said. "But watch your syntax. You can improve on that."

Grimly determined now, I boiled my piece down to three simple declarative sentences devoid of adjectives, adverbs and literary flourishes. On my third attempt the lady rewarded me with a grimace of a smile and spiked my copy on her print shop spindle, which signified that I had passed, just barely, my first trial at arms, that tomorrow my report on the activites of the Stamp Club would appear in the pages of the *Blue and White Daily.* Two semesters later, after many an agonized revision, I was knighted with the job of News Editor.

During her long tenure at what she called "the old pioneer school" Katharine Carr played a key role in the early training of many who later became successful journalists, screen writers and novelists, some nationally known. She once addressed my class as a "pack of illiterate young heathens." But the one admonition that no student of Kiddy Carr ever forgot was "you can improve on that."

The success of *Shortgrass* might have marked a turnaround point for Hal. He had surfaced from the murky depths of self-doubt and despondency to regain his credentials as a leading contributor to America's most popular magazine. His fan mail swelled overnight, along with queries from editors and requests for interviews. In terms of *McGuffey's Eclectic Readers* morality, on which he had been reared, he should have learned a universal lesson: Life is not a bottomless bowl of cherries, but a vale of tears, travail and remorse. He had been granted a reprieve, an opportunity to mend his ways. But he was a mere mortal, beyond redemption, heavenly or otherwise.

His drinking continued apace. He submitted to several more drying out cures and promptly fell off the wagon. He had become a sporadic but incorrigible out-of-the-closet drunkard. Fearful, Sylvia "hid" his gun collection in our secret wine depository. Our costly Hutchinson fire some years earlier had left scars; late night after night she patrolled the house for smoldering cigarette butts, a routine she followed long years after his death. One crisis succeeded another, each more stressful and debilitating for us all than the last.

He had given up hunting but during his "good" spells, between bouts, we continued to camp in the desert. On the seamy urban side he took me sightseeing to a speakeasy, to Reno's Red Light Row, to a gambling joint in Mexicali, all of which he considered part of my education. "If you're going to be a writer," he told me, "you have to see some life in the raw."

We attended sporting events: midget car races, polo at Midwick Country Club, an air show at Mines Field, Los Angeles landmarks of fond memory, and many a Saturday afternoon football game at the Coliseum to watch mighty USC beat up such patsies as UCLA and Oregon State. The event— today we might call it a happening—to which I looked forward the most was the monthly dinner meeting of the Adventurers' Club at downtown hotel Rex Arms, a boisterous affair where, after the guest speaker sat down, members vied with one another in spinning their garish tales. Sylvia, although she never attended (strictly men only), referred to Hal's favorite watering hole as "that gang of drunken old liars."

At the time I failed to realize why Hal so often made me his companion on these excursions, but the answer was simple. He had never known a father or a brother and both his grandfathers had died when he was barely out of diapers; he had been raised in a family "copiously supplied with girls." He wanted to make sure that *his* son had the kind of boyhood that he had missed. On my part, I went along delightedly but also in the role of guardian, to exercise whatever influence I could to help steer him away from what Sylvia euphemistically called "trouble." In short, to keep him reasonably sober.

Only once that I recall did we have a sit-down father-to-son discussion of my future. "So you still think you want to be a writer?" he said shortly before I entered college.

"I don't think," I told him. "I'm sure."

"Well, it isn't always easy, you know," he said.

"You made it. And if you can, I will too," I said with the toplofty superiority of seventeen.

"You probably will. But, Son, writing for a living is a risky business. No security. Writing is like being a Mississippi River boat gambler, only more so."

"I'll never know unless I try, Dad."

Hal sighed. "I've always let you follow your own float stick. But listen to a word from your old man. When you're off there at Stanford, study something practical. Like banking."

Banking? Naturally I disregarded his advice.

I never sat in his den and watched him work, never observed his actual habits. But I know that he worked best alone, without a stenographer or mechanical aids. A tape recorder, dictaphone or word processor would have seemed an abomination. He adjusted easily to minor interruptions, able to return to his desk and resume his train of thought. With exceptions. My Grandma Emma visited us frequently and one day tiptoed past his closed door, turned to Sylvia, who happened to be nearby, put a finger to her lips and stage-whispered "Shhh! We mustn't bother Hal at work."

Hal poked his head out of his den. "Mother," he said in exasperation, "a herd of elephants tramping through here wouldn't bother me. But please don't tiptoe and whisper around the house. I can't stand it!"

Emma doted on him, still spoiled her forty-four-year-old son, basking in her pride in his accomplishments. He was the fatherless boy who, despite all predictions, had made it big. But she agonized over his drinking problems, which were no secret among family and friends. Emma lived on a comfortable fixed income from an annuity set up by Lee Bigger's estate, part of which she shared with less affluent relatives. At this stage Hal, fluctuating between a state of prosperity and semi-poverty (where had all the money gone?), qualified as most needy. Over-generous, concerned about his health—although that word was never spoken aloud—she offered to finance an extensive trip. Hal acccepted with alacrity and, I hope, profound gratitude. The day after I graduated from high school the two of us sailed on a three-month cruise to the South Pacific which, in those desperate pinch-penny days, cost some $3,000.

Our voyage to the fabled isles of Stevenson, Melville and Gauguin took place in the summer of 1932, the nadir of the Great Depression. I was not unaware of the climate of the times. The Dow Jones had sunk into the low 40s. Hal declaimed incessantly against forces he called "wild-eyed socialists" who had brought about the Bonus March in Washington, massive bank failures, soup kitchens, breadlines, the highest unemployment rate in American history. A number of my friends already had known the pinch and bite of ravaged incomes. But in our glorious moment of departure, covered aboard ship by the L.A. *Times*, I felt like the golden boy, a child of fortune immune to the afflictions of ordinary humans. Depression, failure and disaster could never touch me or mine—an ecstatic glow granted to me only that once-upon-a-lifetime.

Hal, suffering from post-hangover despondency, was confused. The second day out he ordered a steward to move our deck chairs away from an overhead ventilator. "Somebody's spying on us," he confided to me. "Listening to my conversation."

I tried to assure him otherwise and when we reached Honolulu wrote back this report to Sylvia: "Dad seems better, more relaxed, the sea air agrees with him. He hasn't had a drink that I know of. Leo Carillo, the actor, is on board and they pass most of the time together swapping jokes and stories about the movie business."

In Honolulu Hal reverted briefly to his first love—wildlife watching. Some friends who lived on the city's edge near Diamond Head told him about a mongoose family that often watered at a backyard pond. Hal had never seen one of these ferret-like rodents. He erected a blind of bamboo stalks in the garden of our surprised but agreeable hosts, rigged up his camera with a trip cord, and spent the better part of four days concealed there in solitary vigil, waiting for a mongoose that never materialized but enjoying himself immensely nevertheless.

On the long voyage south to Sydney aboard a Canadian liner, he improved still more. He lost his pallor, ate three meals a day and limited himself to one nightly highball. But he still insisted that someone was out to "get" him.

"Who?" I wanted to know. "Who's trying to get you? For what?"

"They," he said and lowered his voice. "They've followed me all the way from Hollywood."

"Dad, we're thousands of miles from Hollywood. You're safe here."

"They're right here on board. Watching every move I make." And every night he made sure our cabin door was locked.

Once we reached Sydney and boarded an Australian freighter, his paranoia receded and faded in the rush of new scenes and events. The *Montorro* was a scruffy little vessel that made such Paupa-New Guinea ports of call as Madang, Rabaul, Salamua and Manus, names that became grimly, bitterly familiar to all Americans a decade later. Prohibition did not prevail in these waters and Hal quickly established his beachhead in the bar-salon, drinking and yarning with an assortment of colonial administrators and constables, bush pilots, gold hunters, engineers and plantation managers. Over us all, in the dank tropical heat, hung the sweetish stench of copra—our principal cargo—and the sweat of massed humanity. The "second class" passengers, Stone Age Melanesians a bare remove from cannibalism, were packed from scupper to scupper on the open lower decks, inter-island contract labor to work the coconut groves.

Heady stuff for a young would-be writer who had brought

along in his luggage a single volume collection of Shakespeare's plays.

From a sandy coastal strip at Lae, Hal and I made our first-ever journey by air. It was a white-knuckle flight in a Gypsy Moth four-seater: up the Wampit Gorge through mist-shrouded 13,000-foot peaks, over a divide into the Bulolo River drainage, and down onto a postage stamp field hacked out of the jungle at Wau, where an Aussie-American consortium was bucket-dredging for gold. By air, forty minutes; on foot, eight slogging days through the equatorial rain forest. We were met by a bullock cart driven by a grinning black man with a bone through his nose, and saw the marvels that technology had wrought in this remote outpost of the 20th century.

Our pilot of that day died in a crash four months later.

When Hal returned to Los Angeles in late September, he ignored another request from Lorimer to write a serial about the Pony Express, and by Christmas had turned out an article, *Guinea Gold*, and four animal stories (*Birds of a Feather, Koala, Warragal* and *The Pool*) for a fast $10,000, the maestro once more at the top of his form.

Meanwhile, back at the Farm—a nomenclature to which the Stanford campus had some legitimate claim in its then bucolic setting—I enrolled (tuition: $342 a year) and reported for freshman football practice. There I learned, the first afternoon, that I was too small, too slow and too under-motivated to play at the college level. This was the year in which a group of rabid alumni, frustrated by USC's long dominance of West Coast football, had recruited nation-wide a band of super athletes on scholarships. These became the "Vow Boys," who did indeed defeat the hated SC Trojans four years in a row and played in the Rose Bowl back-to-back.

Stanford was widely, but inaccurately, perceived as an elitist institution, playground for sons of the idle rich. Daddy, so 't was rumored, could buy your way in with under-the-table endowments. It was not truly co-educational; the number of female students was limited to a maximum of 500 by terms of the Stanford family will. This distaff discrimination was lifted the following year, as the Depression deepened and enrollment dropped. Thereafter it became slightly easier to date Stanford girls who, nevertheless, were regarded as uppity and icy iron maidens.

I joined a fraternity known as the "Meat House." During my extended association we had among the membership several all-American football stars, the intercollegiate heavyweight boxing champion, captain of the basketball team, a succession of ICAAAA shotput and discus winners; a number of dedicated party boys; a sprinkling of Phi Beta Kappas and two Rhodes Scholars—a healthy mix. Stanford may not have been Number One during those years or even among the Top Twenty, but it was indubitably competitive, whatever one's speciality or aptitude—scholar, jock or socialite.

During my second quarter I achieved one tiny coup in a series of lectures delivered by the University chaplain, Dr. David C. Gardner—Biblical History. This was rated by the cognoscenti as a can't-miss, leadpipe cinch course and was overrun by half the freshman class. The genial dominie gave a few quizzes that any Sunday Schooler could answer easily, then pitched us a tricky knuckle ball: an assignment to write a ten-page essay on selected passages from the King James version, on which our final grade would depend. I chose to do an exegesis of the Ten Commandments; the reason now escapes me. Dr. Gardner, aware that many English majors earned their cakes and ale by ghost-writing term papers, summoned me to his office for a question-and-answer interview. Had I written this myself? Was I taking remedial Bonehead English? What was my religious background? To this last I had to confess that my father was an atheist, that my missionary-born grandfather had come to loathe all missionaries and their good works. The Doctor laughed and awarded me an A-plus, the only one of my college career.

When I reported this to Hal he commented, "I may be a sinner but the devil doesn't have me by the shirttail yet."

"Do you really believe that God doesn't exist?" I asked.

"If He does exist," Hal said, "I've used His name in vain so often that I'll never make it through the Pearly Gates."

Also during my freshman year I witnessed an historical

event, minor but poignantly symbolic. My step-grandfather Lee Bigger had met and shaken hands with ten Presidents of the United States, from Lincoln to Teddy Roosevelt, but I had never set eyes on one. My opportunity came on election day in November 1932. The thirty-first President, Stanford's most distinguished alumnus, and the First Lady still maintained their official residence on campus. I was among the crowd when the Hoovers arrived at the polls in front of the Women's Clubhouse, watched them—a grave and silent couple, almost as if they knew the outcome—step into the booth, then ride away into the autumn haze and history. The era of FDR and the New Deal was about to dawn.

Like most Republicans of his generation, Hal saw Franklin Roosevelt as a reincarnation of Beelzebub, complete with horns and tail. Breakfasts at home often turned into tirades as Hal, scanning the headlines, would thump the table and denounce "that man in the White House." At one point he grew so irate that, as a form of protest, he converted his spare cash—which couldn't have been much—into gold bars and stashed them in a safe deposit box. When the Democratic-controlled Congress outlawed this practice as "hoarding," punishable by fines and prison, Hal roared, "I told you so! That man's driving the country to ruin!"

All freshmen were required to undergo a year-long twelve-unit course misnamed "Western Civilization," a medley of lectures by professors of varying disciplines on such topics as "Communism," "The Corporate Fascist State," "Effects of the Smoot-Hawley Tariff Bill" and "Adam Smith in the Modern World," an effort by the administration to alert our callow young minds to the economic and political realities of the 1930s. When I carried these gleanings home like cautionary red flags, Hal extended his disapproval to include that bastion of arch-conservative capitalism, Stanford University. "That man!" he growled. "Now he's poisoning our colleges and our kids with his radical crap!"

In Hal's eyes FDR had one redeeming quality: he advocated repeal of the Eighteenth Amendment—Prohibition. On the night of April 17, 1933, I was present at a delirious mob scene on San Francisco's Market Street when a truck came trundling out of a brewery with a load of legal 3.2 percent beer, the first in fifteen years, to be ambushed and sacked like a Gold Rush stage coach. Baghdad-on-the-Bay would not enjoy another such celebration until VJ-Day in 1945.

How Hal observed the occasion I never learned.

15.

ONCE AGAIN HAL was having difficulties launching a new serial, this one to which he had given the working title *Wolf Dog*. When he described the basic story to me I said, "It sounds a lot like *The Cross Pull*."

"Yes, it does," he said. "I guess you can't teach an old dog new tricks. The trouble is, new ideas are hard to come by. As you get older you fall into a rut, repeat yourself over and over, the same old stuff."

At forty-five Hal did look older. He had lost most of his hair, gained ten more pounds, grown careless about his grooming and appearance. Sylvia, by contrast, still slim and vivacious and pretty, looked much as she had ten years earlier, except for an occasional lock of gray hair, which she had "touched up" at the beauty parlor.

"You've said that before, Dad," I told him. "You'll come up with another winner, like always."

"No, it's different this time around. I have to get away from this place, this town. It's getting me down."

He had said that before too, but I didn't remind him.

"Not just another trip," he went on. "For good, I mean. Sell this big house, move out, buy some place in the mountains. Wyoming, maybe. Raise a few furs, have a couple of horses to ride. How does that strike you?"

This was the dream he repeated more and more frequently, the impossible dream of turning back the clock, returning to Wapiti, the scene of his carefree youth, his honeymoon, the source of all his success. But to me Wapiti was only a faint and distant flicker. "Have you talked it over with Mother?" I asked.

"No, not yet. And don't mention it to her. She might not be enthusiastic at first."

Hal knew, and I knew, that Sylvia would resist with all her considerable tenacity any such proposal, now or in the foreseeable future. One three-and-a-half year fling of ranch life among the skunks and sagebrush had been a generous plenty, rich in memory but no experience she cared to repeat in her forties.

"Well," he said, resignation in his voice, "let's wait until I finish this next book, get some money ahead. Then we'll decide what to do."

That could have served as his epitaph, if he had wanted one: FINISH THE NEXT BOOK, GET SOME MONEY AHEAD. His and the epitaph of many a writer I came to know later.

Without fanfare Paramount released a modest budget picture, *The Santa Fe Trail*, featuring Richard Arlen with Rosita Morena, based on Hal's *Spanish Acres*, my favorite of all his books, for the silent and sound rights to which he had received a total of $15,000. A New York *Times* reviewer had criticized the film as ". . . beautifully photographed and has its moments of humor but is emphatically weak in drama." The two of us saw this version one night at a downtown movie palace, one of those rococo relics of the 1920s, a kind of gilded mausoleum with rows and rows of empty seats. Not too long ago there had been Hollywood stars in their limousines, klieg lights, mobs of squealing fans. Now this. Admission, two bits, and "Brother, Can You Spare a Dime?"

Bored halfway through the show, Hal ducked out for a smoke. When the lights came on and the meager audience began straggling up the aisles, he turned to me and said, "Dull as ditch water. No action, all talk. Sounds like a debating society. Did I really write that?"

"Well, they gave you screen credit," I said. "Based on a story by—"

"Pretty scenery, I'll have to admit. They must've spliced in some footage from an old travelogue."

Remembering the debacle of *The Big Trail*, I offered a few words of consolation.

"No," he said, "I'll never understand the movie business. It's like—like—"

"Like *Alice in Wonderland*?"

"Yeah." Hal grinned at that. "And *Through the Looking Glass*. Backwards."

I saw less of my parents now. In my 1931 Model A Ford roadster it was a twelve-hour drive south from Palo Alto to Los Angeles down narrow, bumpy, old Coast Highway 101 with a load of share-the-ride passengers, two in front and two in back in the rumble seat, huddled under a blanket. Cut-rate gas sold for ten cents a gallon. Only rich kids took the overnight Pullman train, the Lark, the essence of luxury. Hal and Sylvia had always encouraged my independence. At the age of eleven they had sent me alone on a 1,000-mile rail journey to my first summer camp, with a change of stations in Chicago. Many a time they had left me behind with relatives, or a maid or a good book to read. The world, Hal often told me, was my oyster. So I never felt homesick or lonely or despondent away at college, unlike some of my peers. One of my freshman friends, brooding over money and poor grades, drove to a secluded spot on Sand Hill Road and put a bullet through his brain.

Nineteen thirty-three marked another change in our family. My grandmothers, Cora and Emma, died suddenly within three months of each other. I was their only grandson, had loved them both, as different as they were in many respects, and I grieved, but more from sorrow for Hal and Sylvia than myself. Death was still remote to me, an abstraction, a loss not to be measured in tears or regrets or might-have-beens. My classmate's suicide—that was real, a tragedy; their's had been the natural inevitable turn of the wheel.

News items from the Stanford *Daily* of that year:

"President Ray Lyman Wilbur said that he would turn his attention to the falling enrollment, down to 2,823, and to the dropping off of endowment increases.

"The Board of Trustees decided that Stanford professors

and instructors whose income was already more than $1,000 a year would receive ten per cent less next fall.

"Palo Alto soft drink proprietors sold 3.2 percent beer, with Stanford students composing most of the trade. One student passed the police sobriety test after he consumed eight bottles (one gallon)."

That summer Hal and I spent two months as non-paying guests at a mountain ranch in southern Oregon recently purchased by one of his more flamboyant E.F. Hutton friends, C. Ray Gilliland. In his youth Gil had been a professional baseball pitcher in the 3-I League. Since then he had become a promoter-speculator in such varied fields as grain futures, furs and vitamin pills, his fortunes rising and ebbing like the tides of Fundy Bay. The year before, he had borrowed a thousand dollars from Hal for some dicey investment, then turned up at our house on Christmas Eve in a new Rolls Royce with beautiful actress Claire Windsor on his arm.

(A non-reader of movie fan magazines, I had nonetheless absorbed a good deal of Hollywood lore and trivia, including many seamy details of the town's most sensational, never-to-be-solved murder, that of director William Desmond Taylor in 1922. I knew that the enchantress sitting in our living room was the last woman Taylor had escorted in his checkered life, dancing in the Ambassador Hotel's Cocoanut Grove, two nights before someone shot him at his nearby "love nest" apartment. No suspicion of complicity ever touched her, but I'm afraid that I stared at Miss Windsor in a state of pop-eyed fascination.)

At the ranch, while I labored on odd jobs, Hal dabbled with *Wolf Dog* and advised Gil how he might convert his timber land into a successful dude resort. And I fell in love again, this time with a busty, blue-eyed blonde several years my senior, a woman of the world I liked to think, lusting after her body and scheming how to lure her into Gil's hay barn or the nearest bed. An opportunity arose one Saturday night when I filched a bottle from Hal's cache and took her to a country dance at the crossroads of Prospect, prepared for any eventuality. We encountered a battalion of randy, woman-starved, young $30-

a-month trainees from a nearby Civilian Conservation Corps camp, one of the New Deal efforts to abate unemployment. Early in the evening a fist-swinging melee erupted on the dance floor, a potential free-for-all. I hustled my lady love out the door, a brave but prudent gallant rescuing fair maiden. Within the next few hours I got drunk for the first time in my life, lost my virginity, and suffered a hangover, a triple play the old 3-I pitcher would have applauded.

When I related a few details to Hal, a long while later, his comment was: "You have to grow up sometime."

One night, shortly before the Christmas holidays that year, I observed another small bit of history that reflected the rage and ugly vigilante temper of the times, a legacy of the Lindbergh case. From a park across the street from the Santa Clara County jail, my roommate and I watched a berserk mob storm the doors, overcome the sheriff and deputies inside, drag out a pair of confessed kidnap-murderers awaiting trial and hang them from two trees. Next day Governor "Sunny Jim" James Rolph, Jr., whose nephew was a friend and classmate of mine, issued this statement: "This is the best lesson California has given this country. We show the country that the State is not going to tolerate kidnaping."

On our next desert camp-out Hal and I spent an afternoon in the ghost town of Ballarat chatting with one of the Mojave's last and most famous prospectors, Frank "Shorty" Harris. Shorty, a snowy-haired wisp of a man only five-feet four, then seventy-six, entertained us with a non-stop account of his exploits. In 1904, for instance, he had discovered the fabulously rich gold outcroppings that became the boom town of Rhyolite, sold his claim for $1,000 and sobered up six days later in a saloon with one quarter left in his jeans to buy "a hair o' the dog."

"I'm gonna make me another strike, yessiree," Shorty assured us. "Then I'm goin' to Paree and dance with them can-can girls and drink buckets of champagne." He died penniless a year later and was buried at his request near Badwater in Death Valley, the lowest point in the United States, his grave marked by a plaque that read: "Here lies Shorty Harris, a single blanket jackass prospector." From some of these elements Hal fashioned what was to be his next-to-last short story for the *Post, Detour.*

The following spring we squeezed in another trip, accompanied by a courtly old gentleman with a sweeping handlebar mustache who was introduced to me by Hal only as "Bear George, he used to hunt grizzlies in Montana."

In the silt of China Lake we dug for and found some tusks of the prehistoric mammoth. Then in a remote corner of the Coso Range we located what is perhaps the finest gallery of Indian petroglyphs in the West, carved in the canyon walls. (Now a part of the U.S. Naval Weapons Center, it is protected against vandals.) At night around the fire Hal and George talked and sipped bourbon while I listened, trying to picture in my mind the first Americans who so long ago had created those mysterious stick human figures, serpents and mountain sheep, suns and moons and indecipherable squiggles. Back in Los Angeles Hal began an article which he never finished. But one of Bear George's tall tales, a saga of his ride for life on the back of his "pet" grizzly, survived almost verbatim in *Wolf Dog*, a choice bit of Americana.

Two weeks after I returned to college, Sylvia phoned me long distance, an unprecedented extravagance for our family in that day and age. "Your father's had a heart attack," she said. "A bad one. We didn't know if he'd live through the night."

I must have been speechless.

"You'd better come home as soon as possible." My mother's voice sounded scratchy and faraway. "He keeps asking for you."

"How—how is he now?" I managed to say.

"Some better, but Dr. Brandel says it's still touch and go." Dr. Harry Brandel, our oldest Los Angeles friend, was a name that Sylvia had plucked out of the directory back in 1917 to circumcise me at the age of two. "Can you leave your classes?"

"Of course. I'm on the way."

"I don't want you driving that car of yours," Sylvia said. "Not with this on your mind. Take the train."

"But—"

"Hal Jr., take the train!"

So I did, my first and last ride on the luxurious Lark.

Propped up in bed, Hal looked gray and shrunken, diminished, but surprisingly cheerful. "You shouldn't have come all this way," he said. "I'm going to be okay. Doc Brandel said so."

We had never been demonstrative. I can't recall ever having kissed or hugged him, even as a child. Now I took one of his hands in both of mine. "Sure you are," I said. "You'll be fine."

"Nothing too serious," he said. "Just my bum ticker acting up again. I'll take it easy for a few days, get some rest."

"Sure, Dad."

"Lying here, I've been thinking. As soon as I finish *Wolf Dog* we'll take another trip. A good one. Africa."

"Africa?"

"That's right, Africa. We've killed off most of the game in this country. But there's still plenty over there. We'd better go before they kill off the rest. Not to hunt, just take pictures. How'd you like that for a graduation present?"

"Sounds terrific, Dad. But I have two more years to go."

"Well, whenever." He waved off that consideration as immaterial. "When I get some money ahead. Then we'll go. Pull you out of school."

"Hal," Sylvia spoke up, "you're talking too much. Remember what Dr. Harry told you."

Hal sighed and closed his eyes and sank back into his pillows. "Thank you for coming, Son. We'll talk some more later."

I noticed a stack of yellow writing paper and an array of pencils on the nightstand beside his bed, and after he dozed off I asked Sylvia if he was trying to write in his condition.

"Not write," Sylvia told me. "Dictate. Whenever he feels strong enough he dictates aloud to me for a few minutes. Then I type it up and read it back to him. Sometimes just one sentence."

"But he's too weak to be working," I protested.

"Try and tell him that," Sylvia said. "You know how stubborn your father can be. He's like a man possessed. He's going to finish *Wolf Dog* if it kills him. The last two chapters."

"Does Dr. Harry know about this?"

"Hal won't listen to the doctor. Maybe he'll listen to you, but I doubt it."

Hal didn't listen to me. Several weeks after I returned to Stanford by Greyhound bus I received a jubilant note in his shaky barely legible script that he had completed *Wolf Dog* and sold it to the *Post* for $15,000.

When I came home late in June he seemed much better, almost back to normal. He could walk about easily, his color had improved, his face fleshed out. After I congratulated him he said, "You'll never guess what I'm working on now. The serial for Lorimer about the Pony Express."

Recalling his earlier reservations, I said, "With all your characters spread out from hell to breakfast?"

He laughed. "Exactly. From Missouri to California and back again. Sounds worse than *The Big Trail*. But I'll make it work somehow. I have to."

On his next house call Dr. Harry took me aside. "I made your acquaintance when you were still using a potty chair," he said. "So now I'm going to talk to you like a second father."

I nodded. "Dad is sicker than he admits. Is that it?"

"Sicker than he knows," said Doctor Harry. "His heart is in sorry shape, small wonder after the kind of life he's led. He's lucky to be alive."

"Can he still work?"

"No more than one hour a day. No excitement. No stress or strain. No travel. Probably he should never again go much above sea level."

"No travel?" I said in despair. "He lives for his trips."

"We'll see. Maybe next fall. An ocean cruise. But nothing strenuous." Doctor Harry patted my shoulder. "Tell Sylvia, if you want, but don't breathe a word to Hal. He's one tough old rooster."

While Hal began his research on the Pony Express—working title *Long Ride*—I cast about for a summer plan of my own. There would be no Africa in our near future, no Wyoming, not even a weekend in the Mojave. More significantly, with Hal so ill our entire family pattern of life would have to change in ways as yet impossible to plan for. I decided not to tell Sylvia yet, but of course she knew. Probably Hal did too. We could only wait and hope, biding our time. We were not a family that prayed, but we were pretty good pretenders.

A job opportunity of sorts opened up when the West Coast Longshoremen's Union, led by Harry Bridges, went on strike, followed by the Seamen's Union, which threatened to develop into a crippling general strike. Hal grumped about "pinkos driving America to ruin" and fretted over money, although both he and Sylvia had received small inheritances from their mothers the year before. Apolitical, indifferent to the grievances of labor, under the spell of Richard Halliburton's bestselling *The Royal Road to Romance*, I saw a chance to become a sailor on the seven seas—a strikebreaker and hated "scab."

I registered with a downtown emergency employment office and sat there for several days with a suitcase between my knees, waiting for my name to be called. When at last it was, I naively asked the supervisor where I would be sent. He shrugged. "Do you want this job or don't you?"

I looked over my shoulder at the hiring hall jam-packed with hundreds of my fellow Americans desperate for work of any kind and mumbled an affirmative.

Two other teen-agers and I were hustled into a freight elevator like bit players from some mobster movie, down to an alley and a cruiser manned by two LAPD cops. We whizzed out through a cordon of jeering, rock-throwing pickets, performed a razzle-dazzle fox-and-hounds gambit through the city streets to throw off possible pursuers, at length reached a fenced enclosure and wharf of the Standard Oil Company of California at El Segundo. Job description: Ordinary seaman, $45 a month and found. Destination: Providence, Rhode Island. Not exactly the fabled shores of the Indies I had hoped for, but a beginning. Fifteen minutes later I was carrying 100-pound bags of flour up a ship's gangway to the galley storeroom.

16.

ABOUT TWO O'CLOCK next morning, limp with fatigue, I watched the lights of southern California dwindle over the stern. Dan Thomson, captain of the 6,000-ton tanker *H.M. Storey*, headed out for Panama with a load of heavy crude and a motley patchwork crew that included several collegians like myself, a couple of winos off the beach and a handful of genuine, down-on-their-luck old salts who knew how to tie a bowline. Skipper Thomson had first gone to sea as a cabin boy in the days of sail. A tall grizzled man with an awesome command of billingsgate, on warm tropical nights he often paced up and down his open topside bridge deck in the altogether and a pair of carpet slippers, muttering imprecations against the unkind fate that had dealt him such a stupid bunch of land-lubber fuck-ups. One of my duties was to stand watch at the compass binnacle from eight to midnight; consequently, I had an opportunity to observe him, with considerable trepidation, at point blank range.

On our first Sunday morning out of port, in lieu of any religious observances, he decided to instruct a few of his very ordinary neophytes in the art of steering a vessel under full steam. He summoned three of us to the bridge, designated me as first guinea pig and positioned me in front of the big wooden-spoked wheel. "Now the ticket here," he said, "is to anticipate. Keep your eye on the compass. When she begins to veer a shade of a degree to starboard, you adjust the wheel a shade to port, which brings us back on line. And vice versa, port back to starboard, steady as she goes, within a range of two, maybe three degrees. You got that?"

"Yes, sir," I lied.

"Sea's calm as a bathtub. No wind to speak of." Thomson pulled a lever which transferred the ship's steering control mechanism from Automatic Pilot to Manual. "She's all yours, boy. Anticipate, then compensate."

I had read of actors afflicted by stage fright on opening night, forgetting their lines, until the prompter came to their rescue. Dan Thomson was my prompter.

"For God's sake, grab it! You're yawing to port!"

The instant I gripped the wheel spokes I suffered an acute attack of nautical freeze. The sea was flat, no breeze, blue skies, nary a landfall or another ship on the horizon. I had the whole Pacific Ocean in which to maneuver this leviathan and God knew how many tons of Cal Standard's petroleum sloshing about in the tanks. But *H.M. Storey* suddenly took on a life of its own, a fractious obstinate personality with a will of iron.

"Starboard, damnittohell! Anticipate!"

Where, I wondered, had this crusty old bastard picked up words like "anticipate" and "compensate?" That was my department—English. I gave the wheel a yank to the right. No, starboard. Or was it? In addition to the compass there was mounted on the forward bulkhead an electric navigational aid with a graduated scale and an orange light. Every time the ship's course altered one degree, either left or right, the light shifted accordingly and emitted an advisory "Ping!"

Lost in a floating pinball arcade of lights and bells and shouted commands, with a deadweight monster that defied my every effort at control, I soon was steering a zigzag course of some thirty degrees' variation, ten times the captain's permissible limit. I managed one frantic glance back at what I had wrought, the tanker's glassy serpentine wake, before Thomson relieved me at the wheel. "What's your name?" he asked.

I told him.

"Evarts, huh?" He gave me his gimlet stare. "I'll never make a sailor out of you, boy. But stand by and pay attention."

Next morning, when I was polishing brightwork near his cabin, he poked his head out and barked, "Evarts!"

I swallowed. "Sir."

"Report to me here at six bells tonight."

Apprehensive, I speculated on what punishments he might have in mind. I had screwed up his official log; my calamitous few minutes at the helm would become part of the company's permanent maritime record. A master with powers as absolute as those of any Medici monarch, he could slam me in the brig, have me keel-hauled or swung from the yardarm—fell fantasies I had acquired from *Treasure Island*.

But the captain was all smiles and gruff affability when I reported after supper. He handed me a recent copy of the *Saturday Evening Post* with *Wolf Dog* and Hal's name featured on the cover. "So your old man's an author?" he said.

With relief I admitted as much.

"Tell me," Thomson said. "Who wrote this? 'The sea never changes and its works, for all the talk of men, are wrapped in mystery.'"

"I don't know, sir."

"Joseph Conrad, that's who. In *Typhoon*. The greatest writer about the sea that ever lived. And I've read 'em all, from Homer to Herman Melville."

I must have been staring at him open-mouthed.

"You think an ignorant old sailor fart like me can't read literature?" The captain brayed with laughter. "Well, you're wrong. Let me tell you something, boy."

And tell me he did. In countless fo'castles and hammocks and bunks on the oceans of all the world, in every conceivable type of ship from windjammer to tramp freighter, Dan Thomson had read the lonely off-watch hours away, learning his trade and climbing rung by rung up the chain of command. Not only that, he had written. From two enormous sea chests packed to capacity, he chose a few journals in which over the years he had kept a daily record of his observations, commentaries and reminiscences, and now began reading selected passages aloud to his captive audience of one.

At the sound of eight bells I squirmed nervously. I was due

—overdue—on the bridge. But Thomson brushed that aside and read on, and on. "There's a thousand stories in there," he said, slapping one of the chests, "and hundreds of novels. If I only had time to write some of them."

At last I discerned the purpose behind this interview and said lamely, "Yes, sir, you must keep real busy running this tanker."

The captain gave me a smile as guileless as a baited hook. "I thought maybe your old man could help me out. Then we'd split the money. Make a fortune."

How many such "share-the-wealth" propositions had Hal received from would-be authors? Beyond number. But never before had I been the middleman, caught between the devil and the deep blue sea, as it were. "Sounds very interesting, sir," I said. "But the problem is, my father doesn't know a thing about the sea. He—he grew up in Kansas."

"Balls o' bullshit, boy, I know enough for twenty men. But he knows how to write." Thomson produced one of his cards, scrawled his signature and handed it to me. "When you're back home again tell him to get in touch. We'll make a deal."

I could only nod.

Having settled that detail to his satisfaction, the captain shifted gears. "Thinking about a career in the merchant marine, are you?"

"Sort of, sir."

"I don't recommend it. Maybe you'll grow up to be a writer like your old man."

On that note we said goodnight.

When I returned from Providence to El Segundo six weeks later with the empty *H.M. Storey* riding high in the water, the captain signed my discharge papers with a "Very Good" notification for character, ability and seamanship. Gross flattery. On the homeward voyage, during much of which I'd slaved in the noxious bowels of the tanks, inhaling vile fumes, hand scraping rust and shoveling mountains of oily sludge, I had abandoned forever my dreams of becoming a sea rover.

Hal never got in touch with Dan Thomson, nor Dan Thomson with Hal. But somewhere, if the old skipper had any relatives, there may still survive in the corner of an attic or a moldy basement two forgotten sea chests full of diaries waiting to be discovered.

During my absence Hal's health had improved, or so he claimed, although his face looked puffy and sallow. He had finished the first chapter of *Long Ride* and was talking about a fall trip, possibly a river run down the Colorado or a car safari to the tip of Baja. Dr. Harry vetoed both these projects and followed up his original suggestion, an ocean voyage. And so it was arranged. Late in September Hal would take a six-week cruise around South America aboard a passenger liner, with the stipulation that he write no more than one hour each day and walk a daily mile around the deck.

"There's no justice," he said to me. "Here you are, got paid for a Caribbean cruise. But me, I have to pay through the nose for mine."

I laughed and showed him the calluses still tender from my labors aboard the *H.M. Storey*. "Earned by the honest sweat of my brow."

"By the time I was your age," he said, "I'd worked an alfalfa stacker, swung a sledge hammer on the Santa Fe, shot ducks for the market till my shoulder was black and blue. What are you complaining about?"

"Dad, you told me once that you'd built a lot of rock walls. Where was that?"

"At Papa Bigger's summer place in Cascade, Colorado. He was crazy about natural rock retaining walls. Papa and I worked like fools." Hal paused. "That's where I first met your mother, by accident, along the creek. My God, she was a pretty woman."

Two evenings before his departure Hal and Sylvia and I took a picnic supper to a beach near Malibu. We had the spot to ourselves, not a light or another person in sight. By the glow of our campfire coals, my mother read aloud the opening of a current novel, *Goodbye, Mr. Chips*, a tale about an English schoolmaster and his lads. This was not Hal's particular brand of tea and he fell asleep on the sand, snoring softly.

Sylvia closed the book. "He's so tired, poor man," she said. "I hope this trip will do him some good."

"I hope so too, Mother," I said. "He needs a long rest. At least he hasn't been drinking lately."

I spent the next night camping with a friend and returned to South Lorraine Boulevard in ample time to deliver Hal dockside at the sailing hour of 5 P.M. And found him drunk. Not tipsy and talkative, but reeling, marble-eyed, almost incoherently drunk. The why, the what, the how slashed through my conscience like ripple-edged knives. Submerged in a gulf of guilt and failure, I asked myself why I hadn't stayed home with him that weekend. Why hadn't I understood his dependence on the bottle? Why, why, why. . . ? What the lousy hell kind of son was I?

Sylvia and her sister Lala, who had driven north from San Diego to see Hal off, were in a state of helpless shock and distress while he stomped about the house in his BVD's, swearing that he'd never catch the boat, that he'd never wanted to visit South America in the first place; it was all some kind of Hollywood plot to get rid of him. Somehow I persuaded my mother and my aunt to go ahead and let me handle the crisis alone.

Sylvia had packed his bags, one till full of cigarettes, writing paper, sharpened pencils and notes on the Pony Express. I manipulated Hal in and out of a cold shower, into clean clothes and primed him with hot coffee. By then it was close on three o'clock. Crossing the living room, he lurched into a small tip-top table and knocked it crashing to the floor. Stunned and perhaps sobered by the wreckage, he mumbled, "That's Sylvia's favorite. From her mother. She'll never forgive me. Never."

"Yes, she will," I said. "She'll forgive you, Dad. Come on, let's go."

In my Ford roadster we raced to the harbor at Wilmington. I steered him through a throng of streamer-throwing, farewell bon voyagers, up the gangway of the S.S. *Malolo* and to his cabin. Someone had sent him a bouquet of roses. Before looking at the card, he said, "You know, Son, nobody ever sent me flowers before in my life."

"You've got a lot of admirers," I said and hugged him. "Have a great trip."

One corner of his mouth lifted in a grin. "I'm just a tourist now. From L.A. to L.A. Going nowhere. But I'll finish that book."

I received a postcard from Valparaiso, Chile: "Between me and the South Pole there's nothing but a bunch of penguins. Love, Dad."

Some days later, while laboring over Chaucerian stanzas in the Stanford Library, I received word from a fraternity brother: Dean of Men, urgent message.

Unsuspecting, I hurried to the Administration Building. The Dean, a compassionate man familiar with adversity, broke the news gently: Hal had died of a heart attack a few hours earlier.

"It-it must be some mistake," I stammered. "My father, he's in South America."

The Dean showed me a copy of a radiogram relayed through Rio de Janeiro.

That night the Richfield Reporter, the West Coast Dan Rather of the airways of that era, led off his ten o'clock radio broadcast with: "Literary circles were saddened today by news of the death of—"

On October 23, 1934, after a brief railside ceremony, at the request of Sylvia and myself, Harry George Evarts was buried at sea in a flag-draped coffin in the South Atlantic somewhere off the coast of Brazil, two months into his forty-seventh year.

A few weeks later Sylvia received his effects from the steamship company, among which she found seventy-nine manuscript pages of *Long Ride*, the novel that never would be completed.

In the volume *Twentieth Century Western Writers*, historian W.H. Hutchinson, biographer of W.H.D. Koerner and author Eugene Manlove Rhodes, wrote this appraisal of Hal's work: "Hal G. Evarts's writing career was a logical extension of his occupational pre-occupation with the out-of-doors West and the wildlife it held. His articles on wild animals and on natural resources conservation entitle him to recognition as forerunner of today's concern with the natural environment."

In fiction "Evarts's contributions to the 'western' genre, *Tumbleweeds*, for example, being in that category established by no better authority than this writer as the 'epic' western. This epic phase began with the 1922 serialization of Emerson Hough's *The Covered Wagon* in the *Saturday Evening Post* and the epic remained a staple in the *Post's* pages so long as George Horace Lorimer, who dominated the fortunes of that great magazine, remained alive. It was, of course, imitated or adopted, as you prefer, by other mass circulation slicks. There was a plot line in these epic westerns and a romantic interest as well, but these were almost subordinate to the vast canvas of the west that contained the epic event, virtually a pageant in itself, that was filled with life and movement.

"It was to this sub-genre, or perhaps the climactic phase, of the 'western' that Evarts applied his knowledge of and affection for the wildlife of the west for the vast land in which it and all things moved by the grace of their gods, and for the real people who he knew lived and often died by the natural resources they conserved or exploited as their natures or their needs demanded. He brought to the task of portraying all these things correctly a solid, driving straight-line narrative, free of the cursive tricks of light and shadow but redolent of prairie and sky, that was most effective in grabbing the reader's attention and holding it. He deserves more attention than he has received from students of the literature of the American west."

Jim Kjelgaard, the late outdoor writer and author of *Big Red*, beloved by millions of young readers, said this: "In my firmly considered opinion the name of Hal G. Evarts ranks with that of Ambrose Bierce, Joaquin Miller, John Muir and Henry David Thoreau. Those five contributed more to virile literature than any other group of men in the United States. Some day he'll take his rightful place among American writers. It will be a high one."

17.

THE LEGEND IS that "real" American men don't cry. Some do. I did. Not in sustained bursts, but often at unexpected moments tears welled up uncontrollably and, if in public, I would pretend to blow my nose or excuse myself to go to the bathroom. Months passed before I could accept, even believe in, the finality of Hal's death. He had played such a cardinal role in my life that I felt bereft, inconsolable, as though some vital part of me were lacking.

I tried to rationalize the manner of his going. He had died while doing what he loved—traveling and writing—at the pinnacle of his career. His burial had been appropriate for a man of his views, perhaps symbolically perfect; from mortal dust to mother sea. During those first weeks I took long solitary walks in the empty hills behind Stanford and read a great deal of poetry, which ordinarily did not appeal to me.

From Philadelphia George Lorimer, Hal's patron saint, wrote my mother: "We could always count on a fine Western story from Hal Evarts. It is hard for me to put into words our feelings about the passing of one who, like Mr. Evarts, has been for so long a time identified with the *Post* and one who was a real source of strength to it."

But how long could he have continued as a source of strength to anyone, least of all himself? Those of us close to him knew that he was headed on a downhill course of demolition. Day after day Sylvia and I lived in dread of some disaster or public disgrace. Would he have ended in an institution, blood brother to the drunken derelicts of downtown Skid Row? He went out a winner, I told myself. Take comfort from that. Granted, he might have written a classic about the Pony Express. A trip to Africa might have produced a series of animal stories from the Dark Continent to rank with his American best. (His final animal story, *The Black Roo*, appeared in the *Post* three months after his death.) But, in the last analysis, only one reality mattered: he was gone. And, for a long time, I would sorely miss him both as a father and friend.

If Sylvia was bitter, and she had reason, she was also fiercely protective. She and I never seemed able to discuss his "weakness" openly and frankly, even after his death. It was a subject we accepted as fact, but avoided. For Hal's part, although he often taunted her as "the little martyr," he was never abusive or threatening or lifted a hand against her.

Not long before her own death, in a rare moment of revelation, she told me, "He punished his body so. He squandered his talent." To everyone, including family, she came to refer to him formally as "Mr. Evarts," never "Hal." Widowed at forty-four, eminently remarriageable, she never had an involvement with another man. Whether or not she too had been smitten by "love at first sight" across a mountain creek, she remained steadfast to her fading memories of him, both the good and the bad.

For now there were practical considerations and decisions to make. Sheltered by the umbrella of Hal's earning power, I had never given much thought to money. Among his assets and liabilities he left a small checking account, a large mortgage, no life insurance and numerous debts. After much soul-searching Sylvia sold a portion of his library to the research department at Metro-Goldwyn-Mayer, rented our house to a screen writer pal of John Wayne's, and moved in with her sister and brother-in-law in San Diego where she lived off and on until her death forty-three years later.

At Stanford in my junior year I reviewed my own financial position: one aging Ford and a savings account of some $1,500, a nineteen-year accumulation of Christmas and birthday gifts from loving relatives—my nest egg for the future, whatever that might be. My first job brought in $15 a month from SERA, the State Emergency Relief Administration, for washing test tubes and beakers in the biology lab. From that I branched out into waiting on table—hashing—at a private girls' school and various campus sororities for three meals a day.

For the summer of 1935 my uncle-in-law, Lester Bradley, who had left the Bank of Italy to become publisher of San Diego's two leading newspapers, hired me as a cub reporter for the *Evening Tribune*. Nepotism, what else? I covered the police beat and municipal courts, observing a parade of pimps, hookers, muggers and petty thieves. I attended my first murder trial, touched my first corpse. And when I returned to college in the fall, I thought of turning to journalism as a career.

That September I had the good fortune to land a job as business manager of my fraternity—room, board and laundry. I never studied banking, as Hal had once urged, but he would have been pleased, I think, to know that I learned the fundamentals of handling sizable sums each month, meeting a payroll and keeping an accurate ledger of accounts. Over the lifelong haul this extra-curricular activity proved to be more useful than any academic discipline.

Stanford, like most universities of that day, private or public, had no program of creative writing. The catalogue listed a single course in the short story, none in the novel, non-fiction or drama. John Steinbeck, who had passed that way ten years earlier without earning a degree, recalled that he got little or no encouragement for his early efforts. A would-be writer, one supposedly qualified, had the option of taking what was loosely termed "independent study" for which he received a plus or minus grade, unit credit but no significant instruction. We few step-children of the English Department met occasionally at the Union for coffee and fifteen-cent malts to bemoan our neglect, like students everywhere. We saw the faculty as highbrow eggheads, dedicated to Serious Literature, scornful of such mass entertainment media as the slicks and the flicks. We were Philistines.

My most unforgettable professor was a woman, as were all my memorable teachers in grammar, junior and senior high school. Novelist Allen Drury, class of '39, described her as:

"Marge Bailey, with her gray hair pulled back in a severe bun, her prominent eyes glaring about the room, deliberately intimidating expression, her invariable Elizabethan red velvet cloak—Stanford's own Dame Edith Sitwell, half of her life's work the creation of Marge Bailey, fearsome myth and implacable legend. She was a brilliant lady, was Marge, respected, admired, feared by generations of undergraduates for her devastating put-downs, her ruthless dismissals of young dreams, her unexpected and equally ruthless encouragements."

Marge gave few written examinations. But one morning she swept—she never walked—into our class room, course #183, 18th Century Lit, and pinned on the bulletin board a full page advertisement from the San Francisco *Chronicle*, some department store copy editor's depiction of women's undergarments: slips, panties, girdles, the works. Not one of us snickered. "Each of you," she announced, "will write 500 words on how you think Samuel Johnson would have reacted to this display." And swept out.

The lady loved good theater.

However Marge regarded my potential, she appointed me to edit the English Club's Literary Year Book, gave me a private office and free rein. I spent much of my final quarter assembling a collection of student stories, essays, sketches and poetry. One of my contributors, a young lady from Wyoming, won first place for the best 1936 college short story published in the United States, a coup for her and Marge Bailey and Stanford U; for the editor, whose contest entry garnered not even an honorable mention, a lesson in humility.

As graduation neared I applied for admission to the Columbia University School of Journalism, counting on my nest egg to see me through a year in New York. And then an opportunity presented itself from a most unlikely and unexpected direction: the movies. Sylvia had sold the screen rights to Hal's *The Painted Stallion* to a newly formed studio, Republic. The executive producer, Sol C. Siegel, offered me a contract at $50 a week to work on the screenplay. Hal's experience on *The Big Trail* had left me leery of the industry but who could refuse that kind of money? In 1936, a pasha's ransom. I drove south to Hollywood and signed the papers. Starting date: July 1.

Three days before I was due to report, an old friend and classmate invited me to his house for dinner. Midway through the meal he cleared his throat and, almost matter-of-factly, asked if I would like to join him on a trip to the Olympic Games in Berlin and a summer tour through Europe. Flattered and dumbfounded, I blurted out some idiotic response to the effect that: "Thank you, thanks a lot. I'd love to go. But I can't. I have a job starting nine o'clock Monday morning."

Long before Hal's death Sylvia had cut me adrift from her tenuous apron strings. She treated me as an adult, even when I merited less, never advising or counseling me unless asked. Not once did she utter that odious phrase: "I told you so." Whatever course of action I might undertake, no matter how hair-brained it seemed to her or in fact proved to be, I could count on my mother's support, then and throughout her life. But on this occasion she spoke up.

"You're being foolish, Hal Jr.," she told me.

"You know how scarce jobs are," I said. "I can't go."

"Yes you can. You'll always regret it if you don't."

She was right, of course. Sanity prevailed. My about-to-be boss, Sol Siegel, was understanding and cooperative; he promised to keep the door open until my return in the fall. Almost everyone, I suppose, can look back over his total experience at whatever age and single out some one incident, decision or happenstance that profoundly affected the course of his life. Thus Jack Bowen's friendship, in the most unpredictable way, altered mine.

Someone—I wish I could remember who—gave me a copy of John Gunther's best seller *Inside Europe*. Then and there my real education began. As Jack and I rolled across the American heartland aboard the Golden State Limited I read with eerie fascination the record of the man whose monstrous crimes would affect the lives and deaths of my entire generation far into the next decade. Where had I been all this time? I asked myself. In a cloister on the Stanford campus, that's where.

Why hadn't I read any newspapers except the sports page

and the comics? Because I'd been too busy reading the great masters. Hadn't my year-long course in European history taught me anything? Yes, history from the Protestant Reformation to the Treaty of Versailles. But that was yesterday. This was now, today, four months after Adolf Hitler had goose-stepped a renovated German army back into the Rhineland. Somewhere east of the Mississippi I underwent a metamorphosis into another fantasy role, that of globe-trotting foreign correspondent.

Jack and I crossed the Atlantic on the elegant French liner *Normandie* but arrived in Berlin too late to buy tickets for any Olympic events. We did, however, manage to catch a glimpse of the main attraction. After waiting for hours on the Unter den Linden, engulfed by the greatest massing of humanity I had seen in my twenty-one years, Der Fuehrer rolled past in his open limousine like some papier-mâché mannequin in a brown uniform and red armband. The crowd loosed an animal roar that must have shaken the Brandenburger Tor.

For a week we stayed in the home of a middle class, ultra Aryan Berlin family—a doctor, his wife and daughter. We ate breakfast in a room dominated by an autographed, swastika-draped photograph of Paul Joseph Goebbels, for whom the daughter worked in the Ministry of Propaganda. Each morning our hostess, an apple-cheeked, grandmotherly little dumpling, greeted us with an upraised fist and "Heil Hitler" salutation. Whenever she spoke of "our leader" her voice quavered and her eyes misted over—with love.

I wrote Sylvia: "The Germans are bewitched by this man, incredible as it seems. If anybody objects to him they don't dare whisper. Fanatics."

Moving on, we traveled first class, staying at the best hotels and dining in sumptuous restaurants in a style befitting two young bloods on a traditional circuit of the Continent. We steamered down the Danube into central Europe and in a Budapest nightclub missed by minutes His Majesty King Edward VIII of England, Mrs. Wallis Simpson and their royal entourage. The washroom attendant gave me a wink and said, "He iss veree dronk, the kink. Almost fell into pisser."

At Sarajevo I stood by a bridge over the Miljacka River where in 1914 a Serbian nationalist had fired the shot that ignited World War I. Among my musings ran the thesis that it could not happen again, not a Balkan assassination nor any other human folly of that magnitude, not in my lifetime. But as much as I wanted to believe this wistful prophecy I discovered that, somewhere between Sarajevo and Berlin, I had lost my conviction.

In late September we turned north through Italy enroute home to the workplace, Jack to enter the family business, I to try my wings in Hollywood. But I had become spoiled, a travel glutton; the countries we had visited only whetted my appetitie for more. I debated with myself and the Protestant Work Ethic: "Who do you think you are, Evarts—Playboy of the Western World? You've had your free lunch. Now grow up. Buckle down. You're not a bubble brain college kid any more. Go home. But—But—" The "buts" won.

During a stopover in Venice I happened upon a Stanford friend in that oasis eulogized by U.S. expatriates, Harry's Bar—"You can't go to Heaven until you've been to Harry's." Ernest Arbuckle, who later would become dean of the Graduate School of Business and board chairman of Wells Fargo Bank, had a knapsack, blanket roll and a dark stubble of beard. "Why the outfit, Ernie?" I asked. "What are you, a bindle stiff?"

"I'm a citizen of the world. On the cheap. Very cheap." He laughed. "I have a job with Standard Oil when I get home."

"I worked for Standard a couple of summers ago," I said. "On a tanker."

"Standard's hired some Arabs to drill for oil in Bahrain," Arbuckle said. "They asked me to take a look."

"Bahrain? Never heard of it."

"Neither has anybody else. Some godforsaken little island in the Persian Gulf. I'm taking the scenic route through Russia."

On the instant, without reflection or weighing pros and cons, I knew I had to see that misbegotten speck myself, for reasons that defied all logic and common sense but suddenly seemed irrefutable. And astounded Ernie Arbuckle by inviting myself to join him.

His reaction: "You sure make up your mind in one helluva hurry."

We discussed it over a drink, decided to merge forces and agreed to meet in Athens four weeks later.

In the 1930s the American dollar was undisputed king of the road. In some countries the exchange of a single ten-dollar traveler's check yielded sheafs of the local currency and leveraged unbelievable purchasing power. One willing to put up with certain discomforts—native hotels and regional food, fourth class rail carriages and steerage ship passage, antiquarian buses shared with livestock and passengers prone to motion sickness, no frills or nights out on the town, skin tight economy—could travel far and wide for a modest cash outlay.

Third World countries did not exist. Much of the world's land mass was divided into crumbling colonial empires—British, French, Dutch, Belgian, Portugese and their territorial satrapies. The Germans had lost theirs at Versailles, the Japanese were busy carving out a new one. The other two heavyweights, not yet superpowers, the U.S.A. and the U.S.S.R., had their "spheres of interest." But all of this geography and realpolitik I had yet to learn. I cabled Sylvia to withdraw my $1,500 nest egg from the bank and send it on. It was the shrewdest investment I ever made.

In Paris, after a farewell bash that included dinner at Maxim's and the Follies Bergère, I poured Jack on the boat train, shipped home my first class wardrobe and bought a more functional outfit—backpack, bed roll, boots and work clothes. On a crisp October evening I left the *Gare de Lyon* aboard the coach section of the Orient Express.

18.

INNOCENTS ABROAD, Arbuckle and I disembarked from an Italian freighter in the Soviet port of Batum at the eastern end of the Black Sea. According to my diary it took the pair of us six hours to clear customs and immigration, on-the-job-training in patience for bureaucratic tribulations to come. President Roosevelt recently had extended diplomatic recognition to the Soviet Union for the first time since 1917, a mini-thaw in relations, so the human climate for U.S. citizens was perhaps less frosty than in previous years. Neither of us had any particular bias or partisanship. This leg of our journey, across the Caucasus via Tiflis, where Joseph Stalin had been a seminary student and later a gun-toting Bolshevik bandit, happened to be the most convenient route to our destination. But we were curious, naturally. And the inhabitants, a polyglot population of Georgians, Azerbaijanis and Armenians, were intensely curious about us. Few Americans came their way. Whenever some Soviet citizen who could speak a few words of garbled English appeared, we became the focus of a crowd. We were questioned about every item of our apparel and possessions, down to the fillings in our teeth. And the inevitable, "Is it true that all Americans are rich?"

The trains ran on time and the plumbing worked. We gorged on black bread and mounds of glorious Caspian caviar, cheaper than chicken or beef. We read English language editions of the Moscow *Daily News* which predicted that Hitler would invade Russia within weeks. We had no hassles with officialdom. I wrote my mother: "Contrary to popular belief, secret agents do not shadow tourists up and down the streets. You can wander almost anywhere and take photographs. But it is a tightly closed society. You can't learn anything they don't want you to know."

Some weeks later on a black December night in the Persian Gulf aboard another freighter, this one British, we watched a distant cluster of lights while the lascar crew dropped anchor and swung out a cargo boom. "That's Bahrain," the captain said. "Arsehole of creation."

Arbuckle, who had presented his V.I.P "To Whom It May Concern" letter of introduction from a Standard Oil executive in San Francisco, said, "I can't see anything from here."

"Better here than there," the captain said. "Bloody damn wogs."

"I have to go ashore," Arbuckle said.

"Ashore? Sonny-me-lad, those bleedin' Muslims would broil your Christian liver and lights for breakfast. Calm your bowels now, and sit tight."

Arbuckle and I sat tight, waiting until the cargo lighter returned empty and the freighter got under way again and the lights of Bahrain fell astern.

Many years, several wars and two international oil crises later, I flew by night over the Persian Gulf and, from the window of a Boeing 747 at an elevation of 30,000 feet, looked down on the orange pillar of flaming gas that was Bahrain, metaphor of a voyage that had come full circle.

In November, we learned, Franklin Rooveselt had thrashed Alf Landon at the polls to win a second term as President. In December King Edward abdicated his throne to "marry the woman I love." These events made no ripples in our world East of Suez. We shared a Christmas dinner of mutton curry in a remote railroad station in the Sind Desert, now part of Pakistan, and on New Year's Eve paid homage to the Taj Mahal in Agra. In New Delhi we parted company to go our separate ways. Arbuckle had commitments, a schedule to keep. I had Hal's code of the old fur trappers: "Follow your stick wherever it floats."

I took what travel agencies today call a "trek"—in my case a

100-mile hike through the Naga Hills into Burma, a route made famous a few years later by General Joseph "Vinegar Joe" Stilwell on his retreat from a crushing defeat by the Japanese ("We got a hell of a beating.") Threading my way across southeast Asia by rail, bus, boat and shank's mare, I arrived in Hong Kong in June, 1937, somewhat surfeited with exotic scenes, not quite broke, but thinking fondly of home. There was a letter from Sylvia at the American Express and a draft for $100. "For heaven's sake," she wrote, "buy yourself some new clothes. You must look like a tramp."

I wrote back that I would catch the next freighter bound for California. A rash promise, as it turned out.

In the southern Chinese city of Canton, I made a brief visit to check on a student exchange program at Ling-nan University. There I met another Stanford friend, Mel Jacoby, who'd been an editor of the *Daily* and was now studying the Chinese language.

"Hey, you can't go home yet," he told me. "There's one trip you *have* to take. Before it's closed to foreigners."

"Where to?" I said.

Jacoby produced a map marked in crayon. "There."

I traced a jagged line north and west, over several provinces and an ominous looking mountain range. "Chungking? That's way out in western China. A thousand miles from here!"

"You bet." Jacoby gave me a triumphant grin. "I did it last fall. Brand new road hacked out by the military. No highway. But you'll see the old China like it was in Marco Polo's day."

He proved correct on all counts. As a detour it was sensational. No lone American would be able to travel that route again for years. I never had a chance to thank Jacoby in person. He became a correspondent for *Time-Life* in the Far East, was evacuated from Bataan shortly before that Philippine peninsula fell to the Japanese in 1942, then died in an accident in Australia. But I still think of the steep, torturous roller-coaster non-highway that became a critical lifeline to China's soon-to-be wartime capital, Chungking, as Mel Jacoby's Road.

The Canadian Mission Hostel, high on the cliffs above the

Yangtze River, buzzed with rumors. For centuries China's feudal warlords had ravaged the land, marching and countermarching. Since 1932 Chiang Kai-shek's Nationalists and Mao Tse-tung's Communists had been locked in a life-and-death struggle for control of half a billion people. And now the mechanized divisions of a foreign invader, Japan, were massed only a few miles outside the walls of Peking itself. In the midst of this complex and accelerating turmoil, the American Legation issued a warning for tourists: Get out.

In Chengtu, provincial capital of Szechuan, I succumbed to temptation one more time.

The director of the Canadian Mission Hospital, Dr. Ted Best, had finagled from the local warlord four hard-to-come-by permits to enter a military buffer zone called Sikang on the Chinese-Tibetan frontier, several hundred miles to the west. (Gossip had it that he'd cured the general's gonorrhea.) At the last minute one of Best's quartet had dropped out, leaving a vacancy. I happened along at the right moment to fill the void, a strange Yank whom the good doctor must have taken on with some misgivings. "The chance of a lifetime," I told myself, not without a twinge of guilt. And, for a future writer, so it was. Later I would write two novels and a score of stories with Tibetan settings.

Among my intellectual baggage I had brought along a set of preconceived notions, largely negative, about missionaries, colored by Grandfather Charles' background in 19th century South Africa. During the previous few months I had stayed with—free-loaded on—a number of missionary families of varying denominations in outposts across Asia; and found them to be, not the zealots I had expected, but warm dedicated men and women fighting uphill battles—and sometimes winning— against poverty, ignorance and disease. Ted Best, gifted physician and linguist, was a prince among them.

From the trailhead at Ya'an our foursome climbed on foot for the next eight days along the Amban Road, the ancient Tea Route that links western China to distant Lhasa. In mountain-girt Tatsienlu (since renamed Kangding), Sikang's multi-racial capital where Tibetan and Chinese cultures overlap and clash, we regrouped for the next stage. Mounted on ponies, accompanied by native guides and a string of yaks to transport our gear, we plodded over two 15,000-foot passes out onto the high Tibetan plateau which, in the brief summer season, was verdant with grass and wildflowers. We spent a month there photographing villages and snow peaks, lamaseries and religious festivals.

Our departure was hastened by the arrival of a Chinese cavalry detachment westbound to put down an uprising of Tibetan dissidents. The commander literally spat on our documents and angrily ordered us to leave his jurisdiction or face arrest. Didn't we know this was a war zone? By the time we completed the long return journey to the end of the government telegraph line, we learned that most of north China was now a war zone. The Japanese had launched a massive invasion on several fronts, were bombing Shanghai and Nanking. I said goodbye to my Canadian friends and made my way back to Chungking in late August.

Chungking was then a small remote city without an airport. Chiang Kai-shek's battered government had closed all major roads to civilian traffic. The only artery of exit was the great river which flowed by Chungking's doorstep. With several other "foreign devils" I proceeded by steamer down the Yangtze Gorge by stops and starts, tying up at dark along the bank, as far as Hankow, where we hoped to catch a southbound train. That night the lights blacked out, sirens wailed, searchlights swept the sky and anti-aircraft guns boomed—my first air raid. Next morning I saw my first masses of fleeing refugees, a sight that was to become commonplace around the planet in the next few decades.

Another of my wartime first-experiences was the welter of rumors, fright tales and conflicting misinformation that swirled about the city like some deadly gas: Enemy bombers had cut the rail line; floods had washed it out; the Generalissimo had commandeered all trains for troop movements. One rumor I doubted but was able to confirm: A commercial airline operated by German Lufthansa had opened a Hankow office only two weeks earlier. As Hal, the consumate gambler, had advised me more than once: "Everybody needs common horse sense but it helps to have a little luck." In this instance I lucked out. For one of two remaining seats I paid fifty of my precious dwindling dollars and next day flew in a twin-engine Junker halfway across China to the safe haven of British Hong Kong.

In October I touched down at home port in Los Angeles again, 15 months after departing for the Olympic Games. I had missed that spectacle but had seen something of John Gunther's Europe on the eve of Holocaust, one corner of Mel Jacoby's China in upheaval and way points in between; altogether too much to assimilate and digest in a single bite. In an article about the trip, I was described by a Los Angeles *Times* reporter as "the son of . . . one of the best known writers this city ever boasted," a tribute that Jayhawker Hal would have found ironic.

Sol Siegel may not have been overjoyed to see me after such an extended vacation but he honored my contract. Republic was one of the middle rank studios, a cut above Gower Gulch and Poverty Row, a consistent money-making producer of entertainment films for the "nabes," *Variety* magazine's term for uncritical audiences in the boondocks. Most of their movies appeared on the bottom half of double feature programs, none won Oscar nominations. Among their frequent performers, not yet celebrities, were John Wayne, singing cowboys Gene Autry and Roy Rogers and the Lone Ranger. I can still hear disembodied reverberations of the theme music from the *William Tell Overture* that thundered out day after day from the sound department across the alley from Writers' Row.

Someone else had written the screenplay of Hal's *The Painted Stallion* which appeared as a twelve-episode serial for the Saturday matinee trade. Starring Ray "Crash" Corrigan, it opened with this prologue: "Westward! The Trail to Empire! From Independence, Missouri to Santa Fe, New Mexico, dogged pioneers fought to penetrate a wilderness of savage Indians, massacres and death. To the heroes of yesterday— those pioneers who braved the perilous trek westward, defeated a hostile wilderness and blazed a glorious trail across the pages of American history."

A movie researcher made this appraisal some years later: "... bogus history, this serial did maintain an historical flavor. Stirring words which in emphasizing our heritage perhaps made history classes a little more palatable and maybe even interesting to young audiences." Bogus indeed! The film version, laid half a century earlier than Hal's story of wild mustangs, had nothing in common with it except the title. If Hal had lived to see this creation, I can imagine that he might have reacted, not with bitterness and disgust, but with a shrug of resignation and some wry comment about "show biz."

Siegel assigned me, as lowest low man on the totem pole, to write treatments for a popular series, *The Three Mesquiteers*. The Mesquiteers, based on characters created by novelist William Colt MacDonald, were a variation of "The Motor Boys Out West on Horseback," adults playing juvenile wish fulfillment roles. "Tucson" was the man of action, "Stony" the romantic interest, "Lullaby" the comic pratfall artist of this unholy trio. The characters remained the same but the actors often varied from picture to picture. Perhaps I did not take my work seriously enough, although I struggled hard to please. I could not seem to put together a winning combination of heroics and hillbilly humor that the series demanded. Much of the time I hibernated in my shoebox of an office, waiting for story conferences that were inexplicably postponed, writing stories of my own on studio time, playing word games with another frustrated junior writer, Stanley Kramer, who later became Hollywood's most successful producer of "message" pictures. At the end of three months Republic did "not renew," the equivalent of being fired—another first in my real world education.

The Evarts family had one more Hollywood brief encounter. A location scout for a major studio—Metro, I believe—selected our Lorraine Boulevard house for some exterior shots in a picture that would be the first starring vehicle for an unknown actress named Joan Fontaine. The story, titled *Maid's Night Out*, called for an upstairs balcony from which the heroine, in the course of her romance with the neighborhood milk delivery man, would descend by ladder in an elopement sequence. I never saw the movie but I read the script; the mystery is how Miss Fontaine's career survived such a turkey. For the use of our balcony, which opened off Hal's last den, Sylvia received a fee of $600. Eighteen months later, on the day Hitler invaded Poland, she sold the house for exactly half of what Hal had paid for it in palmy 1929.

The Depression had not yet run its full course; the aircraft and armament industries were only beginning to tool up. But jobs, although not plentiful, were easier to find than they had been a few years earlier. I went to work in the San Francisco office of the Occidental Publishing Company, an outfit that put out seven anemic monthly trade journals. My job was to cover all bases in the Bay Area to collect news items from, and sell advertising space to, breweries, wineries, candy manufacturers, flying school operators, furniture stores and their suppliers—a route that encompassed some 300 calls each month. My Ford and I, at five cents a mile, were on the go six days a week. In spare moments I hacked out my first book, an adolescent account of my travels illustrated with photographs by my second-hand Jiffy Kodak, which several publishers rejected without comment. The Sunday supplement of the *Chronicle*, however, bought an article on China for five dollars, my first free-lance non-fiction sale.

As an advertising salesman I set no records and early in 1939 I reentered the newspaper business at the basement level as a $15-a-week copy boy on Hearst's afternoon *Call Bulletin*. Each morning at 4:30 I reported to a silent empty city room to refill paste pots, sharpen pencils, prepare blocks of copy paper and, when the bleary-eyed staffers drifted in, served as "gofer" to fetch cartons of hot black coffee from an all-night diner around the corner. Now and then City Editor Fred Walker let me cover a story on my own.

On March 15 Hitler marched into Czechoslovakia. Only the day before I had covered a convention of morticians at the Palace Hotel next door. Dull, dull stuff worth one short paragraph in the *Call*. As a tyro reporter what did I have to look forward to in career terms? More conventions. Speeches. Banquets. For a change of pace, maybe an occasional fire or murder. With the greatest story of my generation about to explode half a world away, here was I, in what many considered America's most glamorous city, filling paste pots and interviewing embalmers. Not a very mature perspective, probably, but one idea obsessed me. When I approached Fred Walker, whom I had hounded for months to land this job, he stared at me uncomprehendingly.

"You *what*?"

"I'm going to Europe," I said. "I think war will break out any time now."

"So do I," Walker said. "But you—You're going to quit, after just three months here?"

"It sounds crazy," I said. "Maybe it is crazy. But I have a little money saved up. Maybe I can catch on over there. It's a gamble but I hope so."

"Foreign correspondent?" Walker was too kindly a man to laugh. "You?"

"I know. I don't have much experience. But I'll learn. This is a chance I can't pass up."

Walker continued to stare at me with a blank look of bafflement, as though I'd lost my marbles. Then he broke into a smile and shook my hand. "Half wish I could go with you," he said. "Good luck and God bless."

19.

MY FORD, VETERAN of many a desert excursion, setting for several boy-girl encounters, sold for $40 to a used car dealer. That sum paid my rail fare by coach across the country to New York, a four-night marathon more comfortable than comparable accomodations on the Orient Express, but less interesting. With shameless effrontery I called in succession on the foreign editors of the Chicago *Tribune*, *Daily News*, New York *Times*, *Herald Tribune*, Associated Press, United Press and International News Service in quest of an overseas assignment. To a man they were courteous and wondrously patient, considering my lack of qualifications. My work history as a cub police reporter, *Western Brewing World* correspondent and *Call Bulletin* copy boy did not make a very impressive resume.

A meeting with another college friend, a photo editor on AP's foreign desk, was more productive. He gave me several items of advice, some addresses abroad and two letters of introduction, then drove me to Philadelphia where, for a fee of $60, I boarded a U.S. freighter bound for London. The only other passenger was a retired West Point colonel who had fought his war in the trenches of the Western Front in 1918. "They tell me that I'm washed up, over the hill, too old to fight," he complained. "But by Gad, sir, I'm still a soldier, able and willing to serve my country in some capacity. So I'll offer my services to our English ally. They understand such matters over there." On our slow stormy voyage we discussed war endlessly, the last one and the one just over the horizon, and the Civil War, in which our ancestors had fought on opposing sides—two hopefuls, two generations, both seeking employment.

In London I found lodging in an inexpensive hotel near the British Museum and made the rounds of Fleet Street. The British may have slept through the Munich crisis of 1938 but now, a few months later, had few illusions. War was imminent and they went about their preparations with grim determination and a uniquely English sense of gallows humor. I wrote two war-related articles which ultimately sold to American markets for a few welcome dollars. I listened to a parliamentary debate in the House of Commons, and had high tea with an MP who sided with Winston Churchill and flatly predicted that Hitler would invade Poland in late summer, once the crops had been harvested.

On the day before my departure, I stopped by the American Embassy and presented a letter of introduction to the Ambassador's secretary. For what purpose I cannot now recall; surely I had no expectations of landing a job with the State Department. A young man popped in the office behind me and the secretary introduced us. "This is young Jack, the Ambassador's son. He's interested in writers."

Young Jack said, yes, that someday he hoped to write some history himself. A Harvard College student visiting his parents in London, anxious to tour Europe, he was curious about me, my background and future plans. We chatted for several minutes and I left, bearing an impression of a bright engaging individual who spoke with a down-East Yankee twang alien to my midwestern ears. Years passed before I realized that "Young Jack" was John Fitzgerald Kennedy, destined to make, as well as write, some history of his own.

Still jobless, in May I arrived in Paris and presented my second letter of introduction. Laurence Hills, publisher of the European Edition of the New York *Herald Tribune*, listened to my by-now-threadbare pitch. Hmmm, he said. From the *Herald's* viewpoint, perhaps more important than newspaper experience was one's facility in the French language. How fluent was I? This was my one slim qualification, my ace in the hole. French had been my minor at Stanford; my accent was atrocious but I could read with passable comprehension. He then gave me a test: translate a paragraph from *Le Temps*, France's most influential newspaper, a copy of which was lying on his desk.

Hmmm. Yes. Well, hmmm. Was I married? Hills wanted to know. Puzzled, I told him no.

"You may think that an odd question," Hills said. "But in fact it's quite relevant to our situation here."

"I don't even have a girl friend back home," I said. "Can't afford one."

He smiled. "We pay European wage scale, lower than American, somewhat on the basis of according to need. So, if one of our people has a wife or dependents, we pay him more than we do a bachelor. A very French arrangement."

"What," I asked, "if one of your people gets married on the job?"

"In that eventuality we negotiate. But it rarely happens. Newspapermen, I have discovered, are a restless clan. Always on the move." He had a long waiting list of applicants, Hills informed me, but something might open up.

Slightly encouraged, I assured him I would keep in touch. In my favor I appeared to have three pluses: I was single, I could read French and I was available to work for peanuts.

One of the addresses my AP friend had given me was that of a *pension* on the Left Bank grandiloquently called the Villa Racine, favored by impecunious young Americans. By way of a grimy courtyard, past the concierge's box and through a gate, one entered an unexpected gem of a garden, an Eden of greenery surrounded by towering soot-stained walls. For the next few months I made my home here in an 18th century house of nooks and crannies converted into a hostelry for paying guests. At the approximate rate of one dollar a day, I had a tiny room abutting the garden, bathroom down the hall, Continental breakfast and two excellent meals with wine at a family style table presided over by Madame, the owner—a bargain and delight by any standards.

This was not the Paris of the golden 1920s, the Lost

Generation era of Hemingway, Fitzgerald and Gertrude Stein. It was a more somber time and place, a city watching the daily headlines with dread apprehension, fearful of each new crisis. But another generation of American writers passed through during that tense summer of 1939, come to inspect the twilight splendor of the Third Republic, some already famous, others to become so: A.J. Liebling of the *New Yorker*; novelist Jerome Weidman; Leigh White fresh from the agony of the Civil War in Spain; Penn Kimball later of *PM* and *Time*. All paths led eventually to the sidewalk Dome Cafe on Boulevard Mountparnasse, literary heart of the Left Bank. There we gathered frequently at dusk around a table or two, shooing off Algerian rug vendors, nursing a five-cent glass of beer or cup of café au lait, speculating, debating, pontificating far into the night. John Gunther, who frequented classier bistros on the Right Bank, was interviewed by the *Herald*. No war this year, he prophesied; not even Adolf Hitler was insane enough to attack La Belle France.

On Bastille Day, July 14, the government staged a magnificent three-hour parade along the Avenue Champs Elysées show-casing the nation's military might: the superbly mounted Garde Républicaine, the Foreign Legion, foot soldiers from Indo-China in jungle camouflage, Spahis from North Africa with their flashing sabers—an imposing panoply of arms that the Parisian public watched in glum silence. An outsider like myself gained the impression that the French were less realistic than their British brethren. They were still suffering from the trauma of the last war, the hemorrhaging of young manhood. Every subway car and public bus had a section reserved for the war wounded. The French did not want another war. *Voilà*, there would be no war.

The English had their Channel for defense; the French had their Maginot Line. Impregnable. No German army would ever again desecrate the sacred soil of France. From the air? *Mais, non*. The French still treasured memories of the gallantry and glory of their 1917-18 ace pilots who had shot the Boches out of the sky in aerial dog fights. Invincible.

From the days of Benjamin Franklin, visiting Americans had

sentimentalized Paris, City of Light and Romance, beloved by writers, artists and musicians. I fell under that same siren spell. Every morning I pecked away on my portable at the Great American Novel, an epic debunking the Great American Game of Saturation Salesmanship. Afternoons I spent on lessons trying to improve my command of French and circulated among the press community in search of a job. Without fail I crossed the city twice a week to remind Larry Hills of my existence. On August 23, by which time my skimpy reserve of dollars had dwindled close to a go-home or go-broke level, the fatal shoe dropped with a resounding crash: Germany and the Soviet Union announced a mutual non-aggression pact, which in effect freed Hitler to launch a one-front war.

That event, the seal of Europe's agony, led to my temporary salvation. Hills offered me a job at 700 francs a week, about $17 at current exchange rates, hardly munificent but adequate for my needs. "Our day city editor resigned to take a job with some radio broadcast outfit," Hills explained, "so that leaves an open slot. Fellow named Sevareid, maybe you know him."

I had met Eric Sevareid a time or two, a personable young man and able journalist. I knew that he was married, that his wife was expecting a child (in fact, Lois Sevareid gave birth to twins several months later) and, mindful of Hills's "wage according to need" policy, suspected that I would represent a considerable saving to the *Herald* payroll. In any event I felt grateful to all involved in my employment, not including Adolf Hitler and Joseph Stalin.

The night city editor welcomed me aboard and suggested that for my first assignment I write an anonymous "letter to the editor" to help fill the deficiency in that column, one of the *Herald's* most popular features. American tourists and Francophiles were departing France by the boatload every day as the war shadows lengthened. But *somebody* had to keep the letters flowing.

What should I write about?

"Anything that strikes your fancy," I was told. "Except war news or politics. Keep it light."

Sure. Keep it light. While outside on the streets of what was then one of the world's largest cities the population had sunk into a swamp of despair. I sat at my newly assigned desk staring at a sheet of blank paper, the bane of every writer everywhere. What fluff could I possibly write on this doomsday that every Frenchman would long remember? And then my mind strayed to a dog named Fifi.

Fifi was a miniature black poodle, reigning pet at the Villa Racine, adored and outrageously pampered by Madame the proprietress. In addition to a shrewish disposition, Fifi had acquired a curious habit that startled new guests: whenever the Villa's one telephone rang in the salon across the hall from my room, Fifi, who snoozed her days away on a satin pillow, would explode into an hysteric rage, yapping insanely and leaping about the furniture, snarling at anyone who tried to calm her. Madame tolerated these tantrums as an amusing foible and shrugged off all complaints.

My next door neighbor, a young American studying psychology at the Sorbonne, resolved to take action and silence our tormentor. "Every time the phone rings," he told me, "that little black bitch goes off like a bomb. I can't take it any longer, can't concentrate, can't get my work done, can't even sleep."

"You'll get used to it," I said.

"Shit I will. You know anything about Pavlov's conditioned reflex experiments on dogs?"

Dimly I recalled my long ago course in Basic Psych. "If you mess around with Fifi," I said, "Madame 'll kick you out in the street."

"Won't lay a finger on her," my neighbor said. "I'll hypnotize her."

"You're going to hypnotize Madame?"

"Not Madame. The goddamn dog. Next Sunday morning when Madame goes off to church."

Dubious but intrigued, I agreed to serve as lookout when the time came.

That was the situation—an experiment in abeyance—when I reported to the *Herald* for my first evening of employment. And, under duress, I wrote a shaggy dog story, providing a solution in which a young psychologist inadvertently hypnotized himself instead of his canine patient. It appeared next morning, drastically edited and cut, in the Mailbag over the signature INSOMNIA, my first fiction to achieve publication for pay.

I often wondered what Hal would have thought of it. He wrote his first dog story, *The Cross Pull*, about a noble beast of the wild. It appeared as a big slick serial, in book form, a smash hit movie and won him overnight acclaim. Twenty years later I wrote my nonsense about a neurotic city-bred poodle. It vanished into a void of deserved obscurity, drew one snide response suggesting that I cut the dog's throat or move.

Within the week I did move away from the Villa, not to escape Fifi but to be closer to the *Herald* building off the Champs Elysées. And so missed the crucial Sunday and test of my friend's hypnotic powers, the outcome of which I never learned. Afterward I wrote many a "letter" to pad out the newspaper and discovered that, during its heyday, the column had carried commentary from such authentic luminaries as Ezra Pound, T.S. Eliot, James Thurber, Thornton Wilder, Eugene O'Neill and James Joyce. At least I could console myself that I was traveling in good company.

After the war Sevareid, in his autobiographical *Not So Wild A Dream*, had this to say about the *Herald*: "... that rather absurd little house organ for the diminishing American colony, which made ample room for the resort and fashion house advertisements and as a kind of afterthought squeezed in the news. The core of the staff was a group of American soldiers from 1918 who had never found their way home again, who had married and raised large families. Madamoiselle from Armentieres was now fat and full jowled and frequently collected her husband's pay at the entrance to the building before he could escape to the cafe on the corner. The publisher of the paper ... desperately played the game of pretending that Europe was secure and serene and that war could not possibly come, and our daily editorial wisely looked on both sides of the Fascist question and saw many virtues in the works of Mussolini and Hitler."

That may have been essentially correct. On the other hand, my immediate boss, Managing Editor Eric Hawkins, in *his* postwar autobiography, challenged Sevareid's evaluation: "A few hungry writers who later made their mark in journalism have criticized our policies, but at the time were happy enough to work for our paper and accept our pay. The *Herald* became an incubator for the most colorful, competent and sometimes crazy newspapermen that ever populated a city room."

On August 24 under screaming headlines like STABBED IN THE BACK and BETRAYED BY RUSSIAN COMRADES the French press, some twenty Paris dailies including the Communist *L'Humanité*, began publishing official government mobilization orders for reserve classes up to age forty-five to report for duty. And for the first time since 1918 military censorship reappeared in the form of blank spaces in every newspaper. Overnight a news blackout laid its pall over the city.

My new bed-and-breakfast quarters on the Rue Washington, a ten-minute walk from the office, catered to Anglo-Saxons, bore the cozy name *Le Home* but lacked the raffish charm of the Villa Racine. I started work at five each afternoon, took a dinner break and labored on till one A.M. when the paper went to press, an ideal schedule that left my days free.

One morning I rode the subway to the *Gare de l'Est*—East Station—in a dingy district of sleazy hotels and bars where I had lived for a short period in 1936. There were no parades here, no marching bands, no banners unfurled, not a single tricolor flag in sight, only queues of grim-faced soldiers—many old enough to be my father, some in their World War I uniforms and crested steel helmets, gas masks and musette bags slung over their shoulders—waiting to entrain for stations up the line. Perhaps most awesome to an American was the relative silence of that enormous crowd. Wives, sweethearts and children clung to their departing men, saying their goodbyes quietly, in hushed voices or with their eyes and hands, displaying little outward emotion. I saw no weeping and few tears, heard no sobs or lamentations. Thus the excitable mecurial French. I almost felt, as did other foreign reporters who covered that scene, as though I were some kind of voyeur, a Peeping Tom who had no right to be present, to witness their hour of naked national grief.

The City of Light shortly followed the news blackout. Citizens were given an ultimatum of hours in which to tightly shutter or curtain their windows; thereafter squads of wardens patrolled the nocturnal streets, hammering on the doors of any building whose occupants failed to comply. One quickly learned how to navigate after nightfall or stayed home. On September 3, the day France declared war, which happened to be my night off, I was caught in a strange working class neighborhood by the first banshee howl of air raid sirens.

I trailed a small orderly crowd to a sand-bagged doorway and descended into a candle-lit wine cellar that must have dated back to Napoleonic times. As a bomb shelter it was far from reassuring but none of my companions seemed nervous. Someone brought out a bottle of *vin ordinaire* and passed it around, somebody produced a mouth harp and entertained us with music hall tunes, this in an atmosphere as casual and relaxed as a neighborhood social. By the time the all-clear sounded half an hour later I, a conspicuous odd-man-out in this Gallic blue collar bunch, had been warmly toasted, somewhat to my embarrassment, as "our brave American ally."

Next night the sirens wailed again. Most of the *Herald* staff, instead of hurrying to our basement shelter, took the elevator to the open rooftop nine stories above ground level to watch the action. But aside from searchlights probing the empty heavens there was none. No planes, no explosions, no ambulances or fire engines careening through the streets. Even the nearby Champs, normally a vehicular cacaphony, was whisper silent. The military had closed it to traffic by parking empty buses at angled twenty-yard intervals, a tactic to prevent Nazi paratroopers from seizing that proudest of Parisian boulevards as an airstrip in the heart of the city. Another false alarm.

While war raged in Poland half a continent away, Paris sank into a fatalistic apathy that came to be known as the "phony war," a twilight zone of wishful thinking and make believe. The blackout was a minor inconvenience. Business proceeded much as usual. Food and gasoline were plentiful; rationing remained a nebulous cloud in the future. Politicians still bickered and jockeyed for power in the Chamber of Deputies. The High Command issued daily communiques full of optimism but bare of specifics, barring all correspondents from the front. Some conservative newspapers hinted that an overall Franco-German peace settlement was in the wind, once the eastern front had been "stabilized."

A story important to the *Herald* and its few remaining subscribers that fall was the World Series, this one between the New York Yankees and the Cincinnati Reds. Our "sports department," an alcoholic octogenarian named William "Sparrow" Robertson, had described the first three games, all won by the Yanks, in his inimitable style, relying on skeletal statistics cabled from our New York home bureau. But the night following the key fourth game Sparrow turned up missing and untraceable, presumably incommunicado in some bar. In that emergency the editor handed me five lines of condensed arcane cableese, an economy measure of those days to cut down the high cost of trans-Atlantic transmission, with instructions to flesh out the numbers and write a blow-by-blow, pitch-by-pitch, I-was-there account of an October classic. In other words—fake it.

Sparrow, whose column *Sporting Gossip* had appeared more or less regularly in the *Herald* since 1921, was depicted by the man who knew him best as: "... five-feet-four inches, beady-eyed and beaky, a holdover from World War I, Sparrow never accepted the existence of World War II. He ignored it. His *metier* was really not sports, but barroom gossip. Drink cadger supreme, master of the misspelled appproach to scrambled syntax and the mixed metaphor." None other than Eugene O'Neill is on record as having said, with tongue in cheek, one supposes, "Why, that man is the world's greatest writer." Whatever his place in literary lore, Sparrow Robertson, who often closed his column after a hard night's pub-crawling with this valediction, "So long, pals, never again," was an original.

I had never seen a professional baseball game, didn't know

the difference between an RBI and an infield fly. But on that interminable night, with the aid of a baseball handbook from the office library, I patched together a creative version of the final game of the 1939 World Series, in which Joe DiMaggio drove in three runs in the tenth inning to win 7-4 and sweep the Reds in four straight.

Outside in the larger world Poland fell and was carved up by Germany and Russia. A white Christmas came and went while the French government slumbered on, secure in its Maginot mentality. By night I performed my routine stint for the *Herald*, by day I prowled the city, Hemingway's "moveable feast." We younger single members of the staff became a rather ingrown cadre, too lowly paid to hang out in bars or pursue Paris' pleasures of the flesh, instead hung out at the office after hours, our private club. We often discussed the fate of a former staffer, Jim Lardner, one of Ring's gifted sons, who had quit the paper in 1937, joined the Republican cause in Spain and disappeared without a trace. Could such a thing happen to any of us? we wondered. In a way, yes it could, and did. A few years later my friend and colleague, George Polk, was murdered by Greek terrorists and dumped in Salonika harbor. He left his name enshrined as the annual George Polk Award, a prestigious honor for the American voted the outstanding overseas journalist of the year.

To usher in the new decade, a few of us gathered at *Le Home* for a celebration, but it was an occasion of ersatz cheer. During the next few weeks, a leaden "no news" period when winter shut down combat on all fronts, I began to reassess my future. Should I cling to my security blanket at the *Herald* and perhaps end up like Sparrow and the other veterans twenty years later, reminiscing in print about "my" war? Did I really want to be a foreign correspondent, having learned by now that as a profession it was glamorous only in the eye of the beholder? Did I want to spend the rest of my life writing about the human condition in terms of an editor's perceptions instead of my own? Day after day I tramped the slushy streets in my galoshes and overcoat, weighing the negatives and positives and imponderables of a career. Hal had often cautioned me:

"It's a gambler's choice." Under a lowering February sky on my twenty-fifth birthday, on a *quai* alongside the Seine, I watched that historic river flow by and came to a decision.

20.

GEORGE LORIMER HAD retired as editor of the *Saturday Evening Post* in December 1936 and died a few months afterward. In his obituary the New York *Times* commented: "... he probably had more influence upon the cultural life of America than any other editor," and called him "the Henry Ford of American literature." The *Herald Tribune*: "Lorimer was the most notable editor of our times. He left a definite imprint upon the lives and thinking habits of what, for want of a better word, may be called the great American middle class."

Almost three years later, the *Post* was still America's most popular and successful magazine, although drifting ever farther to the right of political center. Lorimer's successor editorially opposed American intervention in foreign wars. "Let the Europeans fight their own wars," he proclaimed, echoing the isolationist wing of the Republican Party.

I was not concerned with ideology. I had no lofty illusions about creating art or literature. What I wanted was to reach that great American middle class, all those millions of readers of the slicks. Unlike Hal, I was no natural born spinner of tall tales. He had broken through on his first try. I anticipated no such instant success; to that extent I was realistic. But I had one advantage: I had studied the magazines and, as beneficiary of his experience, knew a few basic principles about the production of popular fiction. I gave myself a make-or-break deadline of two years, by which time or sooner, it seemed obvious that the United States would be drawn into the war, isolationists or no—the unfinished war of my father's generation.

My first act was to consign to the wastebasket my Great American Novel; Sinclair Lewis had written it twenty years earlier, better than I ever could. I set up a schedule, a minimum quota of a thousand words a day and went to work, from 9-to-4 in my ivory tower at *Le Home*, then around the corner to the *Herald* for another eight-hour go at the typewriter, a kind of dichotomous Jekyll-Hyde existence.

The harsh winter of 1940 gave way to an early spring and the Germans, having temporarily secured their eastern front, turned their attention westward and overran Denmark and Norway in April. At the *Herald*, dependent on skimpy French military communiques and foreign reports pulled in by George Polk's short wave radio, we tried to present a comprehensible account of day-to-day developments. Censorship won. Night after night the generals and their press flunkies slashed our front page to ribbons.

Even I, in my role as an occasional contributor to the Mailbag column, once fell afoul of the blue pencil. I had written an innocuous—or so I thought—little fiction about an imaginary children's kite-flying contest in the Bois de Boulogne, describing the balmy weather and merry breezes. The humorless censors ruled otherwise. In their view it disclosed "critical meteorological information" to the enemy.

In my other, private world my first short story—sheer escapism—centered around a Tibetan yak herder, an individual whose skills and personality I had observed first hand on my Asian travels. During the next three months I wrote steadily, a word monger on a binge, some thirty pieces in all, an eclectic assortment of war stories, mysteries, adventure yarns, efforts at humor, life in small town Kansas and romances, especially romances, supposedly gossamer bits of down in which boy-meets-girl, boy-loses-girl, boy-wins-girl, a formula dear to the hearts of slick editors. One area into which I did not venture was that of wildlife, Hal's ticket of admission to the big time.

Over a drink one night an acquaintance accosted me:

"Evarts, you'll never be the man your old man was."

I had no rebuttal. At that muddled stage in my life I doubted if in fact I were even my own man. But, much as I admired Hal's many accomplishments, of one thing I was sure: I did not intend to become a pale carbon copy of Dear Old Dad.

The rough first draft manuscripts accumulated in my suitcase, for my eyes only. I sent none off to New York editors. German submarines patrolled the North Atlantic sea lanes, torpedoing Allied shipping, which made delivery of surface mail uncertain at best. Airmail for bulky manuscripts via neutral Portugal (with obligatory return enclosed envelope) was prohibitively expensive. So I would have to bide my time, untested in the market place.

In May my friend and co-worker Kenneth Koyen and I, frustrated by censorship and months of confinement in the city, decided that we owed ourselves a brief vacation in the country. Given the current stalemate on all fronts, the *Herald* could easily spare us. Koyen, something of a gourmet, chose our destination, a two-hour ride northwest of Paris to a village known for its pastoral beauty and regional speciality of river trout. We caught an early morning bus and rolled out through the lovely green spring. There was little traffic, an occasional cyclist or horse drawn cart. We sped past sleepy hamlets, orchards of ripening fruit, carpet-like pastures and sleek cattle—a classic picture postcard scene of rural France. One could scarcely imagine that not too far away millions of troops faced each other across the most awesome intimidating fortifications ever constructed by man, the foredoomed Maginot Line. The date was May 10, 1940.

We arrived at Pacy-sur-Eure, registered at a small inn and strolled out to see the sights, German Leica cameras dangling around our necks. Within minutes two gendarmes stopped us on the main street and, without explanation, conducted us to the *hotel-de-ville*, seat of municipal government. Behind a closed door in a room with barred windows, a police inspector examined our ID and questioned us at length. Koyen and I, supposing at first that this was just another display of French officiousness, began to sweat. What had we walked into?

"So, *messieurs*," said our stony-faced interrogator, "you claim you are journalists. Harmless American tourists on vacation. If in fact you are journalists why are you here, not at the front reporting the invasion?"

What invasion?

At daybreak that morning, the inspector informed us, the filthy stinking Boches had launched an all-out attack on Holland, Belgium and Luxembourg, the northern gateway to France. What did we say to that?

It was our first inkling that the "phony war" had ended.

Furthermore, he said, the Germans had dropped some French-speaking paratroopers in civilian clothes behind the lines to spy and commit sabotage. This turned out to be a wild never-substantiated rumor. But the French had a war-time itchy finger record of shooting suspected spies. Even women. Most famous case in point: Mata Hari. For our protection, the inspector went on, he must advise us that a few hours earlier two young men had been cornered in a nearby village by a crowd of enraged farmers wielding hay forks and barely escaped with their lives. The pair were actually French citizens, innocent traveling salesmen from Paris but strangers in the district, like ourselves. So take heed.

He removed the film from our cameras and left us alone to contemplate our transgressions. When he returned some while later he said, "*Monsieur*," indicating me with a nod and a hint of frosty smile, "you have convinced me. Not even the Germans would be so stupid as to send a spy who speaks the French language—" he groped for a felicitous phrase "—our language as you do."

With relief and no intended sarcasm I said in English, "Thank you, sir."

The inspector had one shot left in his locker before releasing us. "Gentlemen," he said, "you must agree that it is not an ideal time to vacation in this part of France."

Koyen and I took his hint. We did not wait for lunch and a taste of the renowned trout. We caught the next bus back to Paris and the real war.

The official communiques issued during the first few days

were gibberish. One glance at our office situation map revealed that the French brass were up to their traditional ploys of obfuscation and evasion, if not downright lying. The German grand strategy, code-named Operation Yellow, was as apparent as it was simple and audacious—to ignore the Maginot Line, to outflank it, to end-run around it. That possibility seemed never to have occurred to the French master planners, although the flat open fields of Flanders had been the invasion route for hordes of central Europeans from the time of Julius Caesar. The Germans had no secret weapons. What they did have were new applications of old ones—the stuka dive bomber and the panzer tank column. And the evil genius of a madman in absolute command.

A cynical but widespread perception of the state of French military preparedness went something like this: In 1870, on the eve of the Franco-Prussian War, they were ready for the 1814 Battle of Waterloo, both of which they lost. In 1914, before World War I, which they almost lost, they were ready for the war of 1870. In 1940 they were ready for the war of 1914.

Newspaper readers and radio listeners in distant New York and California were better informed about the great debacle already unfolding than those of us on the spot, in the blind eye of the hurricane. We staffers spent most of our waking hours in the city room, not because we were indispensable, but in the faint fading hope that the High Command might pull some last minute miracle out of the hat to equal that of General Gallieni, who in August 1914 mobilized his famous "taxi cab army" to halt the Germans on the Marne forty miles from Paris. But no heroic savior emerged in this thirty-day Götterdämmerung, only apologists and scapegoats.

In its collective ignorance, lulled by fairy tale government bulletins, Paris remained remarkably calm. The weather continued superb. Parisians picnicked in the parks, sipped aperitifs at the sidewalk cafes, fished along the Seine, crowded into theaters and concerts. The public mood seemed to be: It can't happen here.

The morning of May 16 a pall of smoke emanating from the courtyard of the Quai d'Orsay, the Foreign Office, wafted upriver on the breeze. Rumors spread like wildfire: The government was burning secret documents in preparation to decamp. That evening Premier Paul Reynaud broadcast a denial, but the dike of confidence had been breached. In the ensuing weeks Paris became a hollow shell of a city. An estimated 4,300,000 of its five million inhabitants fled in panic, joining some eight million refugees from Belgium and northern France, clogging every highway and country road in a frantic mass flight to escape the German juggernaught.

A new friend, a middle-aged German Jew from Cologne, who in 1938 had brazened his way across the frontier to freedom with a set of forged papers, begged me for help. Penniless, a stateless person who survived by selling cheap neckties on street corners, he faced the Nazi peril once again. I tried to buy him a black market Panamanian passport. Asking price: $5,000 U.S. dollars, in cash. The most I could afford was a railway ticket to Brittany where, with luck and guile he might be able to reach England. Whether he made it to safety I never learned. Few Jews did.

On June 2 several of our *Herald* cohorts called it quits and left for St. Jean-de-Luz, the southwestern harbor to which the State Department had dispatched a liner to evacuate U.S. nationals. Assured that the paper would continue to publish as long as possible, a corporal's guard of us opted to stay on, not so much out of loyalty but, in my case at least, curiosity. I had come to observe a war and write about it. So far I had only read about it, in garbled dispatches and cryptic handouts. In China I had witnessed the prelude to war but, I now convinced myself, such an opportunity might never come my way again, an assumption that proved incorrect.

Another thunderclap struck on June 10. Mussolini's Italy, wavering junior partner of the Axis, at last chose sides and declared war on France. That was the clincher. A few hours later the French government did depart, unceremoniously and unannounced, folding their tents like nomads in the night—the President of the Republic, the Premier, the ministers and members of parliament and top administrative officials—not in convoy or with military escort, but as an ignoble pack of fugitives by whatever transport they could commandeer or lay hands on, adding to the chaos on the highways. Next day Paris was declared an Open City, a meaningless designation, a plea to the Germans to spare it from the devastation that had laid waste Warsaw and Rotterdam.

Every newspaper shut down, all but the *Herald*. That night into the early hours of June 12, we few diehards struggled to put out a castrated one-page sheet that contained more blank space than print. But, by God, we congratulated ourselves, it *was* a newspaper, the only one remaining in the capital of France!

About 2 A.M. our editor, an Englishman heretofore unflappable from crisis to crisis, called us together. He had come to work for the *Herald* as a reporter in 1915, seen it through the black years of World War I, never missing a day of publication. With quavering voice he read us a cable from New York. The owner, Ogden Mills Reid, ordered him to stop publication, pay off the staff and cease all operations. He, Reid, refused to publish under German occupation or follow the government into exile. For our remnant crew of "colorful, competent and sometimes crazy newspapermen" the ball was over.

Stunned, not quite believing that we had been cut adrift, Koyen and I lingered on the dark street outside the office, listening to the intermittent rumble of German artillery fire north and west of the city. Once again the Champs was blockaded with empty buses and sanitation trucks, a pathetic futile gesture if ever there was one. Even the prostitutes, who cruised this neighborhood on foot at all hours during the blackout, were gone; they too had deserted Paris.

"To hell with it," Koyen said. "No point in staying now. No job, no credentials, we're dead."

I agreed.

"So let's clear out, while we can."

"*If* we can," I said. "We're practically surrounded."

"May be," Koyen said. "But damned if I'm going to stick around and watch those Nazi bastards parade through the Arc de Triomphe."

While we stood there in bleak depression, a familiar, jaunty little figure shuffled out the door, mumbled, "G'night, pals. See ya tomorrow," and vanished into the night.

"Maybe Sparrow's the lucky one," Koyen said. "He's still in fantasy land."

. . .

Eric Hawkins, who returned after the war to resume his editorship, wrote this in retrospect: "... for some weeks Sparrow could not bring himself to believe that there was no more *Herald*. As an American he moved freely through the streets and each day he climbed to the dark and empty news room to his tiny cubbyhole in the rear of the building, and there sat down before his portable to write *Sporting Gossip*. The long dreary afternoons dragged on. He tapped away in semi-darkness. The job finished, he would then walk to my silent office, drop the typewritten pages into my basket and depart."

Sparrow Robertson died of heart failure in the Paris suburbs under the German occupation a year after his last column was published.

21.

DAY AFTER DAY the weather had been splendid, perhaps the finest French spring in a decade—warm, clear and windless. As one Paris journalist lamented: "God must be on Hitler's side because He has provided perfect conditions for a blitzkrieg."

Wednesday morning, June 12, Paris' next-to-last day as a free and independent city, I attended an unlikely event, a wedding in the downstairs sitting room of *Le Home*. My landlady's daughter, a young miss who every morning seven days a week had delivered at my door a breakfast tray of hot chocolate, warm croissants and butter, was marrying her soldier boy in a hurry-up ceremony before he reported back for duty with his unit. I stood witness to the rites, solemnized by the neighborhood priest, whose church had been blocked off by the military for some unknown reason. The groom never saw his bride again. Among other bitter legacies I heard later that he had died in a prisoner-of-war camp of an undetermined disease.

The escape hatch, if one still existed at this late date, could be no more than a narrow rapidly shrinking corridor. Koyen and I gambled on the railway system which so far had outperformed every other branch of government with efficiency and dedication, hauling troops and civilians under heavy bombing. Our first stroke of luck was to find an available taxi; since the exodus began and the subway suspended service, the once ubiquitous cab had become an endangered species. As we rode along the deserted boulevards, Paris seemed like a city decimated by some medieval plague, a memory soon to be immortalized by the music of Jerome Kern, the lyrics of Oscar Hammerstein II and the account of Elliot Paul, another *Herald* alumnus, in *The Last Time I Saw Paris*.

At the *Gare d'Austerlitz* a mob of thousands milled about waiting for what might, or might not, be the last train to beat the encircling enemy pincers, scheduled to depart at 5 P.M. A few days later I wrote my mother in San Diego: "... they sat patiently on battered suitcases and bundles of hastily collected belongings. Their children carried toys and tugged dogs on leashes. In the heat old women were fainting from strain and exhaustion. Boy Scout volunteers were doing their best to help the sick. There were soldiers on crutches and dazed elderly couples and young women wearing black armbands of mourning. One gray-haired woman on a bench who had just received notice of her son's loss in action wept herself to sleep. The station was considered a prime target and every few minutes anti-aircraft batteries all around us opened up. We could see white puffs in the sky and hear the thud of shell fragments on the roof."

We did not know but, at about this time, the first contingent of German ground forces was entering the city's northern suburbs a few miles away.

After nightfall a switch-yard crew assembled enough rolling stock to make up one long passenger train, hours late but under the circumstances a prodigious feat. The routine of ticket punching and reserved seat confirmation no longer prevailed; it was every man for himself. Even so, the crowd did not panic and storm the coaches. Boarding was a brisk but orderly process, an almost surrealistic exhibition of cool under stress, what Hemingway, writing about an earlier war, defined as "guts, grace under pressure." A stranger would not have suspected that for many trapped and desperate Jewish families, catching the Southwest Express on this particular night could make the literal difference between life and death. Koyen and I were among the last to squeeze aboard, elbowing our way into a corridor where we shared standing room only and minimal breathing space, packed together like livestock bound for the slaughterhouse. About ten o'clock, in total darkness, we crept out of Paris.

The journey, normally a six-hour run, took fourteen. We clickety-clacked non-stop through towns and cities, leaving behind on station platforms swarms of cursing fist-shaking Frenchmen who felt, with considerable justification, abandoned and betrayed. But we made several halts in the open countryside, unexplained delays during which one imagined the worst. People spoke, if at all, in whispers. Mothers shushed their crying babies. One man who dared to light a cigarette had it savagely slapped from his mouth. Above the panting of the engine and the midnight drone of crickets in the fields, we could hear an occasional explosion and the roar of planes overhead, whether friendly or hostile nobody was sufficiently expert to judge. Then, with a lurch and rattle of couplings, the train got under way once more.

The ordinarily placid provincial city of Bordeaux had been turned into a madhouse by the invading hordes, all seeking food and shelter and an illusory hope of security. Advance agents of the government had requisitioned most of the hotels. Even the Duke of Windsor, formerly King Edward VIII, and his duchess, fleeing as we lesser mortals, were ousted from their ritzy digs. Groggy after two sleepless nights, Koyen and I found a dingy fleabag of a hotel on a back street, paid an extortionist's price for one night's lodging, or so we understood, and flopped on the bed in our clothes. About 6 P.M. the proprietress pounded on the door and ordered us out. Customers were arriving for the evening trade, she informed us, and her girls required our room. Mortified by our gullibility and naivete, thereafter we slept on the town, in hotel lobbies, public parks and abandoned cars and trucks, or wherever.

William L. Shirer, another former *Herald* reporter, now a correspondent for CBS, described the scene in his *The Collapse of the Third Republic*: "Toward evening of Friday, June 14, the haggard members of the French government straggled into Bordeaux. It seemed to those who wanted to continue the struggle to be the worst possible place for the shaky, harassed government to set up office. It was in a state of chaos. An air of defeatism, of despair, hung heavy over the city. Those who were there that fateful mid-June weekend remembered afterward that one could feel, almost smell the decomposition of the government, the High Command, the Army, the State, the flesh and bones of society, setting in.... Fear spread: fear of being bombed, fear of being overtaken by the advancing Germans, fear for the fate of one's family left behind in the disordered flight. For most this was the end of the road."

For Koyen and me it was a way point. If caught in the German net we, a pair of unimportant unemployed journalists, would be questioned, released and deported. Theoretically. But probably after months of red tape and delay. Two other options, neither attractive, remained: escape by sea or overland through Spain and Portugal. The American Embassy, uprooted from Paris and swamped with weightier matters of state, could offer no advice or aid; the acting ambassador was all but mobbed when he put in an appearance. The harbor was jammed with shipping but few vessels, under whatever flag, chose to risk running the German submarine blockade. A Royal Navy destroyer evacuated a capacity load of British nationals and rumors circulated that a freighter of Liberian registry—or was it a Brazilian tramp, possibly a Costa Rican banana boat?—was taking on passengers at X-dollars per head, only the well-heeled need apply. In the early hours of June 20 the Luftwaffe bombed Bordeaux for the first time, killing 63 civilians and injuring 180.

Out of that tragedy a random encounter turned up the person of Viktor, a White Russian emigre, refugee of World War I, proud owner of a vintage Chevrolet sedan. For an exorbitant fee he guaranteed to deliver us to the city of Bayonne a hundred miles south and close to the Spanish border. Cocky and tough, a driver of Grand Prix class, Viktor somehow whisked us through massive traffic jams, around military checkpoints and down back country roads in the miraculous time of six hours. For a reward I gave him a bottle of cognac I'd been hoarding for months, for some occasion to celebrate. This celebration was premature.

In Bayonne both the Spanish and Portugese consulates were closed, their doors locked and windows shuttered, as though their staffs had gone out of business permanently. Throngs of refugees waited outside in the blazing June heat, dumb with despair, praying that some divine providence would issue them passport visas to salvation. Short of food, many restaurants shut down. Bakers and wine merchants rationed their dwindling stocks. Municipal water service funtioned only one hour out of the 24. The fabric of one of the world's most civilized nations was unraveling before our eyes. Then came the finale, the *coup de grace*: in Bordeaux the French government announced its unconditional surrender to Hitler. We could expect German tanks any day, any hour.

One absurd moment of black humor underscored the insanity of it all for me. A *type* in a chauffeur's uniform lounging against a gleaming Rolls Royce limousine beckoned me over and, with a ferret's grin, held out a set of keys. American, wasn't I? He could tell by my clothes. His boss, he said, had skipped the country; he personally had no use for a limousine. So maybe we could make a deal, a trade—my passport for the Rolls. What flashed through my mind at that instant was the immortal Jack Benny gag: When confronted by a thug with a gun and the demand, "Your money or your life," Benny responds, after a delicious pause, "I'm thinking it over."

For lack of any better alternative, Koyen and I moved on to the court of last appeal, the seaside town of Hendaye where we looked across the Bidassoa River to the hills of Franco's Spain, the Promised but Forbidden Land. Head-on, eyeball-to-eyeball we confronted an early version of Catch 22: To enter Spain one must have a Spanish visa. To get a Spanish visa one first must have a Portuguese visa. To get a Portuguese visa one first must have a Spanish visa. Checkmate. The frontier, guarded by green-shirted, tricorn-hatted Falangist militia, had become a mammoth human dam.

Among the several hundred Americans impounded there like flood debris a new rumor surfaced. A stranger who claimed to be some kind of official had arrived in town with an offer of help. Not only that, he had called an emergency meeting. Skeptical but at land's end, we poured into one of Hendaye's faded resort hotels.

A harried-looking young man introduced himself as a consular official from the U.S. Embassy in Madrid, sent to negotiate our exit from France and transit through Spain. The situation, he said, was sticky. Spain, now an Axis ally after three years of devastating civil war, did not welcome foreigners. But Spanish officials, under pressure from Washington, reluctantly had agreed to grant passage to bona fide, documented American citizens. This meant, explained our would-be liberator, that he must take all our passports back across the frontier for examination—a security check.

"Security, hell!" said a voice from the crowd. "Turn my passport over to a guy I never saw in my life? You must think we're nuts."

There was an angry buzz of agreement.

"But," said the young man, "here are my credentials. You have to trust me, all of you."

"Trust, my ass!" said the voice. "Anybody can buy fake credentials."

I took another look at the young man and pressed closer. Something about him seemed familiar. And then, larger than life, coincidence struck, a happenstance that no self-respecting fiction writer would dare use in a story. "Your first name's Tom," I said. "You were a vice consul in Teheran, Persia, back in 1936."

"That's right," he said. "How do you know?"

"We played a softball game on Thanksgiving Day. Alborz College campus. Diplomats versus the Missionaries. I think your team won."

"By God, we did! Twenty-something to nothing." He laughed. "I was the pitcher, that's why I remember."

"Small world and all that stuff," I said. "Can you really get us out of here?"

"Have you got any better offers?"

And so the impasse was resolved.

Minus our passports, feeling naked and vulnerable despite reassurances, our contingent stood in a drizzle on the Bidassoa international bridge for hours that night. I caught a cold. Koyen was luckier; he fell into conversation with a young lady who later became his wife. Eventually the frontier guards raised the barrier and we straggled through. For us fortunate few the war was over. For now.

The Spanish detained us for another two weeks in the ancient Basque city of Bilbao, then sent us on by rail to Portugal. The Duke and Duchess of Windsor had preceded us and were already on the high seas bound for New York. I never did catch up with them.

In Lisbon we boarded the U.S. liner *Manhattan*. Huge American flags had been painted on her sides and at night a special array of lights blazed from bow to stern, apprising every U-boat captain in the mid-Atlantic that we were an unarmed neutral. Our crossing was not exactly a carefree pleasure cruise. But Koyen had his bride-to-be. I had my typewriter and manuscripts. And a mother lode of raw material.

22.

IN NEW YORK the *Herald Tribune* offered both of us jobs on the metropolitan desk. Koyen accepted. I declined, an opportunity that a year earlier would have seemed beyond my reach. A writer I'd met on board ship, a young talent who had sold his first story to the *New Yorker*, gave me the name of his agent. Ironically, he never sold another story to *any* magazine, a one-shot phenomenon not uncommon in the literary steeplechase.

On a steam bath August afternoon in midtown Manhattan, I waited in the agent's outer office in a state of nervous funk, three of my virginal manuscripts in a manila envelope on my lap. A stocky character with a guardsman's mustache, wearing a black overcoat with upturned velour collar and a black fedora, barged through the door. Out of the side of his mouth he growled, "Whadya hear from the mob, baby?"

A play actor Mafia don out of a bad gangster novel, I wondered, or some kind of crazy?

The startled receptionist glanced up, stared and burst into giggles. "Oh, Mr. Saroyan, you're so funeee!" she simpered. "Go right in. He's expecting you."

Saroyan? William Saroyan? *The Daring Young Man on the Flying Trapeze* Saroyan? Boy, oh boy! This was really a major league operation.

Funny Mr. Saroyan did not reappear. He must have exited by another door. Or maybe he went down the fire escape. But presently I was introducing myself to one Harold Matson, crisp, courteous and business-like. He repeated my name and said, yes, he knew my father's reputation as an author, then excused himself to answer the telephone. In a two-minute conversation he sold the latest Horatio Hornblower novel to the *Saturday Evening Post* for $40,000 for his client C.S. Forester, and turned his attention back to me.

Had I sold any magazine fiction? Noooo, but, confidence at ebb-tide, I showed him my wares. Matson gave them a glance and quizzed me about the war in France. What had happened over there? How come? The world's supposed finest army had collapsed like a house of cards. Why? It was a question I would be asked innumerable times in the next few months. I had no definitive answer then nor do I now.

Forty-eight hours later Matson phoned me at my hotel. Two of my stories, he reported, were forgettable, amateurish, non-commercial duds. But one, about a Tibetan yak herder, had some merit. Had I mined the authentic-sounding details out of the *National Geographic* in a public library? I told him where. So, he said, it's much too wordy, cut the story by a third and send it back. Maybe we could do some business. We did. Harold Matson and his associate Don Congdon represented me for the next forty years.

Before leaving New York I called on one of Hal's old friends, Erd Brandt, his agent along with brother Carl, now a senior fiction editor of the *Post*. Did he have any advice for a beginner?

Write a good story, he said.

Any *specific* advice?

Well, Brandt said, think of the editors of the *Post*, or any other national magazine, as hosts. Once every week they threw a party and invited a bunch of selected guests—the writers. The guests were a mixed crowd, strangers to each other. Maybe some of them had rotten table manners or mangled the King's English. No matter, not if they were lively and interesting and pepped up the party. What the hosts did not want, would not invite, were the bores and the stuffed shirts and the pompous, certified party poopers. Did I get the picture?

"To make the *Post* guest list then," I said, "a writer has to be interesting?"

"And entertaining," Brandt told me. "Reading *Emily* Post won't help."

I learned later that Erd Brandt had delivered that same brief sermon to scores of writers, for the good of their literary souls.

When I returned to San Diego, where my mother now lived, I received a flurry of publicity and several invitations to speak at men's service clubs on what the press solemnly referred to as the "Fall of France." San Diego was and is a Navy town. To my astonishment I discovered that a number of prominent citizens, both military and civilian, harbored a conspiracy theory to explain the French debacle: It was a Communist plot.

At one post-luncheon question-and-answer session, a man stood up and informed me that the French had lost the war because all the French railway workers belonged to a Commie trade union and went on strike on secret orders from Moscow.

Not so, I said. There was no strike. The railways did a magnificent job under enormous pressure.

It was common knowledge, insisted this self-annointed authority, that Stalin made a deal with Hitler to tie up every train in France and stop all troop movement.

Could be, I said, but I had ridden the last train out of Paris and nobody stopped that one, Commies or Nazis.

Some time later, after I had applied for a reserve commission in Naval Intelligence, I learned from an impeccable Navy source in Washington that I had been turned down because I was considered "too liberal."

I worked a 9-to-5 schedule, six or seven days a week, turning out one 5,000-word short story every two weeks, sometimes more—an intensive, self-instructional crash course in the communication arts. Every month or so Matson, without comment or criticism, sent me a list of my manuscripts and the magazines that had rejected them. It was what golf hackers call a "humbling game." On my twenty-sixth birthday, exactly one year after the birth of this venture, my wandering Tibetan yak herder found a home, in the Toronto *Star Weekly* for a price of $75. Hal had received that identical sum for his first story back in 1919.

In one of his rare advisories Matson wrote: "Send me more like this one."

Time for taking stock. Why did *this* story, my first bumbling effort, win acceptance while none of the others had? I received a clue from a friend of a friend, the fiction editor of *Collier's*, the *Post's* most successful rival. Kenneth Littauer told me: "You're trying to write too much, too fast. I see no reason why you can't learn this business. Study the markets and slow down." Cautionary words, which I did not appreciate at the time.

But there was a lesson to be learned here, if I could marshal enough objectivity. For one, I realized I was writing too many different kinds of story, the scatter gun approach. Example: my they-gotta-meet-cute-boy-girl romances bored me; undoubtedly they also bored the editors, my hypothetical hosts. I seemed to write with more conviction about outdoor themes and situations, perhaps a heritage from Hal. Also, most importantly, I began to understand that stories were people, people were stories. I had been writing plots, tricky and convoluted, with surprise endings made popular by O. Henry two generations earlier. My Tibetan had been real; almost by accident I had captured some of his flesh and blood dimensions on paper. Plot grew out of character, not vice versa, a simple but fundamental truth I had been slow to grasp.

After that I began to sell with regularity to the better pulps such as *Argosy* and *Adventure*, often using a foreign setting. One sale in particular, *Everest Tiger*, which developed out of a climb through the Himalayan foothills with a Sherpa guide, bolstered my morale. The editor raised my price to $125 and featured my name on the cover.

I became engaged to the light of my life—not a blonde this time, but a blue-eyed redhead—who shared my interest, among others, in France. She had spent her third college year as a student at the Sorbonne and spoke the language with a purity which I could only envy. I gave her one of Grandfather Charles' South African diamonds but our engagement promised to be lengthy. On my earnings from the pulps I could barely support myself, let alone a wife.

In April 1941 the Axis powers dismembered Yugoslavia. I wrote several war stories laid in the Balkans and sold them all, but a breakthrough into the slicks still eluded me. On December 7, Pearl Harbor day, war at last came home to southern California, fearful of an imminent Japanese invasion. By then I had been rejected by the U.S. Army, Army Air Corps, Navy and Coast Guard respectively, not because of my purported liberalism. The medics all pronounced me a healthy 1A specimen, except for one defect: my lazy, amblyopic right eye refused to distinguish the topmost single letter on the examination chart. So by night I served as a volunteer air raid warden in my blacked-out La Jolla neighborhood and by day continued to write.

The embryo of my next story was a chance conversation aboard a train with a frightened teen-ager an hour or so before he reported for basic training at the San Diego Marine Corps Depot. *Suppose*, said my imagination: Transpose this innocent, all-American fuzzy-cheeked farm boy to Yugoslavia. Now he's a Serbian peasant, different culture, different language, but no different under the skin, a youth caught up in events beyond his comprehension. He's completed his training and, before being sent into combat, is granted a three-day pass to visit his war bride, from whom he's received no word in months. Why no word? Because his home lies on the far side of a zone now occupied by enemy troops. What then? Suppose this, suppose that. How would this kid react?

It seemed like a simple straightforward story of character development, no better or worse than many I had turned out with high hopes. Four months after Pearl Harbor Erd Brandt wrote me a congratulatory letter. The *Post* was buying *Short Leave* for $500. He signed it *in loco parentis* which I translated loosely as "in place of your father."

On the strength of that I married my girl. The big slicks, I convinced her, were the gateway to success and a bright tomorrow.

When the story appeared, the *Post*, on its *Keeping Posted* page—a department featuring biographical squibs about contributors to the current issue—printed this under the heading *Old Blocks and New Chips*: "Apparently contributing to the *Post* is getting to be a thing that runs in families like going to Yale or being born into the Navy. Now we are printing the first *Post* story by Hal Evarts, Jr., son of the man who wrote those famous *Post* serials of a generation ago, ***Tumbleweeds***, ***Moccasin Telegraph*** and a host of others.

"Our department of archives and human documents has dug up the story of how Evarts Senior came to write his first story for the *Post*, and although Evarts Junior may not know it, he was mixed up in that sale himself—despite being only three at the time.

"In a thumbnail autobiography written for the *Post* in 1920 the elder Evarts says, 'The life story of a writer would be incomplete without some reference to his first work'—and proceeds to tell all about it. At the age of eleven he came into possession of a large notebook, intended for the neat setting down of school work, which he speedily filled with the names, habits and other bits of information about birds. When the book was seized upon by his teacher to be given a grade at the end of the school year all hell broke loose, and the book was returned to the Evarts family as evidence of their son's unprecedented sliding from the studious paths of grace.

"It was years before he looked at it again. Finally a box of his youthful treasures was sent to his three-year-old son (our new *Post* author). A few hours later Evarts Senior noticed scraps of paper floating widely downwind, and investigation proved them to be the last tattered fragments of the book of boyhood nature lore, torn into shreds by chubby three-year-old fingers. The recollection of all that the old book had meant to him led to his writing another, and this time a more adult one.

"To quote the elder Evarts again: 'The *Saturday Evening Post* lived up to its policy of holding out a helping hand to the unknown author.' We hope the author's son will vouch for the fact that the *Post* is still holding out the same hand."

I so vouched, with a fervent amen, and sold the *Post* one more story before the Army reduced its physical requirements to the lowest common denominator and tapped me on the shoulder. Emerging from the mystic maze of the military classification system, I wound up with a desk job in a limited service, housekeeping detachment at Fort MacArthur, California, a dead-end catchall for the lame, halt and blind. In several attempts I failed to achieve the minimum passing score on the rifle range. Firing a right-handed, bolt-action, antique Springfield, I either overshot or undershot every target from distances of 50 to 200 yards, a hoisted red-flag humiliation known as "Maggie's Drawers." As a prototype member of the gang that couldn't shoot straight, I seemed destined to sit out World War II shuffling papers on the sidelines.

But the Army, in due time and with Byzantine circumvolution, matched my square peg with a square hole. I was assigned, wonder of wonders, to the only combat job for which I remotely qualified—reporter and recorder—and shipped back to Europe with the 89th Infantry Division, the "Rolling W," first American division to cross the Rhine Gorge under fire.

I returned to Paris after VE-Day, as a GI sergeant, five years since I had left, to the same second story office at the *Herald* building, 21 Rue de Berri, where I spent several weeks writing the combat history of my outfit for USFET, United States Forces European Theater. The pay was better but I was no longer twenty-five years old and a starry-eyed idealist. I had seen my generation's war, too much of it, including the charnel house of Ohrdruf concentration camp, which the 89th "liberated." Perhaps in the interval I had come of age.

Illogically, my first post-war story, my first fiction in three years, written after hours in the old *Herald* office, was an unabashed romance wherein a GI met and fell in love with a French shopgirl. Matson sold it to the slicks without revision. So maybe my characters were growing up with me.

Most of the general circulation magazines survived the war, as I did, in reasonable health. But in the late 1940s and into the 50s they began to falter and fall: *Liberty, American, Collier's,* the pulps along with the slicks, monthlies as well as weeklies, like so many dominoes in a row. Then *Look, This Week* and eventually *Life*. In 1968 the *Post* published its final emaciated issue and succumbed after a frantic struggle, another casualty of changing public taste, outmoded technology and poor management. Ghosts of George Horace Lorimer! Erd Brandt's genial party-giving hosts had closed their doors and would entertain no more. The writers, those beguiling guests around the banquet table, would have to find their sustenance elsewhere. If any culprit were singled out to blame for the demise of the Big Slicks, it would have to be a small box with flickering electronic images that I and millions of other visitors to the New York World's Fair in 1940 gawked at for the first time, that *enfant terrible*—television.

Many older writers, unable to adjust to shifting markets, folded with the slicks. Younger writers, if they were nimble, quick and adaptable, suffered a lower mortality rate. Some had part time jobs or outside income or were clever enough to marry money. But for most of us free-lance relics, it was often a financial struggle. I was fortunate to have a patient loving wife and a mother who wept with happiness and pride when I sold my first story and cheerfully typed all my manuscripts, as she had for Hal. Altogether, for husband and son, Sylvia with her primitive hunt and peck system copied forty-two novels and upward of 500 short stories and articles, which must be some kind of single family record.

One question arose from time to time: Did I suffer from the "famous father" syndrome, feel awed and overshadowed by his reputation, driven by a compulsion to succeed? No. Hal wrote perhaps the best animal stories of his era, certainly the most popular. I never wrote one, for the simplest of reasons—I lacked his expert knowledge. In the one field in which we did overlap, that of the historical West, we employed different techniques and styles and points of view; there was no familial similarity or basis for comparison. Probably I earned more money overall, but in inflated dollars. I sold more books, because I lived longer; he died before the advent of cheap million-print paperbacks. And in time I too arrived in *Who's Who*. I felt no sense of inferiority, I think, because in the sudden-death world of popular fiction, possession of a so-called family "name" cuts no ice nor colors editorial decisions on authorship. (The exception that confirms the rule: unless you happen to be the son or daughter of the President of the United States.) One is only as good as his latest story, which has to stand on its own. Talent does not necessarily flow in blood lines.

A friend, a successful writer for the slicks, a high school dropout like Hal, once criticized me early in my career: "Sometimes you write like you've been scared by a college education. Your old man knew better." Meaning that I used too many obscure words, a pedantic showoff. I got the message.

I identified with Hal, but never saw myself in the role of rival or competitor, playing some childish game of catch up.

Hal summed up his philosophy of literary inspiration this way: "It (inspiration) can be summoned only by the association of ideas, by fishing for related factors in the stream of past experience and observation, adding the fragmentary catch of facts from present research, and assembling these odds and ends and bits in a more-or-less presentable whole. It is the process utilized by every mortal, according to his talents, and applied to the matter at hand, whether that be a business problem, the painting of a picture, writing of a story, pleading of a case in court or peeling a banana. The notion that one must go out on the mountain, there to sit with folded hands and blankly receptive mind until some mysterious agency alights upon his shoulder and whispers sweet words of wisdom in his ear—the popular conception—is applesauce."

Applesauce or art, who is to say? Perhaps a measure of both.

From a distance I sold to Hollywood with limited success— to motion pictures and television. In 1959 I wrote my last magazine story, which had a Tibetan background similar to that of my first sale 18 years earlier, and sold it to the ailing *Post*. But times, and world history, had changed. In my first version the villains had been Japanese; now they were Chinese—Communists. The Cold War, the Bomb and the Tube—the last affordable on budget terms to every low-income American family—had doomed the slicks. The wonderful innocent optimism which outlasted boom-and-bust, Prohibition and the Depression, Adolf Hitler and Korea, was no more. The audience that suppported two generations of my family had faded, like one of Hal's nostalgic heroes, into yesterday's sunset.

. . .

On November 18, 1985, fifty-five years after its world première in Hollywood, a resurrected version of *The Big Trail* played a one night stand at the Academy of Motion Picture Arts and Sciences Samuel Goldwyn Theater in Beverly Hills, as part of a "Fifty Years of Films from the New York Museum of Modern Art" tribute to the industry. Among the packed house audience were several descendants of the star, John Wayne, and of the author, Hal G. Evarts.

Kevin Thomas, film critic of the Los Angeles *Times*, wrote: "Preserved in a conversion to CinemaScope, *The Big Trail* is a splendid entertainment in which Raoul Walsh takes full advantage of the wide screen and deep focus to tell Hal G. Evarts' story of a wagon train's adventure-filled journey from Missouri to Oregon. The result is an epic film with a visual texture so rich and graphic as to look like a series of authentically detailed etchings of the Old West.... the film's look and feel seem way ahead of its time."

The famous "fight" scene between Wayne and villain Ian Keith was left on the cutting room floor. But Louise Carver's super mudhole floperoo survived intact and, as it had more than half a century earlier, brought down the house.

EULOGY

IN TODAY'S SIMPLE burial service of the seas, whether you, Hal Evarts, can remember us as we remember you, we cannot know. Whether your final journey has been over an interminable ocean, stretching between invisible shores, we cannot know. Anyway, old friend, it has been great to know you, and the noble heart which always beat true to those you loved. Sincere tokens of loyalty brought you many friends, from great and generous minds, and no enemies. There was not a melancholy soul among them. Diligence, vigilance, tenderness and patience, combined with a heart of gold, created in you one of God's nobility. So, farewell, old friend, with Fate's benison and benediction. Sleep in the deep.

—COLONEL CHARLES H. HASKELL
UNITED STATES ARMY

At sea, 500 miles north of
Rio De Janeiro, Brazil
October 23, 1934.

BIBLIOGRAPHY

UNPUBLISHED SOURCES
The Library, Special Collections, University of Oregon, Eugene.
   Evarts, Sr., Hal G. Papers.
   Evarts, Jr., Hal G. Papers.

PUBLISHED SOURCES
Abbott, Lemuel A. *Descendants of George Abbott of Rowley, Mass.* Boston: T.R. Marvin & Son, 1906.
Albright, Horace M., with Cahn, Robert. *The Birth of the National Park Service.* Salt Lake City: Howe Brothers, 1985.
Allen, Frederick Lewis. *Only Yesterday.* New York: Harper, 1931.
Berg, A. Scott. *Max Perkins, Editor of Genius.* New York: E.P. Dutton, 1978.
Bigger, Leander A. *Around the World With a Business Man* (4 vols). Philadelphia: John C. Winston Co., 1909.
Brent, Bill. *They Don't Make 'em Like That Anymore.* Arizona Days and Ways Magazine, June 5, 1966.
Boone, J. Allen. *Kinship With All Life.* New York: Harper & Row, 1954.
Burdsall, Richard L. and Emmons, Arthur B., 3rd. *Men Against the Clouds.* New York: Harper, 1935.
Burt, Struthers. *Powder River, Let 'er Buck.* New York: Rinehart, 1938.
Corle, Edwin. *Desert Country.* New York: Duell, Sloan & Pearce, 1941.
Evarts, Hal G., Sr. *On Inspiration's Trail.* Philadelphia: Saturday Evening Post, Curtis Publishing Co., Aug. 21, 1926.
——. *The Log of The Big Trail.* Los Angeles: Fox Film Corporation, 1930.
Eyles, Allen. *John Wayne and the Movies.* South Brunswick: A.S. Barnes, 1976.
——. *The Western.* South Brunswick: A.S. Barnes, 1975.
Fenin, George N. and Evenson, William K. *The Western, from Silents to Cinerama.* New York: Orion Press, 1962.
Fox, Stephen. *John Muir and His Legacy.* Boston: Little, Brown, 1981.
Friedrich, Otto. *Decline and Fall.* New York: Harper & Row, 1970.

Goetzmann, William H. and William N. *The West of the Imagination.* New York: W.W. Norton, 1986.
Halliwell, Leslie, *Mountain of Dreams, the Golden Years of Paramount.* New York: Stonehill Publishing Co., 1976.
Hawkins, Eric, with Sturdevant, Robert N. *Hawkins of the Paris Herald.* New York: Simon & Schuster, 1963.
Horwitz, James. *They Went Thataway.* New York: Dutton, 1976.
Hurst, Richard M. *Republic Studios—Between Poverty Row and the Majors.* Metuchen, N.J.: Scarecrow Press, 1979.
Hutchinson, W. H. *The World, the Work and the West of W.H.D. Koerner.* Norman: University of Oklahoma Press, 1978.
Idriess, Ion L. *Gold-Dust and Ashes.* Sydney: Angus & Robertson, 1933.
Kirkpatrick, Sidney D. *A Cast of Killers.* New York: E.P. Dutton, 1986.
Lingenfelter, Richard E. *Death Valley & the Amargosa.* Berkeley: University of California Press, 1986.
Matthews, Leonard. *History of Western Movies.* New York: Crescent, 1984.
Parrish, Robert. *Growing Up in Hollywood.* New York: Harcourt Brace Jovanovich, 1976. Reprint, Boston: Little, Brown, 1988.
———. *Hollywood Doesn't Live Here Anymore.* Boston: Little, Brown, 1988.
Paul, Elliot. *The Last Time I Saw Paris.* New York: Random House, 1942.
Potomac Corral of the Westerners. *Great Western Indian Fights.* Garden City: Doubleday, 1960.
Schulberg, Budd. *Moving Pictures.* New York: Stein & Day, 1981.
Sevareid, Eric. *Not So Wild a Dream.* New York: Atheneum, 1976.
Shankland, Robert. *Steve Mather of the National Park Service.* New York: Knopf, 1951.
Shirer, William L. *The Collapse of the Third Republic.* New York: Simon & Schuster, 1969.
Singer, Bruce. *100 Years of the Paris Trib.* New York: Harry N. Abrams, 1987.
Stedman, Raymond, W. *The Serials, Suspense and Drama by Installment.* Norman: University of Oklahoma Press, 1978.
Swindell, Larry. *The Last Hero, A Biography of Gary Cooper.* New York, Doubleday, 1980.
Tebbel, John. *The American Magzine, a Compact History.* New York: Hawthorn Books, 1969.
———. *George Horace Lorimer and the Saturday Evening Post.* New York: Doubleday, 1948.
Tomkies, Mike. *Duke, the Story of John Wayne.* Chicago: Regnery, 1971.
Vinson, James, editor. *Twentieth Century Western Writers.* Detroit: Gale Research Co., 1982.

Walsh, Raoul. *Each Man in His Time*. New York: Farrar, Straus & Giroux, 1974.
Weld, John. *Young Man in Paris*. Chicago: Academy, 1985.
Zolotow, Maurice. *Shooting Star, A Biography of John Wayne*. New York: Simon & Schuster, 1974.

BOOKS BY HAL G. EVARTS

The Cross Pull. New York: Alfred A. Knopf, 1920.
The Bald Face. New York: Alfred A. Knopf, 1921.
The Yellow Horde. Boston: Little, Brown, 1921.
The Settling of the Sage. Boston: Little, Brown, 1922.
Fur Sign. Boston: Little, Brown, 1922.
The Passing of the Old West. Boston: Little, Brown, 1923.
Tumbleweeds. Boston: Little, Brown, 1923.
Spanish Acres. Boston: Little, Brown, 1925.
The Painted Stallion. Boston: Little, Brown, 1926.
The Moccasin Telegraph. Boston: Little, Brown, 1927
Fur Brigade. Boston: Little, Brown, 1928.
Tomahawk Rights. Boston: Little, Brown, 1929.
The Shaggy Legion. Boston: Little, Brown, 1930.
Shortgrass. Boston: Little, Brown, 1932.
Wolf Dog. Garden City, N.Y.: Doubleday, Doran, 1935.

SPECIAL ANIMAL SERIES
Jerbo the Jumper. Racine, Wis.: Whitman Publishing Co., 1930.
Kobi of the Sea. Racine, Wis.: Whitman Publishing Co., 1930.
Phantom the White Mink. Racine, Wis.: Whitman Publishing Co., 1930.
Swift the Kit Fox. Racine, Wis.: Whitman Publishing Co., 1930.

ANTHOLOGIES
Clarke, Francis E., compiler. *Wild Animals (Koala).* New York: Macmillan, 1939.
———. *Great Wings and Small (Fine Feathers).* New York: Macmillan, 1940.
Mason, F. van Wyck, compiler. *The Fighting American (The Sioux* from *Fur Brigade).* London, Jarrolds, no date.

MANUSCRIPTS — *Published*
"What Next," *Country Gentleman,* April 12, 1919.
"Hal G. Evarts," *The Editor,* August 25, 1919.
"The Big Bull of Shoshone," *Saturday Evening Post,* November 1, 1919.

"The Bald Face," *Saturday Evening Post*, November 15, 1919.
"Straight and Narrow," *Sunset*, November, 1919.
"The Cross Pull," *Saturday Evening Post*, 4 parts, November 22-December 13, 1919.
"Protective Coloration," *Collier's*, December 20, 1919.
"The Black Ram of Sunlight," *Saturday Evening Post*, February 7, 1920.
"Hobgobblins of the Trail," *Collier's*, March 6, 1920.
"The Black and Cinnamon Twins," *The Popular Magazine*, March 7, 1920.
"Who's Who—and Why," *Saturday Evening Post*, April 3, 1920.
"Dude Wrangler," *Saturday Evening Post*, May 1, 1920.
"The Stayer," *The Popular Magazine*, June 7, 1920.
"The Palmated Pioneer," *The Redbook*, July, 1920.
"Dog Town," *Saturday Evening Post*, August 14, 1920.
"Convincing A Lady," *Collier's*, August 14, 1920
"The Yellow Horde," *The Redbook*, 3 parts, August-October, 1920.
"Savagery," *The Premier*, November, 1920. *The Redbook*, January, 1921.
"Old-Timer," *Saturday Evening Post*, 5 parts, February 19- March 19, 1921.
"Traveling Otter," *Saturday Evening Post*, April 23, 1921.
"Swamp Colony," *Saturday Evening Post*, May 14, 1921.
"The Glutton," *Saturday Evening Post*, June 25, 1921. *The Windsor Magazine*, November, 1923.
"The Vanished Squadrons," *The Redbook*, August, 1921.
"End of Steel," *Saturday Evening Post*, 2 parts, October 8 & 15, 1921.
"Fur Sign," *The Country Gentleman*, December 17, 1921.
"The Settling of the Sage," *The Redbook*, 5 parts, October, 1921-February, 1922.
"Tumbleweeds," *Saturday Evening Post*, 4 parts, September 2-September 23, 1922.
"The Drop-In," *The Redbook*, January, 1923.
"The Nibblers," *Saturday Evening Post*, January 13, 1923.
"Timber-line Trails," *Saturday Evening Post*, January 20, 1923.
"The Mountain Wilderness," *Saturday Evening Post*, January 27, 1923.
"Desert Playgrounds," *Saturday Evening Post*, February, 1923.
"Mountain-Lying-Down," *Saturday Evening Post*, March, 1923.
"Sierras by Campfire and Pack," *Saturday Evening Post*, April 21, 1923.
"The Last Stronghold," *Saturday Evening Post*, May 12, 1923.
"Census of a Section," *Saturday Evening Post*, June 2, 1923.
"Secret Ambitions," *Public Ledger*, Philadelphia, Pennsylvania, June 23, 1923.
"The Last Straggler," *Saturday Evening Post*, July 4, 1923.
"Sandrock Folk," *Saturday Evening Post*, August 4, 1923.
"Fur Supply," *Saturday Evening Post*, October 27, 1923.

"The Timber-Line Cycle," *Saturday Evening Post*, November 3, 1923.
"Duck Lore," *Saturday Evening Post*, November 10, 1923.
"Spruce Jungles," *Saturday Evening Post*, November 17, 1923.
"The Spread of the Coyote," *Saturday Evening Post*, December 15, 1923.
"Overlapping Flowering Periods," *Saturday Evening Post*, January 5, 1924.
"Color Phases," *Saturday Evening Post*, March 22, 1924.
"The Wild Ass and the Tame," *Saturday Evening Post*, March 29, 1924.
"Concerning the Remnants," *Saturday Evening Post*, September 6, 1924.
"The Final Rally," *Outdoor America*, December, 1924.
"Everyday Trap Sets," *Saturday Evening Post*, 1924.
"Allies Now—The $ and Sentiment," *Outdoor America*, February, 1925.
"Spanish Acres," *Saturday Evening Post*, 5 parts, June 27-July 25, 1925.
"A Chinaman's Chance for the Elk," *Saturday Evening Post*, September 5, 1925.
"The Painted Stallion," *Saturday Evening Post*, 3 parts, September 26-October 10, 1925.
"Hal Evarts Eats His Lunch," *Outdoor America*, February, 1926.
"Grazing Control," *Outdoor America*, May, 1926.
"Kenai," *Saturday Evening Post*, June 19, 1926.
"On Inspiration's Trail," *Saturday Evening Post*, August 21, 1926.
"Feathered Foragers," *Saturday Evening Post*, October 2, 1926.
"Hal G. Evarts—His Page," *Outdoor America*, February, 1927.
"Camera Hunting With Hal G. Evarts," *Outdoor America*, March 1927.
"The Blue Bear of Yukutat," *Saturday Evening Post*, April 30, 1927.
"The Red Raccoon," *Saturday Evening Post*, May 14, 1927.
"A Disciple of Solomon," *Saturday Evening Post*, May 28, 1927.
"Kobi of the Sea," *Saturday Evening Post*, June 4, 1927.
"The Moccasin Telegraph," *Saturday Evening Post*, 5 parts, July 23-August 20, 1937.
"Chaparral," *Saturday Evening Post*, October 8, 1927.
"Restocking the Coverts," *Saturday Evening Post*, October 15, 1927.
"Renegade," *Outdoor Life*, 2 parts, October, 1927.
"The Border Jumpers," *Saturday Evening Post*, 3 parts, November 5-19, 1927.
"Deer Tracks in the Snow," *Saturday Evening Post*, December 3, 1927.
"The False Status of Bruin," *Outdoor Life*, January, 1928.
"Prairie Blizzard," *Saturday Evening Post*, February 25, 1928.
"Seeing is Believing," *Saturday Evening Post*, March 3, 1928.
"Fur Brigade," *Saturday Evening Post*, 6 parts, April 21-May 26, 1928.
"The Most Vicious Bird I Know," *Country Gentleman*, July, 1928.
"Cruising the Kenai," *Outdoor Life*, August, 1928.
"Salt Marsh," *Saturday Evening Post*, September 15, 1928.
"Mixed Bags," *Saturday Evening Post*, September 29, 1928.

"Elk Steaks," *Saturday Evening Post*, October 20, 1928.
"The Post Office at Dry Fork," *Saturday Evening Post*, November 3, 1928.
"Sage," *Saturday Evening Post*, December 1, 1928.
"Trout Meadow," *Saturday Evening Post*, March 16, 1929.
"Tomahawk Rights," *Saturday Evening Post*, 4 parts, April 6-26, 1929.
"Ride and Tie," *Saturday Evening Post*, May 25, 1929.
"The River Bottom," *Saturday Evening Post*, July 6, 1929.
"Tide Flats," *Saturday Evening Post*, September 14, 1929.
"Snowhide," *Saturday Evening Post*, October 12, 1929.
"The Dethroned Monarch," *Saturday Evening Post*, October 19, 1929.
"The Shaggy Legion," *Saturday Evening Post*, 6 parts, November 30, 1929-January 4, 1930.
"Phantom of the Aspens," *Saturday Evening Post*, April 19, 1930.
"Back-tracking on Early Game Trails," *Saturday Evening Post*, May 24, 1930.
"Comedian of the Wild," *Saturday Evening Post*, August 23, 1930.
"The Rustler of Sentinel Knob," *The Blue Book*, November, 1930.
"Short Grass," *Saturday Evening Post*, 5 parts from May 21, 1932.
"Guinea Gold," *Saturday Evening Post*, February 4, 1933.
"The Pool," *Saturday Evening Post*, March 11, 1933.
"Warragal," *Saturday Evening Post*, July 8, 1933.
"Fine Feathers," *Saturday Evening Post*, November 11, 1933.
"Koala," *Saturday Evening Post*, January 27, 1934.
"Detour," *Saturday Evening Post*, March 17, 1934.
"Wolf Dog," *Saturday Evening Post*, 5 parts, July 14-August 18, 1934.
"The Black Roo," *Saturday Evening Post*, January 26, 1935.
"The Last Move," *The Redbook*, no date.
"The Fatted Calf," *The Redbook*, no date.
"Who Write the Country Gentleman—Out-of-doors with Hal G. Evarts," *Country Gentleman*, no date.

— *Unpublished*
Back to the Land.
The Best Animal Family Man.
Celluloid Cowboy.
Crossing Trails and Celebrated Liars.
Crow Chief and Others.
Early Fur Traders of the West.
Erosion From Overgrazing.
Fairview News Items.
The Final Rally.
Flappers—How They Got That Way.
General Conservation Issues.
Horns.

How's the Road?
Jackson Hole Elk.
Killing Dogs Versus Raiding Coyotes.
Last Two Strike.
Long Trail of the Tortoise°.
The Main Traveled Highway to Heaven.
A Man Called Smith.
Perfection by Poison°.
Rattle and Drum°.
Report on the Kaibab Deer Herds.
The Stricken City.
What of Our Fur?

°Submitted to editors but rejected, the only rejections in his career.